Rapture
PRACTICE

Rapture
PRACTICE

A TRUE STORY BY

AARON HARTZLER

LITTLE, BROWN AND COMPANY

NEW YORK ✶ BOSTON

Little, Brown and Company

Hachette Book Group
237 Park Avenue, New York, NY 10017
Visit our website at www.lb-teens.com

Little, Brown and Company is a division of Hachette Book Group, Inc.
The Little, Brown name and logo are trademarks of
Hachette Book Group, Inc.

First Edition: April 2013

The definitions of *rapture*, *belief*, *genesis*, *exodus*,
revelation, and *acknowledgments* are used by permission.
From *Merriam-Webster's Collegiate® Dictionary*, 11th Edition
© 2012 by Merriam-Webster, Incorporated.

The publisher is not responsible for websites (or their content)
that are not owned by the publisher.

Library of Congress Cataloging-in-Publication Data

Hartzler, Aaron.
Rapture practice : a memoir / by Aaron Hartzler. — 1st ed.
p. cm.
ISBN 978-0-316-09465-8
1. Hartzler, Aaron. 2. Christian biography—United States. 3. Teenagers—
Religious life. 4. High school students—Religious life. I. Title.
BR1725.H2425A3 2013
277.3'083092—dc23
[B]

2012028746

10 9 8 7 6 5 4 3 2 1

RRD-C

Printed in the United States of America

For Ann Maney,
whose faith helped me start.

For Nathan Hatch,
whose love helped me finish.

And for Alice Pope,
who helped with everything in between.

Author's Note

This book is a memoir. It reflects my present recollections of specific experiences over a period of years. Dialogue and events have been re-created from my memory, and in some cases have been compressed to convey the substance of what was said or what occurred.

With the exception of my immediate family, the names and identifying characteristics of most people have been changed. Several characters are composites of different individuals, the conversations we had, and the kisses we shared. (Yes. Be warned: There is kissing.)

I hope reading this memoir will inspire you to tell your own story. We can never have too many stories—especially about high school.

Here's mine.

RAPTURE

noun \ˈrap-chər\

1: an expression or manifestation of ecstasy or passion

2a: a state or experience of being carried away by overwhelming emotion; **b:** a mystical experience in which the spirit is exalted to a knowledge of divine things

3 *often capitalized*: the final assumption of Christians into heaven during the end-time according to Christian theology

PART I

BELIEF

noun \bə-ˈlēf\: a state or habit of mind in which trust or confidence is placed in some person or thing

Something you should know up front about my family:

We believe that Jesus is coming back.

We believe heaven is a real place with gates of pearl and streets of gold, just as hell is a real place of eternal fire and torment. From Adam and Eve to Jonah and the whale, from Jesus rising from the dead to the book of Revelation, we believe that every word of the Bible is true—every story, every miracle, every event happened exactly as it's written.

So when I say we believe that Jesus is coming back, I don't mean metaphorically, like someday in the distant future when the lion lies down with the lamb and there is peace on earth. I mean literally, like glance out the car window and, "Oh, hey, there's Jesus in the sky." There will be a trumpet blast, an archangel will shout, and Jesus Christ will appear in the clouds. We believe that people all over the world who have been born again by accepting Jesus as their personal savior from sin will float up into the air to meet him.

We call this event the Rapture. We believe that it could

happen at any moment and that only God the Father knows when that moment will be.

It could happen today.

It could happen tomorrow.

It could happen before you finish reading this sentence.

It's only a matter of time.

GENESIS

noun \ˈje-nə-səs\: the origin or coming into being of something

CHAPTER 1

I am four years old, and Dad is teaching me to play dead.

"Remember, when I pick you up, you have to stay limp like a rag doll," he says. "If you swing your arms or kick your legs onstage, the audience will know you're alive."

Dad is directing a play at the Bible college where he teaches. He has cast me in the role of a little boy who gets struck and killed by a Roman chariot while running across the street to meet Jesus. The chariot wreck happens offstage. Dad explained it would cost too much money to have a horse gallop across the stage pulling a chariot, which was disappointing; however, I do get carried on dead, which I find very exciting. This excitement makes it challenging to keep still.

Tonight, we practiced my seventeen lines at the dining room table, then moved into the living room to work on being dead. I lie down on the couch, close my eyes, and feel Dad's arms slide under me. Slowly, he lifts me into the air. I concentrate on letting my limbs dangle loosely while Dad walks around the living room.

"Great, Aaron!" he says. "You're really getting it. Now, keep your eyes closed, but don't frown."

I've been thinking so hard about not kicking my legs I've scrunched up my forehead. When he mentions it, I can feel the tension between my eyes. Slowly, I let my face relax.

"That's it!" Dad says. I can tell he's pleased. It makes me want to smile, but I don't move a muscle because *I'm dead*. Dad walks around the living room one more time, then gently lays me back down on the couch. When I open my eyes, he is grinning at me.

"Good job, son!"

Rehearsing for the play is the most fun Dad and I have ever had together. He is very encouraging and has a lot of great tips on how to look as authentically dead as possible.

In the weeks before opening night, Mom sews me two identical pale green linen tunics with dark green satin trim. She distresses one of them with scissors and a cheese grater, then smears it with dirt and red paint so it appears to have been worn by a small boy who met an untimely demise beneath pointy hooves and chariot wheels.

Finally, the big day arrives, and when I come offstage from my last scene before the chariot wreck, Mom and one of the girls in the play cover me in dirt and wounds made of lipstick and greasepaint. Once they are done roughing me up, I stop to take a good look at myself in the mirror. My eyes are blackened, and blood appears to be seeping out of my hairline, spilling from gashes on my arms and legs and dripping through the tattered tunic. The effect is startling.

I make a mental note against death by chariot.

The student who carries me on "dead" is very strong, and I can feel his biceps bulge under my shoulder blades when he picks me up. I remind myself not to smile, and completely relax in his arms.

My eyes are closed, but I feel the heat of the bright lights on my face when he steps through the curtain onto the stage, and I can hear people in the audience gasp. I love the sound of that gasp. It means what I am doing is working.

After the curtain call, Dad assures me I was very convincing as a little dead boy. Grandma confirms this by running up and clutching me wildly to her bosom.

"That was terrible!" she tells Dad. "I never want to see Aaron dead again."

On the way home, I can smell the red greasepaint still caked in my hair as Dad tells me what a good job I did. "Aaron, your facial expressions and vocal inflections were excellent," he says, beaming. "Jesus is coming back very soon, and there are so many people who need to be saved. Folks who won't go to church will come to see a play. We are using quality biblical drama to reach lost souls for Christ."

Acting is an amazing gift Dad has given me. It allows me to be close to him in a whole new way—like I'm his partner. It makes us a team. Even better, my acting pleases Jesus, too. What I am doing onstage is not only *good*, it's *important*.

When we get home, Mom hustles me into a steamy bath and shampoos the greasepaint out of my hair. The warm water turns dark crimson and leaves a ring around the white tub. Mom gives me one last rinse under the showerhead to wash away the makeup, then wraps me up in a thirsty towel. I smile as I watch the bloodred suds circle the drain.

I can't wait to play dead again tomorrow night.

CHAPTER 2

"Boys and girls, I am *so excited* that you could make it to Good News Club today!"

I am six years old, and this is how Mom gets the ball rolling at the Bible club she hosts in our family room every Thursday after school. She is pretty and petite, and her light Southern accent wraps pure love around the words "boys and girls," like butter dripping off a crescent roll at Thanksgiving dinner. Kids from all over the neighborhood flock to our front door for a taste of that warmth. We may be the only house in Kansas City that doesn't have a television set, but we've got something better: my mom. Once everyone is settled on the couch or the carpet, she bathes us all in her billion-watt smile and kicks things off with a question:

"Who can tell Miss Belinda what the Good News is?"

Hands fly up all around the room with shouts and moans of enthusiasm. My friend Krista waves like a flag in a hurricane, trying to get her hand higher than her brother's. A homeschooled boy who lives down the block bounces up and down in his seat, shouting out answers over the noise. Mom spreads her hands wide and calls for silence.

"Oooooh! Boys and *girls*. I *forgot*, I *did*! I forgot to tell y'all a *secret*!"

A hush falls over the family room. Everyone leans forward. *What could the secret be?*

"Miss Belinda has funny ears. When I ask a question, I can only hear you if you raise your hand and then sit very still until I call on you." Mom clasps her hands across the skirt of her denim jumper and waits. I love watching her in action each week. She's a pro at crowd control, and always happiest when she's teaching a group of children about Jesus. Her face lights up like she's about to offer you the most incredible gift you have ever received, and if you asked her, she'd tell you that's exactly what she's doing. It's a gift anyone can have, free for the taking:

Eternal life.

"Now. Let's try this again," Mom says. "Boys and girls! Who can tell Miss Belinda what the Good News is?"

Hands shoot up from ramrod-stiff arms. Everyone is silent, but the tension of limbs straining toward the ceiling threatens to pop shoulders from sockets. Mom's eyes twinkle, wide with amazement. She makes a show of seeking out the quietest, most earnest would-be answer-giver, but I have a hunch she's already chosen someone.

"Oh…*my. Yes!* Boys and *girls*! You are making this a very difficult decisi—*Randy!*"

Mom calls on one of the unchurched children in our

midst. Randy's drug-addled mother ran off shortly after his birth, leaving him with his aging grandparents on the next block over. One wall of his bedroom is lined with shelves filled floor to ceiling with He-Man action figures. There is something truly intriguing to me about the rippled plastic stomachs and fur-trimmed bikini briefs of the men who inhabit the Castle Grayskull. I often ask if I can go visit Randy, but Mom is firm.

"Aaron, honey, it doesn't please the savior to play with little plastic men who look like demons." She smiles and squeezes my shoulder. "Besides, sugar, *Jesus* is the Master of the Universe."

Randy doesn't know very much about the Bible. In response to simple questions like "What is the Good News?," he often waxes on at length about characters from Greek mythology. However, in the spirit of ongoing outreach to this poor, lost boy, Mom continues to call on him each week and ignore his answers about Atlas and Cronus.

"You see, Randy," Mom says, "those tales about Zeus are only made-up *stories*, but *Jesus* is *real*. He was an *actual person* who walked on earth just two thousand years ago, and the Bible, God's holy word, tells us the Good News is that Jesus died on the cross for our sins, rose again, and is coming back very soon to take everyone who believes in him up to heaven."

Each week, Mom patiently explains the Good News, and each week Randy nods and smiles with a quizzical look that says it all: He doesn't understand how the stories he knows are different from the ones Mom tells him.

"We'll talk about that more in a *minute*." Mom smiles. "Right now, we're gonna get things started off with a *song*."

In a way, I understand Randy's confusion—I don't know who Atlas is just like he doesn't know who Jesus is—but the songs we sing at Good News Club help explain the plan of salvation. Sometimes, the Gospel message can be more easily understood when set to a catchy tune.

The illustrated song Mom chooses from her stack of visual aids is my favorite. It's called "Countdown!" Rendered in bright shades of purple and red, the front cover is emblazoned with a picture of the Apollo spacecraft hurtling toward the moon. She asks for a volunteer to help her turn the pages so everyone can see the words. Once more, hands are held high and waved with excitement. It isn't so much about holding the song—it's being chosen that feels good. Mom picks Krista, then calls me up to the front as well.

"Aaron is going to help us sing, too, because there is a very special ending to this song, and we'd like to show y'all what it is."

The anticipation in the air is electric. As I take my place up front next to Mom, she winks at me. "Ready?"

I smile back, and Mom gives a quick nod as the signal to begin.

The tune is peppy and joyous, all about how Jesus has gone to outer space to prepare heaven for every Christian who has trusted him as savior. We sing at the top of our lungs about being ready for Jesus to come back, and watching the clouds for his return, and we count backward during the chorus: "Ten! Nine! Eight! Seven! Six! Five! Four! Three! Two! One..."

As we repeat the final line of the song, our voices get softer and softer, and I show the other kids how to crouch closer and closer to the carpet. By the end, we are almost whispering: "The countdown's getting lower every day...." Then there's a tense moment of silence before we yell "BLASTOFF!" and spring from the floor, hurling ourselves into the air as high as we can.

In this moment, as I fly toward the bumpy popcorn texture of the family room ceiling, the excitement swells in my chest. I love this song so much—not only because we get to jump at the end but also because it explains the way my family lives.

This song reminds me why we don't have a TV, or go to movies, or listen to rock music; why Mom never wears pants—only skirts and dresses. It's all because Jesus is coming back, and each of these things is another way we can be different from the world around us. When unsaved people see that our family is different, they will want to know why, and we'll have the perfect opportunity to share the Good News.

I've already trusted Jesus to be my personal Lord and savior. The day I prayed and asked Jesus to come into my heart I was born again. Now I don't have to worry about being left behind when Jesus comes back to take all the Christians to heaven. I can't wait to be caught up in the twinkling of an eye to meet the Lord in the air.

As I fly toward the ceiling in Good News Club, I am

grinning so hard my cheeks hurt. I can't help but smile. I have been chosen by God to help spread the Good News, and it feels good to be chosen. Our whole family is on God's team, helping to rescue souls from an eternity in hell. We are headed to heaven, and no movie, TV show, or Top 40 hit could ever compare to the things God has planned for us there. It's my job to tell as many people about Jesus as I can. Helping Mom with Good News Club is one of the ways I can do that.

Each time I sing "Countdown!" I get goose bumps. What if Jesus came back right as I yelled "BLASTOFF!" and jumped up in the air? I bet I'd keep right on going! I'd zip through the ceiling, and the living room above us, then shoot out the roof to meet Jesus in the clouds!

Today, that doesn't happen. As my sneakers land on the carpet again, I look around and see all my friends laughing and grinning. Mom squeezes my shoulder and whispers "Thank you!" for my help leading the song. She smiles at me as I take a seat on the floor, next to Randy. I'm not the slightest bit disappointed I didn't get whisked away to heaven this time. Whether it happens today, or tomorrow, or a year from now, I know one thing for certain: Jesus is coming back, and I'm ready whenever he is.

In the meantime, Good News Club is excellent practice.

CHAPTER 3

The Memphis skyline looms above Interstate 40, just across the Mississippi River, which meanders past my window, a wide, wet border between Arkansas and Tennessee. As Dad guides our station wagon onto the Hernando de Soto Bridge, we start the countdown:

Ten!
Nine!
Eight!
Seven!
Six!
Five!
Four!
Three!
Two!
ONE!

We all cheer as the car passes under the big sign in the middle of the bridge that reads TENNESSEE: THE VOLUNTEER STATE WELCOMES YOU, and then Mom leads us in a chorus of the hymn we sing at church as the ushers walk down the aisle to start passing the collection plates:

> *Praise God from whom all blessings flow*
> *Praise Him all creatures here below*
> *Praise Him above ye heavenly hosts*
> *Praise Father, Son, and Holy Ghost*
> *Aaaaaaaaaaaa-men!*

The nine-hour drive from Kansas City to Memphis is a long haul, but worth it. As we drive past the buildings downtown, I know we're only twenty minutes away from Nanny and Papa's house, where the TV is always on and there's sugar-sweetened cereal in the pantry.

Nanny comes out on the porch when she sees the station wagon pull into the carport. There are hugs and kisses, and a twinkle in her eye.

"I declare, children. I went to the A&P to get groceries, but I didn't know which cereal y'all liked, so you'll have to come back with me to pick it out." I cheer along with Josh and Miriam as Nanny takes our new baby brother, Caleb, from Mom, and Dad drags duffel bags and suitcases into the house.

When we get to the grocery store, most of the employees know Nanny by name. They greet her as we walk through the door.

"Hey, Miz Davis."

"Hey, y'all." Nanny smiles and wheels a cart past the

checkout lanes. "These are my grandchildren from Kansas City. We're headed down the cereal aisle to go toy shopping."

Mom doesn't buy sweetened cereal at home. "You can concentrate better at school if your blood sugar doesn't crash midway through the morning," she tells me. The Cheerios and Wheaties on our breakfast table never have special prizes in the box, but at Nanny's house Mom makes an exception, and the milk in our bowls turns brown with chocolate or pink with food coloring. "Every now and then won't hurt," she says, smiling.

Each of us gets to choose a box of any kind of cereal we want. The Apple Jacks have a rubber stamp set that comes with every letter of the alphabet and an ink pad, so that's what I pick—I'm seven now, and know how to spell better than Miriam or Josh. When we get home, Nanny pours it all out in a big Tupperware container so I don't have to wait for breakfast to play with the prize, and I set to work hand stamping a copy of the Bible verse she has pasted on the refrigerator door: Ephesians 5:18: "Be filled with the spirit."

The next morning at breakfast, I fill up on a bowl of buttery grits with salt and pepper while Nanny makes eggs, biscuits, and gravy for Papa, Mom, and Dad. Grits are my favorite, but I finish them fast so I can move on to Apple Jacks. Mom smiles and nods at my empty bowl, then Nanny rinses it out and fills it with cereal. The crispy coating on the bright orange loops scrapes the roof of my mouth. The taste is so sweet it's like having dessert for breakfast.

Nanny kisses the top of my head as I crunch, then sits

down at the table with a cup of fresh coffee. Her lipstick leaves a red smudge on the rim of her mug. She doesn't wear any other makeup on a daily basis, so the lipstick is important. "I need just a touch," she says, "so folks won't think we're Pentecostal."

Nanny winks at me and squeezes my hand. "Your uncle Bill is bringing Sadie over later." Sadie's my favorite cousin, but we only get to see each other a couple times a year— usually over Christmas and during the summer. "Last week Sadie had this little brown stuffed animal with her," Nanny says. "It was a doll of that E.T. fella from the new alien movie."

E.T. is everywhere. He was all over the cereal aisle yesterday at the A&P. He smiled down from every bottle of Pepsi when we walked down the soda pop aisle. He was on all of the backpacks and notebooks up at the front of the store by the register, and on the billboard in the parking lot.

Nanny shakes her head. "Aaron, I declare that little creature is the ugliest thing I've ever seen. I said, 'Well, Sadie, did you tear all the feathers off that poor bird?' She said, 'Oh no, Nanny. This is E.T. He's from space.'" Nanny laughs and takes a sip of coffee. "I told her he looked like a plucked turkey."

I picture E.T. with a large, feathery tail and think about that boy on the bicycle flying toward the moon on all the backpacks and Pepsi bottles. He doesn't look like a Pilgrim to me, and I'm confused about how he fits into the Thanksgiving story.

Uncle Bill and Aunt Janice arrive that afternoon, and I

give Sadie and her sister a big hug. When the adults go inside to chat, I boost Sadie up to the lowest branch of the middle tree in Nanny's front yard.

Nanny sees us from the kitchen window and pokes her head out the storm door. "Children, y'all be real careful climbing that tree. Don't want to end up in the emergency room."

We smile and call out "Yes, ma'am," then climb to the highest branches that will hold us, far from the reach of our younger siblings. This is the perfect place for trading stories and telling secrets.

"Have y'all seen *E.T.* yet?" Sadie gushes. "Daddy might take us again next weekend. Are y'all still gonna be here? Maybe we can all go together!"

I'm quiet for a second. "We don't go to the movies."

Sadie frowns. "You've never been to a *movie?*"

We've never talked about this before. The whole idea of a movie theater is still new to me, and Sadie's disbelief makes me feel ashamed somehow. My cheeks get hot. I bite my lip and shake my head.

"Why?" she asks. It's as if I've told her we live in an igloo on Mars.

I shrug. "Dad says even at good movies there are advertisements for bad ones before it starts. You never know what's going to pop up on the screen."

Sadie frowns. "I've never seen a preview for a bad movie when I go to the theater."

"You haven't?"

Sadie shakes her head, and for the first time, I wonder if my parents might be wrong about this.

"What's it like?" I ask her.

"Going to the movies?"

I nod. Sadie cocks her chin to the side and purses her lips. I can tell she's thinking about how to explain it to me.

"Well, it's sort of like church," she says, "only there are no windows, and instead of a pulpit at the front, there is a giant screen where they play the movie. Everybody has their own chair with a cushion on it instead of sitting on the same pew, and when they turn off the lights, it gets real dark—like on Sunday nights at church when the missionaries bring slide projectors to show us pictures of the little huts where they live in Ecuador."

Sadie smiles, like she has saved the best part for last. "Plus, you can get a big Coke and a bucket of popcorn or some candy from the snack bar," she adds.

This is a brilliant plan. I imagine the ushers at church putting down their offering plates and passing out buttery popcorn and cold sodas instead. Sitting through a long sermon would be so much easier with concessions.

After dinner, I am still thinking about *E.T.* and the movies. Uncle Bill and Aunt Janice are Christians, and I know Sadie loves Jesus, but she can do things Mom and Dad say aren't pleasing to the Lord. Nanny is working at the hospital tonight, and Dad is helping Mom give Miriam and Josh a bath. Papa is sitting in his recliner, watching wrestling on TV and crocheting.

"What are you working on, Papa?"

"I'm making an afghan," he says with a wheeze. His breathing is heavy. Papa smoked cigarettes for a long time until he asked Jesus into his heart a few years ago. The doctors say he has emphysema now.

I sit down on the couch, watching Papa's nimble fingers work the little hook. It flies in and out of the blue yarn, creating delicate loops that form intricate chains, all linked together and spilling across his lap onto the parquet flooring.

"How did you learn to crochet?" I ask.

"My sisters taught me," he says. "When I was a little boy up in the mountains, we'd get snowed in for weeks." He pauses to catch his breath. "Didn't have a TV back then."

We don't usually have a TV at our house, either. Besides being a teacher at the Bible college, my dad is a minister, and every now and then he's asked to preach a sermon at different churches. Sometimes he preaches about ways we can keep our thoughts pure, like not watching television.

"We pulled the plug on our TV when Aaron was a toddler," Dad says from the pulpit. "*Sesame Street* was sponsored by the letter *G* for 'Go-Go Dancer,' and when my wife turned it off, Aaron cried like we'd stabbed him."

I always laugh along with the audience when Dad tells stories about us kids. He's pretty funny when he preaches, but he's not joking around when it comes to TV.

Last year, Dad rented a television set for several weeks at Thanksgiving time so we could all watch the holiday specials. We had to ask permission before we could turn it on, and he or Mom always watched it with us. We got to see *The Sound of Music* and *Mary Poppins*, and Dad watched a lot of football and basketball games with Josh and Miriam. I wanted to watch figure skating on ABC, but Dad kept clicking back to the games. He said the female figure skaters were immodestly dressed.

I glance up from Papa's afghan and see a woman wearing a bikini on the screen. She is walking around the wrestling ring in high heels. I feel a little bit guilty for staring. Dad wouldn't want me to look at her, because she's not wearing enough clothing. When there were girls on the beer commercials during the games, Dad would always say "sick" under his breath and change the channel.

Papa doesn't seem to notice that the woman in the bikini is immodestly dressed. A large man wearing tight red underwear struts into the ring. He has dirty blond hair and yells into the microphone through a shaggy mustache. His muscles remind me of Randy's He-Man figures, but he's different somehow—sweaty, angry, loud. Something about him is scary. I'd rather watch figure skating, but it's summertime, so there probably isn't any to see.

I get my blue schoolbag in the corner and pull out the pot holder loom I got for Christmas last year. Then I sit on the end of the couch closest to Papa's recliner. My loom is a square, plastic frame with little pegs that stick up on all four sides. I stretch brightly colored nylon bands across the frame from left to right, then weave other bands over and under from top to bottom with a little hook that looks a lot like Papa's crochet hook. I gave Nanny the first pot holder I made last Christmas, and she hung it up on the cabinet door because she said it was so pretty she couldn't bear to use it. Papa says I have a good eye for color.

Papa and I work with our hooks while the loud men on TV toss one another across the screen. When I finish my pot holder, Papa helps me weave the edges as I slip each loop off the loom.

"Will you teach me how to crochet?" I ask him.

"I reckon," he says with a pant. "Tomorrow, I'll see if I can find another hook." He smiles at me, and I smile back. I feel like I belong, sitting here next to Papa. This is what men do together—watch wrestling and make things from string.

"Hey, Aaron." Dad's voice makes me jump. He is standing in the hallway behind where Papa and I are sitting. "Will you come back here a minute, please?"

I put down my pot holder and follow Dad back down the hall. Mom is in the back bedroom putting Josh and Miriam to bed. Caleb is already asleep, so Dad whispers.

"What are you doing out there with Papa?"

"He's crocheting. I've been making a pot holder."

"What are you watching on TV?"

"Whatever Papa's watching," I hedge. Dad's not a fan of wrestling.

"Well, I don't want you watching wrestling," he says. "It's not pleasing to the Lord."

"Then how come Papa is watching it?"

25

"This is his house, and Papa is in charge of what he watches," Dad says. "I'm in charge of what you watch."

I know better than to talk back, so I don't argue when Dad walks me out to the living room to say good night to Papa, then helps me run a bath. By the time I'm clean and ready for bed, Papa has turned in for the night, and the TV is turned off.

Mom comes to tuck me in on the couch with a big red pillow and an afghan with zigzag stripes that Papa crocheted.

"Can we go see *E.T.* with Uncle Bill and Sadie?" I ask her.

"No, sweetheart. You know we don't go to see movies in theaters."

"But *E.T.* is a *good* movie."

Mom runs her hand across my forehead, pushing my bangs over. Her hand is cool on my skin and smells like the gold Dial bar soap in Nanny's front bathroom. "Last time your dad and I went to the movies was right before you were born," she explains. "It was a John Wayne film, and it was supposed to be a good movie, too."

"But it wasn't?"

She shakes her head. "There was a lot of cursing and fighting, and women who weren't wearing any clothes."

Mom says God's Holy Spirit convicted her heart in the theater. "I sat there thinking, 'If Jesus came back right this minute, I would be so ashamed for him to find me watching this.' I promised the Lord right then and there I would never go to see another movie in a movie theater, because I don't want to bring dishonor to the name of Christ."

I don't want to see a movie that dishonors Jesus, either. I want to figure out how the little Pilgrim boy on the bicycle rescues the alien turkey. It doesn't seem to me like this is going to hurt anybody.

"Can I *ever* go see a movie?"

"Aaron, one day you'll be all grown up, and you'll have to decide what is right for you." Mom's voice is low and serious. She looks directly into my eyes. "I hope when that time comes, you'll make the decision not to go see movies, but it will be up to you. One day when we get to heaven, we'll have to give an account to God for each thing we've done—every word and thought and deed. You'll have to answer for yourself then."

The idea of talking to God about every single thing I've ever done worries me. Mom kisses away the frown on my forehead. "We will always love you, honey. No matter what." Mom prays with me. She asks God to give me sweet sleep, then tucks me in and goes to bed.

Now it's only me in the living room in a race against the clock to see if I can stay awake until Nanny gets home from work. If I'm still up when she arrives, she'll make us a snack in the kitchen. As I try to keep my eyes open, I hear the tick-tock of Papa's clocks. There are several in the living room and kitchen that he winds every few days with a little key, and now, in the stillness, I can hear their steady rhythms in the air. It sounds like a countdown.

As all the clocks chime the half hour at eleven thirty, I hear Nanny's car pull into the carport. She opens the front door, puts down her purse in the kitchen, and peers around the corner into the living room.

"You awake, sugar?" she whispers.

"Yes, ma'am!" I say softly.

She comes over to the sofa in her white uniform and kisses me on the cheek. She smells like coffee and Oil of Olay.

"You want to come down to McLemore's market with me? We need some milk for breakfast tomorrow."

"Yes, ma'am, but I need to get dressed." I am wearing one of my uncle's old T-shirts to sleep in. It is bright green, with the 4-H cloverleaf on the front, and hangs to my knees.

"Oh, you're fine." Nanny grins. "We'll wrap you up like a papoose." She pulls the afghan around me like a cape, and we laugh in the car all the way to the market. "Your mama would kill me for not putting shoes on you," she says.

Nanny carries me into the corner store and sets me down on the counter. She grabs a gallon of milk and a box of Little Debbie Oatmeal Creme Pies ("mud pies," she calls them), pays for both, and then bundles me back into the car. My feet never touch the ground.

We eat mud pies and drink milk at the kitchen table. I love talking to Nanny, especially when it's just the two of us. Even when it's late at night and she's worked all day, she's never too tired to talk with me. She tells me stories about her grandma back in the mountains of Virginia, and how when Nanny was a little girl, they used to talk together like we do.

"You'll be all grown up before you know it," she says. "That's why we're makin' memories now. You and I will always be close, no matter what, 'cause we'll have our memories right here in our hearts." She pats her hand on my chest, then pours some more milk as I finish off my mud pie.

When Nanny tucks me in on the couch, she says a prayer.

"Father God, I ask your blessing on Aaron. Keep him safe, and let him know how special he is to me. Come quickly, Lord Jesus. Amen."

She kisses my cheek. "You are so precious to me, darlin'. I'll never stop loving you."

As I drift off to sleep, I think about Nanny and Mom. Both of them said they'd always love me, but Nanny didn't mention anything about hoping I wouldn't make bad choices. Papa and Nanny love Jesus, and they don't think it's wrong to have a TV set or watch wrestling, just like Uncle Bill doesn't think it's wrong to take Sadie to the movies. It seems like other people love Jesus in lots of different ways and have different rules about what's right and what's wrong.

Nanny asked Jesus to "come quickly" when she prayed, and as I listen to the seconds tick off around the dark living room, I hear a different kind of countdown. I feel like I'm in a hurry to grow up—a race against the schedule of heaven. For the first time, I hope the Rapture doesn't happen *too* soon. There are so many things I want to do before I go to heaven, like drive a car, and act in another play, and go to the movies.

I whisper one more prayer to Jesus before I drift off to sleep: "Please don't come back *too* quickly." Then I pull Papa's afghan tight around my shoulders and close my eyes.

CHAPTER 4

Four years later, Jesus still hasn't come back, and I still haven't been to the movies. I am, however, on my way back to church for the second time today. My family goes twice every Sunday, and usually once again on Wednesday night.

I'm eleven years old, and this morning I got all dressed up in a tie and a blazer for an hour of Sunday school followed by the worship service. It honors the Lord to dress nicely for church. Dad calls it "looking sharp," as in, "Wow, Aaron. That tie looks sharp!" When we finally got home a little after noon, we changed out of our sharp clothes into something softer. There was roast beef, potatoes, and carrots in the Crock-Pot, and Mom's homemade rolls for lunch.

This afternoon, I practiced the piano and read a book Mom gave me for my birthday. It's a novel about a boy named Alexi who lives behind the Iron Curtain in Russia. His family has been exiled to Siberia for believing in Jesus. Alexi is trying to decide whether he should help smuggle Bibles from a secret printing press to other Christians around Russia, or hide his faith and become the school's star hockey player. As he sets out with a suitcase of contraband Bibles, I hear Mom call up the stairs.

It's time to get dressed for church. Again.

The best part about Sunday night church is that I don't have to get as dressed up as I do on Sunday morning. I don't have to wear a tie, only a collared shirt, and usually khakis or, once in a while, jeans if they don't have patches or holes. Tonight I put on the blue corduroy pants and matching argyle sweater vest I got for my birthday. They go perfectly with my boat shoes. Dad is knotting his tie in the mirror at the bottom of the stairs, and as I walk past him toward the front door, he calls my name.

"Aaron, where are your socks?"

I look down at my feet, then back up at him, like he's asked a trick question.

"These are Top-Siders," I say. "You don't wear socks with boat shoes."

I smile as I hurry to pick up my Bible from the coffee table, trying to mask the fear in the pit of my stomach. If I can get to the car fast enough, maybe Dad won't insist on ruining my perfectly planned Sunday night outfit.

"Well, we're headed to church, son, so go put your socks on."
Too late.

"Dad." He turns to look at me when I say his name. I am struggling to keep my voice from betraying my complete dismay. "You don't wear socks with Top-Siders. It isn't stylish. It's dorky."

A look of genuine confusion passes over his face. "Aaron, it looks dorky *not* to have your socks on," he says. "We're going to worship the Lord. Go do it right now or we're going to be late."

I cannot believe this is happening. "Fine. I'll change shoes."

As I head back up to my room, Dad's voice stops me.

"Don't change shoes," he says. "We don't have time. Just grab some socks and put them on in the car on the way."

My frustration spills over. "But, Dad! No one wears socks with boat shoes." I feel tears welling up in my eyes. Mom appears from the kitchen with her purse and my youngest brother.

"What's the problem?" she asks.

"I asked Aaron to put on his socks, and he's being disobedient."

"Honey, we wear socks to church," Mom says. "Obey your dad. Hurry so we aren't late."

She heads out the door with Caleb and calls Miriam and Josh to the car from their football game in the front yard.

"I'm not wearing these shoes with socks," I say. "It's not cool."

"Son, you're more concerned with following the fashion trends of a sinful world than you are with obeying your father."

This seems like a gross mischaracterization of the situation to me. "It's just *socks*," I try to reason, but it comes out as more of a yell.

Dad doesn't yell back. He only shakes his head, crestfallen.

"Aaron, it isn't just socks. It's rebellion. This is something that I have asked you to do, and you're more worried about what other people think of your outward appearance than you are about what God thinks of your heart."

I feel like my head will explode. How did this happen? One minute I'm on my way out the door to church wearing something I feel good about. The next minute I'm arguing with my dad about being rebellious. Over socks?

"Dad, just because I don't want to wear socks with my boat shoes doesn't mean that I'm being rebellious." I'm not wearing a tie, but there's a knot at my throat, one on the inside that makes it hard to speak.

"Aaron, God gave me the responsibility of training you. Your job is to obey me. Ephesians says honoring your father and mother is the 'first commandment with promise.' You know the verse. What are the promises?"

I sigh. "That things will go well with me, and that my days will be long upon the earth," I say from memory.

Dad nods. "When I ask you to do something and you disobey and talk back, you're being rebellious. You're being like Satan. Before God cast him out of heaven, he was Lucifer, the angel of light who said 'I will be *like* the Most High.' You're saying you'll decide what's best for you."

"Dad," I plead as the tears run down my face. "I am not acting like Lucifer. I will change shoes. Please don't make me wear socks with my Top-Siders."

"Son, I want you to prove that you can submit to me by wearing socks with those shoes. It won't kill you. I promise."

"But, Dad—" I slump down on one of the stairs that leads to my bedroom.

Dad doesn't raise his voice. I feel his hand on my shoulder. His words are soft and full of compassion.

"Son, I need your eyes."

I know better than to ignore this request. I look into Dad's eyes.

"I love you very much, Aaron, but I want you to go upstairs and get some socks right now, or when we get to church, I'm going to take you downstairs to the boiler room and blister your bottom."

I don't want to be spanked, especially not at church.

I walk up the stairs and get the socks.

The music pastor is already leading the opening hymn as we walk into the auditorium and take our place in a pew near the front on the right. I'm relieved we don't have to talk to anybody before the service but can't help feeling the eyes of the congregation on my ankles as we traipse down the aisle. I know this is absurd; none of my friends care that much about clothes. That's the thing that makes me so upset when Dad says I'm worried more about what other people think than about what God thinks. It's not that I'm worried about what other people think. I just *like it*. I like feeling well dressed. I like it when my clothes look like the outfits on the guys in the JCPenney catalog.

Dad is the one who taught me we should dress up for church because it honors the Lord, but when he quotes that verse about God looking at our hearts instead of our outward appearance, I feel like he's not making sense. If God doesn't care about what we look like on the outside, then who am I really wearing socks for, besides Dad? I can't imagine that God, the creator of the universe, cares much about my socks either way.

I shove my feet under the pew. I'm relieved no one else can see my socks from here, but I still hide my feet under the pew so I can't see them, either. Looking at the socks in my boat shoes makes me feel angry all over again, and I don't like feeling angry.

The assistant pastor of our church is preaching tonight. When he came to our church with his family a couple of years ago, Mom explained that he was a Messianic Jew. "Pastor Schwartz is Jewish by birth, but he's accepted Jesus as his Messiah."

Last year, Mom and Mrs. Schwartz hosted a Passover dinner at our house. We read the story of the first Passover, in Exodus, and I was especially glad we didn't have to smear any sacrificial blood on the front door trim to keep the angel of death from killing the firstborn son—namely, me. Then we ate a strange meal of hard-boiled eggs and bitter herbs and tears (parsley dipped in salt water) while Pastor Schwartz and Dad read Old Testament verses of Hebrew prophecy and explained that the prophecy symbolized by the food item we were eating was fulfilled in Jesus, who was the true Messiah.

Tonight, I listen to Pastor Schwartz's sermon for a couple of minutes because I have to take a few notes in a half-size, three-ring blue canvas binder Dad gave me when I was in first grade. He calls it my "Life Notebook," and it has half-sheet notebook paper and dividers in it. One of the dividers is labeled QUIET TIME. I'm supposed to read the Bible every day and then write down what truth I found in that passage and how God used it to speak to my heart.

Another tab is labeled SERMON NOTES, and I'm supposed to take notes on what the speaker is preaching about. I write down several of the first things Pastor Schwartz says. He's talking about how God knew he would have to send Jesus to die for our sins before he ever created the universe, and that each one of us who is born again was "preordained" to be saved. This means God knows long before we are born whether or not we will ask Jesus to be our savior. The assistant pastor is using this word *preordain* a lot, so I write it down.

After a while, I get bored and start drawing wedding dresses.

I always think about weddings in this church auditorium, mainly because I've been to so many of them here. Dad performs lots of ceremonies, and Mom is often asked to sing. I love weddings, especially the bridal gowns. Tonight, I draw several dresses with sweetheart necklines, probably a little lower than Mom would think is modest. The one I like best has a princess waistline and a full train, with Camelot sleeves. I've learned the different names for these styles from reading the descriptions of the dresses in the bridal section of the JCPenney catalog. Camelot sleeves have been very popular lately at our church.

Finally, the sermon is wrapping up, and I decide to jot down a couple more points in case Dad wants to see my notes later. Pastor Schwartz is talking about how to handle it when Satan tempts us to doubt God's word. He reads the story in the Gospel of Mark about the father who brings his demon-possessed son to Jesus for healing. Jesus tells the father that all he must do for his son to be healed is believe. The father says to Jesus, "I believe; help thou my unbelief."

I like that Bible verse. The man seems to be saying, "I believe close to ninety percent of the time, but every once in a while I have these questions, these little things that don't make sense," and he's asking Jesus for help with that tiny ten percent.

After the closing hymn, the assistant pastor encourages us to be there next Sunday night, when a missionary family from New Guinea will talk about their work in the bush.

My family will be back again before next Sunday night. On Wednesday night, my parents will come for the weekly prayer meeting. The choir practices that night, too, and the kids who aren't old enough for youth group yet go to special meetings. The girls attend Pioneer Girls, and I join the rest of the guys in Boys' Brigade. Boys' Brigade is like a Christian version of Boy Scouts. In addition to tying knots, we memorize Bible verses each week to earn special pins and badges for our uniforms. My dentist leads the Brigade. He's very jolly, without being fat, and last week I learned how to change a tire.

After the final prayer, I tell Mom that I'm going to the bathroom and will meet the family at the car. I head straight for the parking lot, hoping no one will notice my dorky socks.

It's a long wait. Dad and Mom always have lots of people to talk to after the services at church. Everybody loves my parents. People are always asking both of them to speak at various events or Bible studies and asking Dad's advice about things. Finally, they make it to the car, too.

On the way home, Dad talks about the missionary family who will be at church next Sunday. He knows them and has asked them to speak at one of his classes at the Bible college while they are in Kansas City this week.

"I'd love to take our family to the mission field for a year," he says. "Wouldn't that be a fun adventure?"

Josh and Miriam shout their enthusiastic agreement from the fold-up seat in our station wagon's way back. I am not sure whether it would be fun or not. I like my school and my friends. I like our house. I like being able to visit Nanny at Christmas and over the summer.

Dad has been talking about taking us all to the mission field since last year, when he and Mom took a group of students on a ten-day mission trip to Costa Rica. A thought has been floating around in my brain since their return. I've been trying to ignore it. Like the socks I'm wearing right now, it's something I can feel but don't want to look at. Tonight, that word I wrote down in my notebook makes this thought finally take the shape of a question and tumble out of my mouth.

"What happens to the people who never get to hear about Jesus before they die?" I ask. "Like a tribe in a jungle that missionaries don't even know about yet?"

Dad glances in the rearview mirror. "Well, son, we believe they'll go to hell."

"But that's not fair," I say.

"No, it's not." Dad sighs in agreement. "It's not fair that we know about Jesus and don't go to tell them. That's why it's so important for our church to send missionaries to spread the Good News."

This is not what I meant at all. Sometimes, Dad has a way of reframing things that confuses me.

"Do you think maybe the Lord will call you to be a missionary one day, Aaron?"

I don't answer right away. I know how proud it would make Dad for me to go into "full-time Christian work." He wants me to be a missionary, or a music pastor, or a Christian schoolteacher when I grow up.

"I really want to be an actor."

"Well, son, you could be an actor for the Lord," he says. "Be the English and drama teacher at a Christian school and direct all the plays, or start a Christian drama group and go perform at churches all over the country."

This is not the kind of acting I am talking about. I want to be in plays and movies, like Julie Andrews, and live in Hollywood or New York. I let this go and try to get back to the point I was making about unsaved people going to hell.

"In the sermon tonight, it sounded like if someone is living in a jungle and they don't hear about Jesus before they die, it was preordained that they go to hell."

"Think of it like this, Aaron," Dad says. "Imagine a big gate that leads into heaven, and on the front side as you walk up, it says 'Whosoever will may come.' And on the back of it, after you walk through the gate, it says 'Chosen in Christ before the creation of the world.'"

I picture this gate with the signs on each side. I sort of squint as I try to understand this. "So, everyone has a choice to walk through the door of salvation, but God knows ahead of time who will make that choice?" I feel like I'm doing a brainteaser from the big book my teacher keeps on the shelves by the beanbag in our classroom.

"That's right!" Dad says.

"So, God knows what choice everyone is going to eventually make before they make it?" I ask.

"Yes, honey. Our God is omniscient," Mom says with a smile. "He knows every time a sparrow falls from the sky. He can hear your every thought."

"But that means God already knows who is getting into heaven and who isn't."

Dad nodded. "Yes, son, he does."

"So, why even give us a choice in the first place?" I ask. "Why the big test?"

"God wants us to make a *decision* to love him," Dad says. "It's why he gave Adam and Eve free will in the Garden of Eden. Sin entered the world when Adam and Eve believed the serpent's lie and disobeyed God. That's why we are all born sinners. We have to make the choice to repent and believe in Jesus."

Mom nods her head in agreement. "Sugar, God doesn't want to be worshipped by robots."

I am quiet for a minute as we pass a big movie theater. Families are walking out of the building toward their cars, and I wonder which movie they saw. If I had a choice, I'd go to the movies on Sunday night instead of church. I'll bet no one cares whether you wear socks at the theater.

A pang of guilt shoots through my stomach for even thinking that, but I can't help it. The whole thing about God knowing exactly what will happen but giving humans a choice to believe in him—even though he knows many won't or, worse, *can't* because no one has told them about Jesus—it seems like a bad plan. Like socks with boat shoes.

Dad's question about whether I want to be a missionary feels so silly now. If God already knows which people will get into heaven and which people he'll send to hell, then being a missionary seems like a waste of time. The people who are going to be saved are going to get into heaven whether I am the person who tells them about Jesus or not, right?

Has God created a bunch of people *knowing* he'll have to send them to hell to burn in torment for all of eternity? That would just make God a jerk. Surely, that can't be right. *Can it?*

My head feels foggy. I take a deep breath and say a silent prayer. *God, help me understand.*

"Tell me again," I say. "How do we know *for sure* that the Bible is true?"

Without hesitation, Mom and Dad reply instantly as one voice: "Because it says it is."

Their answer feels like sand slipping through my fingers. My stomach leaps the way it does on the first drop of the Orient Express at Worlds of Fun.

"Are you okay, Aaron?"

Dad is looking at me in the rearview mirror. I realize I am frowning, and quickly relax my face as I did when I was a little boy playing dead.

Don't move a muscle.

"Yes, sir," I say, and turn away from his gaze to look out the window.

But I am not fine. I simply don't know what else to say. As our car navigates a busy intersection, I have the sudden urge to double-check to make sure my father is still in the front seat, driving. When I see him there, it does not quiet the racing of my heart, or soothe the panic in my stomach, or calm this fear I cannot shake—that no one is at the wheel; that at any moment we might spin wildly out of control.

CHAPTER 5

"Boys and girls, let's get things started off with a song!"

It's Thursday afternoon following sock Sunday. Once more Mom greets each kid who comes for Good News Club with a hug and a smile. Once more we sing "Countdown!" Once more I show the other kids how to jump up in the air.

I can't jump as high as I did when I was younger, because I'm taller now and I can touch the ceiling of the family room, but today it's not my height stopping me. Something else is different, too. I try to figure out what it is as we finish the song, and Mom directs us all in reading aloud the Bible verse printed in the back of the rocket ship songbook: John 14:3: "And if I go and prepare a place for you, I will come again, and receive you unto myself; that where I am, there ye may be also."

I glance over at Randy, who smiles at me as we sit back down.

A few weeks before, Dad talked about Randy from the pulpit during one of the seminars he teaches for parents and Christian schoolteachers about how to raise godly children.

He explained to the congregation that Mom is a missionary right here in our family room, spreading the Good News around the neighborhood. Dad said how sad it was that when Randy first came to our house, he had never heard the name of Jesus.

"That poor boy owns every satanic toy you can buy, but he doesn't have a Bible," Dad said with a sad shake of his head. "Randy is one of our American heathens."

When Dad said the word "heathens," I got this image of Randy with a bone through his nose, wearing a grass skirt while dancing around a fire in the jungle, and a thought went through my head:

What if Randy isn't preordained?

What if he isn't one of the people God knows will get into heaven? What if he doesn't understand about the Good News *because he can't?*

Mom begins today's Bible story from the New Testament, about Jesus calming the storm with the words "Peace! Be still!" The picture of Jesus she holds up is beautifully drawn. His eyes are kind, his hair whipped back by the storm, his arms outstretched, his handsome face set firm into the wind and rain.

"Boys and girls," Mom says, "Jesus can bring peace to each one of our hearts like he calmed the angry sea two thousand years ago." She quotes Philippians: "'And the peace of God, which passeth all understanding, shall keep your hearts and minds through Christ Jesus.'"

I search for a peaceful place in my heart as she teaches, but all I can think about is Randy, dressed like a native from a tribe in the jungle, and my fear that he might be one of the people God knows won't accept Jesus. For that matter, what if *I'm* one of those people? What if I'm not *really* saved?

This idea sends a chill down my spine.

I remember sitting on the couch between Mom and Dad when I was almost three years old and asking Jesus to come into my heart. Mom wrote down the words I prayed that day in the front of my little New Testament.

How do I know that I meant it? How do I know that it worked?

Dad says the way you know someone is truly born again is if his or her actions are Christ-like. If a person displays the fruit of the Spirit in his life: love, joy, peace, patience. There's a whole list in Ephesians.

I take a quick inventory as Mom wraps up the Bible story:

I love my parents and my brothers and sister. I am kind to my friends. I help Mom teach Good News Club. On Sunday, I wore socks to church and submitted to my dad. But there are other things, too. Things Mom and Dad don't know about, like the music I listen to late at night under the covers with my clock radio. I must be saved, because this is the Holy Spirit of God convicting me about listening to music my parents wouldn't want me to. And the Holy Spirit only lives inside true believers. At least that's what Dad says.

I just wish I could know *for sure*.

For the first time, as I look around Good News Club

at all the kids watching Mom teach, I am not thrilled and excited about the Rapture. Instead, I feel a desperate sense of urgency about Jesus coming back.

And something else:

Dread.

That night, no matter how hard I pray, I can still feel the fear in my stomach.

Once I hear my brother's breathing level out on the other side of the room, I slide my clock radio off the nightstand and into bed with me. I turn the volume knob all the way down, spread part of the sheet over the radio, and switch it on. The sheet protects my face from the warm, hard plastic as I press my ear directly over the speaker. I can barely hear the sounds of 88.5 KLJC, Kansas City's home for "beautiful, sacred music."

This is the radio station operated by the Bible college where Dad teaches. The call letters KLJC stand for Knowledge of our Lord Jesus Christ. I turn the dial away from 88.5 until I hear the faint sounds of 98.1 KUDL.

Dad teaches that the moral decline of society today started with rock music and something he calls the "counterculture of the fifties and sixties."

"Elvis 'the Pelvis' Presley and the Beatles came armed with the music of rebellion," Dad says. "The emphasis of the rock drumbeat on the two and four count of every measure imitates sexual relations between a man and a woman. It's the same noise that Moses heard when he came down Mount Sinai with the Ten Commandments."

Dad considers any song with prominent drumbeats to be rock music, and frequently refers to this passage in Exodus when Moses finds the Israelites having a big celebration and worshipping a golden calf. Moses heard the music from this party and said, "The sound of war is in the camp."

Anytime we pass the music department at Walmart and Guns N' Roses is blasting, Dad says, "The sound of war is in the camp." This is why I keep the volume down and cover my radio with my ear to muffle the sound.

When the dial reaches KUDL's nightly "Kuddle Count-down," Whitney Houston is singing about how children are the future. As I listen, my eyes fill with tears. I know what I'm doing is wrong, but something about her voice sounds like relief. It soothes the fear in my chest and the doubt in my stomach.

Sometimes the singers on KUDL mention heaven, too, only it's not far away in outer space. It's a place you can visit right here on earth when you hold someone special in your arms. Bette Midler, Linda Ronstadt, Taylor Dayne, Chaka Khan, Richard Marx, and the guys from Chicago and REO Speedwagon all sing about love and longing with a choked sob in their throats. These are epic ballads with guitars and sax-ophones, a blazing key change in the middle, and a soaring high note at the end, songs that make me think of figure skaters spinning across the ice. I press my ear even closer to the speaker and imagine where the triple axels should go.

As I listen, all my worries about the Rapture and whether Randy will get into heaven fall away. The someday Whitney sings about isn't after we die—it's when I grow up. These songs aren't worried about eternity at all. They are focused on the here and now. I know this is one of the reasons Mom and Dad don't want me to listen to this music.

But I can't help it. I've already heard this music, and I love it.

After Whitney, Phil Collins sings a duet called "Separate Lives." The man and woman in this song love each other but for some reason can't be together. As I listen, hot tears of frustration fill my eyes and spill onto the sheet that covers the radio. I love my parents, but the things we want seem so different sometimes. I feel guilty, almost like I am betraying them, but instantly feel relieved that I feel guilty, because this must mean I'm saved. The Holy Spirit is doing his job to convict my heart of my sin, but I don't turn the radio off.

Instead, I decide to turn off my mind. I try to focus on the music, to let these melodies about love drown out the fear in my brain. Even this reminds me of a Bible verse: "Perfect love casts out fear." Maybe perfect love songs cast out fear, too. I smile to myself as this thought crosses my mind. Here in the songs I'm not supposed to like is one more reminder of all the things Mom and Dad have taught me.

I listen to music for a long time that night, until the plas-

tic of the radio grows hot against my ear, and the songs of
KUDL sear a melody on my heart.

Chad Paddle occupies the seat in front of me on the school
bus, and when he sees the lights of the squad car out the back
window, he calls to his mother at the wheel.

"Mom! A cop is pulling you over!"

We don't call policemen "cops" at our house. Mom says
it's disrespectful.

"They are officers of the Lord, who have the responsibility of keeping us safe," she says. "They deserve our gratitude
and respect."

Mrs. Paddle calls for all of us to be quiet, and a hush
falls over the bus. She wasn't driving too fast, that's for sure.
Sometimes it feels like it takes an hour to drive the two miles
from the Christian school we attend to our street corner. I
lean forward to hear what the policeman will say, and catch
a flash of his hat and mirrored sunglasses as he peers in Mrs.
Paddle's front window.

"Are you aware you're driving down the street with your
stop sign out?"

"Oh! Oh, no, Officer, I was not. I am so sorry." Mrs. Paddle is flustered.

"Well, ma'am, you're causin' a little confusion among the
motorists who are following you. If you could be a little more
mindful of that, we'd all appreciate it."

Causing a little confusion. The cop's understatement makes me giggle, and as the sound of my own laughter rings in my ears, I know I've made a mistake.

"Are you a *girl*?"

Chad Paddle narrows his eyes and peers at me through his glasses. He's the only boy in school who has more freckles than I do. I feel my cheeks sting and my stomach turn. I hate it when this happens.

The expressive vocal inflections that Dad says make me a good actor also apparently make me sound like a girl. I can't hear it in my head when I'm talking, but I'm always shocked by any recording of my own voice. Mom says my voice will change soon, and telemarketers will no longer assume I'm "the woman of the house" when I answer the phone.

"No," I say quietly to Chad, "I'm not a girl."

I sit back in my seat and stare down at my backpack to avoid eye contact.

"'Cause you sure *sound* like a girl," Chad says. The mocking tone in his voice makes me want to crawl under my seat. I wish he'd turn around, but I'm trapped.

"And you have big girl lips."

I've heard this before, too. I'm not sure why it's so bad to have full lips. I'm not sure why it's so bad to be compared to a girl. Why is that a put-down? I *like* girls. I like to talk to them and hang around them at recess. We play four square a lot while the other boys are playing kickball and basketball. I don't understand what's so bad about having qualities that some girls have.

But it is. I know it is. It feels like I've been kicked in the stomach.

Chad makes up a song about how I'm a girl, and as he sings, I look around to see if anyone is listening. Most of the other kids are in their own conversations. My sister, Miriam, is up front with her friend Kelly. Josh is in the back with Kelly's brother, Kevin. No one to hear.

Or to help.

Finally, the bus pulls up to our corner, and I cross the lawn and go into the house with Josh and Miriam. The smell of wet paint tickles my nose at the front door and draws me downstairs. I hear music coming from the laundry room, where I find Mom holding a wet roller and listening to KLJC.

Mom loves the laundry room. When people ask her if she has a job, she always replies with a smile and a twinkle in her eye. "Yes, I do. I work around the clock at home as a domestic engineer. I am a wife and mother, and my family is my full-time job."

Mom quit college in her senior year to have me, and she doesn't regret it.

"The work I do in the kitchen and the laundry room is the ministry the Lord has called me to. Even matching socks is very important," she says. "As I fold each pair, I pray for the little feet that go into those socks."

Today, the work Mom is doing in the laundry room does not involve laundry. She's painting the gray cinder blocks on the wall behind the washer and dryer a startling shade of white, almost shocking in its brightness beneath the fluorescent lights. When I ask her why, she fixes me with a knowing gaze and quotes a Bible verse.

"Aaron, 'Men love darkness better than light because their deeds are evil.'" She turns and rolls a wide swath of pure white across the dingy gray.

It's the way Mom quotes that verse—the tone in her voice. I know something is wrong. She reaches over and turns down the clock radio she's listening to. It's my clock radio, and it hits me in a flash: We aren't talking about the random evil deeds of generic men in unspecified darkness. We are talking about *my* evil deeds in *my* dark bedroom.

"Aaron, I went and got your radio this morning so I could listen to some music down here while I painted, and when I plugged it in, it wasn't tuned to KLJC."

My stomach sinks. I'd forgotten to tune the dial back from KUDL when I fell asleep last night.

"Before I started painting, I was folding your socks," Mom says, "and as I folded your socks I prayed, 'Oh, Heavenly Father, help my precious Aaron to have feet that run after righteousness.' Then I went upstairs and found your radio tuned to a rock-and-roll station."

There is paint on her fingers and pain in her voice. She wipes her hands on a rag.

"My precious son, who are your feet running after?"

The answer is simple: Peter Cetera.

I know there is no way to explain this to Mom. How can I tell her that 98.1 KUDL isn't a rock-and-roll station? How do I explain the difference between rock music and "adult contemporary"? Peter Cetera is burning up the charts lately with a duet called "The Next Time I Fall." His partner on this track is a singer named Amy Grant.

Even though she's a Christian singer, KLJC doesn't play Amy Grant's music anymore. I read all about her in the manila folder I discovered in Dad's file drawer. It is full of articles photocopied from magazines with parts highlighted, and notes about how ungodly Amy Grant is. She told *Good Housekeeping* about a time when she and a friend went to a topless beach, and in another interview she admitted she loves having a glass of red wine in a warm bath on her ranch outside Nashville. There were lots of other things highlighted, too, about her plunging necklines and penchant for leopard print.

When I asked Dad about it, he explained that if Amy Grant really was a Christian, she wasn't showing the fruits of the Spirit. She was allowing Satan to ruin her testimony for the Lord Jesus.

"Amy Grant isn't purposefully different from the world," he said. "She wants her music to sound like rock music. Plus, she drinks and does things that aren't a good example of Christ-like behavior."

The clock radio has little white paint spatters on it—spray from the roller.

"Do your feet run after righteousness, Aaron?" There are tears in Mom's eyes. "I called your dad at his office and told

53

him you'd been listening to rock music. He is so grieved. It was like somebody had died."

When Dad comes home, he and Mom call me into their bedroom. Dad doesn't spank me. Mom doesn't take away my clock radio. They simply ask a question:

"Why?"

I am no match for the disappointment in their eyes, and my own fill up with tears. What can I say to make this better? These are the people spending their lives trying to bring me up according to all the commands in God's word. They follow all the rules Dad teaches other parents. Now I'm the kid who is proving to be the exception to their rules. They've done everything right—so why am I already straying from the path?

Dad has an answer for me, one I've heard before. "Rebellion."

He brings up Lucifer again, and how God kicked him out of heaven for deciding to make his own decisions.

There are tears in Mom's eyes. "Aaron, the only thing I want in the whole world is for my children to love Jesus, to be used mightily by God."

Dad nods. "Son, God's word says that when there is unconfessed sin in your heart, God can't hear your prayers. Let's pray together and confess your sin of deceit and disobedience to the Lord. Ask his forgiveness so that you can be a clean vessel he can use again."

I can't bear to see this hurt in their eyes. I want this to end. I nod, and bow my head. "Dear Heavenly Father, I'm sorry for disobeying Mom and Dad and listening to rock music. Please forgive me and help me not to be deceitful."

As I pray, I make sure to use the right vocal inflection, to give the right gravity to the words, to talk slowly and humbly. I try to sound truly sorry, but now I'm lying again.

I don't want to disobey Mom and Dad, but the truth is, I don't think what I did was wrong. As much as they believe this music is rebellious, I don't. That's the funny thing about belief: No one else can do it for you. Turns out, no matter how much I want to, I can't make myself believe something I don't. It's not that I *want* to lie; I don't feel that I have a choice. I know I will always love songs like this. They don't make me feel separated from God. These songs make me feel at peace inside, the way I've always been told the presence of God will feel.

"The Next Time I Fall" is a song about being better at love, about trying again when you get it wrong. It doesn't sound like the music of witchcraft or rebellion. It sounds like the opposite of war in the camp. It sounds like peace on earth.

When I finish praying, Dad starts. "Father, we love Aaron so much. Please give him a heart for you, Lord. Help him stand strong against the temptation of Satan, so you can use him to build your kingdom. Help Aaron see how much we love him...."

Mom and Dad make these rules because they love me, but this doesn't feel like love. This is where I get confused. I know in my head they love me no matter what, but the look in their eyes, the desperation in their voices, the tears stream-ing down Mom's cheeks—all I can feel is their disapproval.

Dad often quotes a verse in Hebrews that says how God is "the same yesterday, today, and forever." My parents believe right and wrong are absolute, and I will never convince them otherwise. I know I will never change their minds about this music. I will never be able to share with them how it speaks to my soul, how it makes everything inside me feel a little bit better.

While Dad prays for me I know I am stuck. I can't stop listening to these songs, but I can't bear to feel my parents' disappointment, either. *Will I always have to choose between the two?* The fear wells up in my chest as the doubt creeps into my stomach. I open my eyes and glance down at the clock radio.

So much trouble over a song…

I get lost for a moment in the memory of Peter Cetera and Amy Grant singing about doing better next time. The tune grows louder until it drowns out Dad's voice and Mom's tears, and suddenly I realize this song that is the problem holds the answer.

Next time, I'll know better what to do.

I did it wrong this time. I got caught. Next time I won't let that happen. Next time I'll change the station back. I'll be sure I don't slip up. No more driving down the road with my stop sign out. No more confusion. From now on, I'll take extra care to be the son they need me to be.

At least while they're watching.

I can't change what I like, but I *can* do a better job of loving them—of protecting them.

When Dad finally says "amen," he and Mom hug me for a long time. Then I climb the stairs to my room with my clock radio and a new resolve.

CHAPTER 6

"What are those pictures of the chicken on your bunk?" Jason asks. I'm fifteen years old, and we've just gotten out of the showers at the bathhouse near our campsite. He's shaving while I put gel in my hair.

"It's an object lesson I'm going to teach the kids at the campfire this week."

"Object lesson?" he asks.

"Like a parable," I explain. "An earthly story with a heavenly message."

Jason is nineteen. He has blond hair and blue eyes. We're both standing at the sinks wearing only shorts and flip-flops. He rinses his razor under the faucet, then lifts his chin and slowly draws the blade up toward his square jaw.

"And in this earthly story, a *chicken* has a heavenly message for us?" he asks.

"Well...yes," I say with a grin. "Cluck-elujah, amen."

Jason leans on the sink with both hands and laughs. "You're hilarious, Hartzler."

I'm the youngest counselor at Timberlake Ranch Camp this summer. Founded by a former student of my father's, Timberlake is built around a Wild West theme in the sprawling woods along the Platte River bottoms and boasts many campsites. Some have cabins on stilts, while others are built like forts or shaped like covered wagons. In addition, there's a working ranch operation with a stable full of horses, a three-story waterslide, and a team-building obstacle course called Armageddon Island, which features physical challenges based on scriptures from the book of Revelation.

All the other counselors here this summer are in college, but when Gary, the camp director, called Dad last month looking for a student who could lead Bible time each night for the first and second graders in the covered-wagon camp, I got the job. I've taught Good News Clubs and vacation Bible schools with Mom for years now. I'm a pro. I haven't stopped listening to KUDL, but if teaching kids about Jesus were an Olympic event, I'd be a medal contender. If God is keeping score, that's got to count for something.

"Saw you talking to Allison again after lunch."

Jason has been trying to get me to ask Allison out all week. She's eighteen, tall and pretty, with bright eyes that narrow when she's about to make a joke. Nobody but me seems to remember I'm only fifteen. Everyone treats me like I'm another one of the college students. The only dates I've ever been on were with girls from church to the banquets at my Christian high school in Kansas City. Maybe Allison would say yes if I asked her out. I'm curious.

What would it be like to kiss a college girl?

Maybe the reason I don't have a girlfriend is because I've never really gotten to be alone with one.

"Did you know Allison's the Nebraska state Suffolk queen?" I ask Jason, rubbing sunscreen onto my face. Being outside most of the week has made my freckles go crazy. "Her sheep won the blue ribbon at the state fair. She has a sash and everything."

Jason snorts and shoots me a sideways smirk in the mirror. It makes me feel good when I crack him up. We've been sharing one of the covered wagons this week, and every night we lie awake and talk for hours before we fall asleep. Jason grew up in a little town way out in the middle of Iowa. His dad is a pastor, and we have a lot in common. He's been telling me stories about how he used to sneak out to drink beer and hook up with girls when he was in high school. I know Mom and Dad wouldn't approve of this, but it feels so good to meet somebody who grew up with the same rules I have and is making his own decisions.

"Where are we eating tonight?" I ask.

"I heard something about a steak house," he says.

It's Friday, our last night of counselor orientation. We have tomorrow off, and then our first batch of campers shows up on Sunday. We're driving into town tonight to have dinner with the other counselors. Jason drives an old sports car from the 1960s that he's restored and painted candy-apple red. It's so glossy it looks wet.

"Can I ride into town with you tonight?" I ask.

Jason turns and looks at me, perplexed. "Of course you're riding with me. You don't have to ask."

I smile as he turns back to the mirror and finishes with his razor. He splashes water on his cheeks and blots his face dry with the towel that was slung over his shoulder. There is something effortless and attractive about this movement, and I notice how different our bodies are. Namely, I am tall but very thin. Jason's muscles make him look like an advertisement for shaving, or for drying your face—or for manliness in general.

On the way into town, he cranks up the stereo. The speakers in his antique car are brand-new and thump with every lick of bass. He's got music I've never heard of by a singer named Roxette, and his favorite song is a pounding anthem called "The Look."

I love this music, and a smile spreads across my face as I realize I'll be able to listen to whatever I want to for the next six weeks. My parents are three hundred miles away in Kansas City. I don't have to ask their permission about anything, or worry about them finding out if I don't.

The song reaches a crescendo and suddenly cuts out. Jason pumps his fist in the air and counts "two...three...four..." and then bangs on the steering wheel as the music explodes through the speakers again at full force.

The warm, humid air whips through my hair, and as we pull up to the restaurant and see the other counselors getting out of their cars, I can't help feeling a surge of excitement that I'm finally grown up. This is what it feels like to be my own person, to have my own friends, to listen to my own music. I'm laughing and talking and feeling…free. I don't have to hurry home. I don't have to worry about curfew or explaining to Mom and Dad whom I'm going to meet where.

This is the first time I've ever been completely on my own.

After we eat, our whole group takes a stroll around the tiny, quaint town of Central City, Nebraska. Allison catches up to Jason and me with Melody, a tiny college gymnast whose blue eye shadow has metallic flecks in it. She's telling me a funny story about campers from last summer when I look up and realize that our big group of counselors has stopped.

We're all standing in front of a movie theater. In fact, we're in a line at the box office.

The theater is a historic building with a ticket booth on the sidewalk and a neon sign above the marquee that spells out the word STATE. One by one, each of our group takes a turn at the window. As I watch, my palms get sweaty. Melody is still talking, but I can't hear anything she's saying as Jason buys a ticket. He's my ride. Am I going to sit on the curb for two hours while he watches the movie?

This is that moment, the one Mom talks about—the moment when I have to decide for myself which choice I'll make.

Mom and Dad will never know you disobeyed them.

The voice in my head is loud and clear, but then my conscience kicks in. It's a tiny whisper that answers back:

God will know you disobeyed.

Mom and Dad are hundreds of miles away in Kansas City, but it feels like they are right here looking over my shoulder. Mom says the Holy Spirit is the still, small voice inside me who helps me resist temptation. He knows *everything*. Every word. Every action. Every thought.

Sharing your brain with God can be handy when you need to pray in a hurry:

God, help me to remember the formula for the circumference of a circle.

God, help me not to mess up on the piano solo I'm playing in church.

God, please don't let Dad take us to Panama next year to be missionaries.

It can also be exhausting. At moments when decisions need to be made quickly, the idea that God can hear my every thought always gets in the way and gums up the works. It makes some decisions very difficult, especially this one.

"You comin', man?" Jason asks.

I smile but say nothing.

"I'm going to go in and save seats," he says. As he holds open the door for Melody and Allison, he jerks his head toward them and grins, mouthing the words *Hurry up!* over his shoulder.

I watch them disappear into the theater with the other counselors, and for a moment I stand alone on the curb. My heart is racing. My mouth is dry. Finally, I square my shoulders and step up to the ticket window.

"One for *Hunt for Red October*, please."

Unless Jesus comes back in the next two minutes, I am going to break one of Mom and Dad's biggest rules. My cheeks are hot. I feel out of breath. A drop of sweat trickles down my back, but the girl behind the glass doesn't even look up at me. She has no idea what is happening in my head, what a big deal this is for me. She couldn't be less interested.

I slide a five-dollar bill under the window. She hands back a small yellow ticket between neon nails so long they curve.

"Enjoy the show."

I take a deep breath.

I take a look over my shoulder.

I take the ticket.

Ever since *E.T.*, I've always known that one day I'd break the movie rule, but I sure didn't see it coming *today*. In all my midnight imaginings of this moment, I never considered it might happen at a historic theater in Nebraska, but as I walk through the front door, I realize something:

This place is perfect.

There is a sense of history here—the dark wood and plush velvet curtains hold a grandeur that matches the momentousness of the event. I feel a surge of excitement. This is dangerous but thrilling. For the first time in my life, I am actually living something I've dreamed about, learning that a midnight imagining can leap out of the darkness and splash across the hi-def, full-color, Dolby surround-sound screen of your life in a place where you least expect it. Like Nebraska.

My fingers are sweaty around the little yellow ticket as I walk from the box office across the lobby toward the

64

door that leads into the theater. My knees are shaking, so I pause briefly by the concession stand, but not because I want popcorn.

You can still walk out. You can sit on the curb and wait for Jason.

Is this the voice of God's Holy Spirit encouraging me to do the right thing? I don't want to wait on the curb. This is my chance. Mom and Dad will never know.

Dad's voice pops into my head: "Integrity is doing the right thing even when God is the only one watching."

Well, God and, in this case, the popcorn guy.

"Our Almighty God loves you so much he keeps track of the hairs you lose," Mom likes to remind me. "He knows the secrets you'd never tell anyone else."

Since I was a little boy I've believed that God is omnipresent, but for the first time, it strikes me as *odd*. Is it *weird* that I think there's an invisible being listening to every thought I have at every moment? Do I really believe if I walk into this theater, God is going in with me? Do I think God cares whether I go see a movie?

I know Mom and Dad care. They would say this is a choice between honoring them and disobeying them; that pleasing God in this case means obeying them—sitting on the curb for a couple of hours and missing the movie.

"Want anything, man?" The popcorn guy sounds impatient.

I want parents who don't think going to see a movie is a big deal.

I shake my head. "No. Thanks."

Popcorn Guy heads outside for a smoke. I feel so frustrated—
with the situation, with my own indecision.

I want to go to this movie.

This thought isn't the voice of God, or Mom, or Dad. It's
my own voice. I recognize it instantly, and the moment I do,
all the other voices in my head flip off like a switch. Stillness
drops like a curtain across the space between my ears. The
silence is deafening.

Now I can hear the other sounds in the room: Jason and
Allison laughing around the corner in the theater, the hum of
the ice machine behind the concession counter. In the lobby
of the State Theater in Central City, Nebraska, for the first
time ever, I feel completely...

Alone.

It only lasts for a split second. Popcorn Guy walks back
in from his smoke. I tell him I've changed my mind. I order
a big bucket of popcorn with lots of butter, and a large Coke.
Then I slip the yellow ticket stub into the hip pocket of my
jeans and step inside the theater.

"Boys and girls, how many of you live on a farm?"

Hands fly up around the campfire. Not surprising.
Nebraska has a lot of agriculture.

"Well, our story tonight is about a boy named Jimmy, and
he lived on a farm, like a lot of you do. One of Jimmy's chores
was to gather the eggs laid by his favorite hen, Speckles.

Speckles was a beautiful bird, and Jimmy loved her more than anything else in the whole world. He took her fresh water and food every day, and Speckles would cluck and come running when she saw him."

I always modify the story to fit the audience. If it's mainly girls, I play up the petting and nuzzling. Girls like a pretty Speckles, so I describe her two-toned coppery feathers in detail. If the crowd is mostly boys, I go heavy on the "pals" part of the story. There is a lot of playing in the fields, and tree climbing. There are adventures for this chicken that are undoubtedly beyond the realm of most commercial egg-laying operations.

Jason is grinning and hides his face at this part of the story. It's ridiculous, and he knows it. I don't mind. I'm telling a good story. This is the hook.

"One morning, Speckles wasn't in the henhouse, and Jimmy couldn't find her anywhere!"

There are gasps from the girls in Melody's covered wagon. I see her put an arm around one of them and reassure her. A little boy from Jason's cabin shouts out, "Oh, no!"

After telling about Jimmy's exhaustive search for his hen, I show the picture of Speckles sitting on a nest hidden in the tall grass along the fence on the back forty. There is palpable relief around the campfire, and then excitement as Jimmy goes down to check on Speckles's nest each day for weeks until one day the eggs hatch. Jimmy is thrilled, and he plans to move Speckles and her chicks back to the henhouse the next morning.

That night, Jimmy wakes up to a great commotion, the smell of smoke, and the light of tall flames leaping up from the field behind the barn. Lightning has ignited a grass fire, and Jimmy has to work through the night with the farmhands and his dad, hauling water to put out the fire.

The next morning when Jimmy goes to the place where Speckles's nest had been, he finds only her charred remains. As he starts to cry, Jimmy nudges her body with his foot, and six fluffy chicks begin to peep, wobbling out from beneath Speckles's lifeless wings.

"You see, boys and girls," I explain, "when Speckles smelled the smoke and saw the flames racing toward her, she realized that there was no escape. She gathered her chicks under her in the nest and spread her wings over them. As the flames passed over her body, Speckles made the greatest sacrifice of all for her chicks. She covered them with her feathers so that they would be saved. She died so that her children could live."

Tears fill my eyes as I say these words. There is something about this story of sacrifice that quickens my heart each time I tell it, and breaks me open inside. This is the heavenly message of the "object lesson." This is a parable about one person loving another enough to die.

No one around the circle of logs at the campfire is smiling anymore, not even Jason. Melody and the girls on the log next to her stare up in rapt attention. I can see their eyes glistening in the firelight as the Nebraska sky turns deep shades of indigo behind me, the sun's last rays shooting over the tops of pine trees at the edge of the clearing ringed by our covered-wagon cabins.

I quote my favorite Bible verse to the boys and girls, from Psalms, chapter 91: "'He that dwelleth in the secret place of the most High shall abide under the shadow of the Almighty.... He shall cover thee with his feathers, and under his wings shalt thou trust.'

"Boys and girls, just like Speckles spread out her wings to cover her chicks, Jesus spread out his arms and allowed Roman soldiers to nail his hands and feet to a cross."

The children are silent as I tell them how God the Father requires a blood sacrifice for the forgiveness of our sins—the things that we have each done wrong. God cannot allow sin into heaven, and I quote the book of Romans: "For the wages of sin is death, but the gift of God is eternal life through Jesus Christ our Lord."

I explain atonement—how God sent Jesus to die so that we could live forever. Jesus took our place on the cross and paid the price of our sins. His death spares us from the eternal death of a fiery hell, just as Speckles spared her chicks from the flames.

"Boys and girls, who can tell me what the Good News is?"

Hands fly up all around the circle. A little boy shouts out, "Jesus is coming back!"

I smile and nod. "Yes! That's part of it. He's coming back because he is risen. Jesus died, just like Speckles, but the Good News is that, unlike Speckles, Jesus didn't stay dead!"

I use the same breathless excitement Mom uses as I

explain that Jesus rose from the grave on the third day, conquering death and making it possible for everyone to have eternal life. "All you have to do to go to heaven when you die is pray and ask Jesus to forgive your sins."

I ask all the boys and girls to bow their heads and close their eyes.

"If Jesus came back right this minute, would he leave you behind or take you to heaven?" I ask. "If you don't know whether you're going to heaven or hell when you die, you can be certain before you crawl into your sleeping bag," I assure them. "If you'd like to talk to a counselor about accepting Jesus as your savior, raise your hand right now."

In the orange glow of the flames at the center of our circle, I see hands fly into the air all around—little hands reaching up toward me to ask for help, to find comfort, to be saved from the fire.

When the boys in our covered wagons are settled into their bunks for the night, Jason finds me by the dying campfire and sits down on the log next to me.

"Nice work tonight," he says.

"Thanks." I smile and peer back into the flames.

"You really got into that story. The kids loved it. You're good at that."

He's right. I *am* good at it. More than once Dad has told entire churches full of people how proud he is of me when I help Mom teach Good News Club, how I win boys and girls to Christ; how if you train your kids right, they'll be able to train others.

But what am I good at, exactly?

This is the question that nags at me as I sit in the dark next to Jason, staring into the low flames. The story of Speckles hasn't changed since the first time I told it in Good News Club several years ago, but I have changed. Tonight as I looked into the eyes of the children watching me talk about flames and hell, I realized Speckles's sacrifice isn't beautiful.

It's horrible.

I must've really scared the little kids around the campfire. If *I'm* afraid of hell, imagine how terrified they must be of it. Eternal torment and crucifixion are heavy issues to raise with first- and second-grade campers. That's why I was trained to do it with an object lesson about a little boy, his pet hen, and the day she became an extra-crispy value meal in order to save her offspring.

I know it's dark enough that Jason probably can't see the tears streaming down my face, but I keep staring into the fire just in case. I don't really care if he sees me crying, but I am glad that if he's noticed, he hasn't said anything. If he asks me what's wrong, I don't think I can tell him.

The truly sad part of the Speckles story—the part I realize now has always made me cry—isn't her selfless act; that's the basic instinct of an animal protecting its young. The heartbreak I feel is because we never find out what happens to Jimmy. All we know is that he loses the thing that is most precious to him in the whole world. From his perspective, the idea of atonement seems horrifying. It seems like the worst idea ever.

I feel like everyone else is satisfied with the leap comparing Speckles to Jesus, but I'm not. A rope of fear tightens around my stomach—fear that his atonement doesn't apply to me. I desperately want to feel the comfort of that psalm about being covered with big wings. There seems to be a promise of safety nestled in those feathers, or maybe it's a promise of flight.

As I stare into the fire, I say a silent prayer to that God with the big wings of protection: *Help thou my unbelief.*

But it feels silly, like a spark from the popping logs that shoots into the darkened sky, then vanishes into nothingness.

The air between Jason and me feels electric. I am sitting on a log at a campfire in the middle of the woods, next to a college student who is so much cooler than I am. I am crying, and he is pretending not to notice, and I think this may be the nicest thing any guy has ever done for me.

I remember how last Friday night it started to rain as we sped home from the State Theater, and Jason turned up the music. As Wilson Phillips sang about arrows through hearts drawn on a misty window, I held on to my little yellow ticket stub and felt like my life was finally beginning. I wasn't the guy who is a whiz at teaching Bible stories to kids, or who plays the piano in church, or who makes my dad proud.

I was just *myself.*

I'm not sure how long I can go on making my parents proud. For the past fifteen years, I've been to church three times a week and attended a Christian school Monday through Friday. I've learned enough to know the atonement Mom and Dad believe in is absolutely free for the taking, but that gleam of pride in their eyes comes with some strings attached. I have a hard time telling the difference between their love and their approval, and when my actions don't live up to their standards, I feel like I've lost both.

The choice that gnaws at my stomach isn't between heaven and hell. I have a hunch that God isn't disappointed with me, but my parents are a different story. I know in my head that Mom and Dad love me, but I can sense in my heart that I'm going to have to choose between their approval and making my own decisions—doing the things that feel right to me.

I can't find the words to tell Jason any of this. So we sit here in silence and watch the campfire shoot sparks into the sky until all that remains is a molten mound of glowing embers. I sneak a quick swipe at my face in the darkness and dry my cheeks with my hand. Then we stand up and head back to the covered wagons we call home.

"We've got the next two nights without campers," Jason says. "I was thinking maybe we could drive in to Grand Island for dinner tomorrow night."

"Excellent," I say, and smile. "That'd be really cool." Jason's car seats only two. It'll just be us.

"Want to do anything special?" he asks.

I smile at him in the moonlight. "Let's go see a movie."

CHAPTER 7

Our waiter is tall and handsome, with dark hair. When he drops off my Diet Coke, I notice he's wearing a silver ring on his left index finger. It's a wide band brushed to a dull sheen. After he takes our order, Dad thanks him, then grasps Mom's hand and addresses his four children.

"Kids, we came to a nice restaurant today because it's Aaron's sixteenth birthday." He turns to me, smiling like he does when I play the piano in church, his eyes shining with pride and affection. "Son, we want to consecrate your young adult life to the Lord Jesus Christ, and the Olive Garden seemed like just the special place to do that."

"Oh, Aaron," Mom gasps, "do you know what I was doing at this exact moment sixteen years ago today?"

"Lamaze breathing?" I know it's a rhetorical question, but I can't resist. Mom can tell you where we were and what we ate for dinner on almost any random date for the last twenty years.

"Oh, no, honey." She laughs. "I was all finished with labor

by this point. I was holding you in my arms and thanking God for my firstborn son."

"Aaron, you have grown into a good-looking young man," Dad says, "and soon Satan will begin to shoot his fiery darts of sexual temptation your way."

As the words "sexual temptation" tumble from my father's lips a little too loudly, our waiter appears. I see him freeze briefly, then recover and place a large bowl of salad and a basket of garlic breadsticks on the table as Dad continues.

"Aaron, your mother and I have gotten you a very special birthday gift that will be a symbol of your commitment to physical purity."

I glance up, hoping that by some miracle the waiter has missed this comment, but he is looking right at me, and I feel my cheeks flush. I drop my gaze and try to distract myself with a sip from my straw, but my glass is already empty.

"I'll be right back with a refill for you," the waiter says. He has bright, kind eyes. "Can I get you anything else?"

I shake my head no, and he heads toward the kitchen.

"Let's pray and bless the food," Dad says, "then Aaron can open his gift."

We all hold hands in a circle around the table, bow our heads, and close our eyes. Dad begins to pray in the middle of the Sunday afternoon Olive Garden lunch rush.

"Lord, we want to thank you for this special time and for Aaron and what a fine young man he is growing up to be...."

As Dad continues to talk to God over our bottomless basket of breadsticks, I can sense the other diners in the restaurant staring at us. It always feels weird to hold hands and pray in public. As usual, that feeling is followed by a pang of guilt for feeling weird about it. As a Christian, this is one of the ways I can show my faith to the unsaved world. It is a simple, quiet act that speaks volumes: Our family believes in Jesus Christ. We pray over meals in restaurants.

Usually, I keep my eyes closed and just pretend that if I can't see the other people, they can't see me, but today is different. I sense someone approach the table, and I open my eyes to see our waiter standing behind Dad with a fresh Diet Coke, waiting respectfully for us to finish praying. This time when our eyes meet, I don't look away.

Neither does he.

I smile and shake my head. *Can you believe this?* I silently telegraph to him over my father's bowed head. He winks at me and smiles.

I don't mind praying. I just wish we didn't have to make such a big scene of it in public. Why can't we pray in the car before we come into the restaurant? Usually, prayer is this thing we do in private—a personal conversation between us and God. Jesus even taught a parable about not praying on the street corner like a Pharisee but showing you are repentant and humble by keeping your prayers out of sight. Restaurants require a prayer of the evangelical variety, it seems. Praying in restaurants is all about other people seeing us do it. It's our faith on offense. One more way we can prove we're not ashamed of Jesus; one more way to spread the Gospel; one more way to show we are different from the unsaved world, when all I really want right now is not to stand out.

"...so we thank you for all your blessings to us but most of all for the blood of your son, Jesus. And it's in his name we pray, amen."

Dad wraps up his prayer and the waiter delivers my Diet Coke. "Here you go." He smiles. "I'll be right back with your food."

I watch him walk away as Mom reaches into her purse and hands me a tiny wrapped package. I am excited, but I'm not sure it's the present. Something about the moment I shared with the waiter made me feel like an understanding had passed between us.

I tear the paper from the present and feel the flocked fabric of a small, velvet-covered box. I'm pretty sure I know what this is, and when I pop open the box, I am not surprised. Inside is an eighteen-karat gold signet ring etched with a large *A* in the kind of calligraphy I saw once in a picture of a Gutenberg Bible.

"Wow," I say. "Thank you."

Dad's voice is husky with emotion. "Son, every time you're alone with a young lady from now until the day you get married, this ring will be on your finger to remind you of your promise to the Lord Jesus Christ to remain morally and physically pure until your wedding night."

"Oh, darling!" Mom is smiling, her eyes bright with tears. "Think how happy you'll be in the honeymoon suite on the night you're married when you'll be able to slip this ring off your finger and give it to your new bride—the best wedding gift of all: your virginity."

"Wait, let me get this straight." Jason is laughing so hard there are tears running down his cheeks. "You're supposed to give it to your wife when you get married? On your wedding night?"

We are in the dinner line at the Bible college cafeteria. It's Friday night, and I got permission from Mom and Dad to spend the night in Jason's dorm room tonight. When I lifted my green melamine tray onto the rails along the hot-food line, he noticed the gold ring on my left hand.

"Yeah," I say. "It's supposed to remind me not to do anything impure with girls."

Jason wipes his eyes and nods. "Well...that's cool, man. I mean, I guess that's a good thing."

Conversations about sex always take this weird turn with Jason. He's had sex, but he wasn't supposed to, and somehow feels he has to encourage me not to do it before I'm married, either. Technically, he's doing the right thing—the thing my parents would want him to do. The rules at the Bible college and my Christian high school are the same: If it's discovered you've been having sex, you get kicked out. Every once in a while somebody gets kicked out for getting pregnant, or getting someone pregnant. The message is always made clear: God will forgive these individuals if they repent, but they can never be virgins again. There's a great sadness around the loss of virginity, the loss of a potential intimacy with one's future spouse. As Dad says, "If you disobey God's plan by not waiting for marriage, you'll never know the special joys of only having been intimate with one other person."

The funny thing is, when I look at Jason, I want to be just like him. I don't feel like it's a sad thing that he's not a virgin. I don't think he does, either. I feel like he's part of a cool club I'm not supposed to want to join. Of course, I've never even had the opportunity to join it. I've hardly even come close. I kissed a girl who was working in the camp kitchen while we were at Timberlake last summer, but only once, and that was the week my parents showed up to take me home.

I left camp in a hurry. Right before the last two weeks, my parents arrived unannounced. They were *concerned*. I'd been too hard to get in touch with, and there were rumors I was running around with some college students of questionable integrity. I hadn't saved a cent of the money I'd been earning, and they'd heard about the magnetic earrings Jason and I had worn back to camp one weekend.

They didn't ask me if I wanted to leave; they simply announced they were taking me home. So I packed my stuff and climbed into the car. It wasn't up for discussion—just like the ring they gave me last week.

The ring itself doesn't bother me. It's not like I'm getting lots of offers to rush out and have sex. Even if I was, I'm not certain I would want to. Still, there's an annoying thought that buzzes in my ears like a mosquito each time I glance down at my left ring finger. Whether or not I will wait until I am married to have sex was never up for discussion.

There's something I've heard countless times at church and my Christian school since I was a little boy: "God says it. I believe it. That settles it." I know my feelings about issues like this don't change the truth of God's word—or Mom and Dad's opinion about what's best for me. I look around the cafeteria and realize none of these Bible college students are supposed to have sex before marriage, either. We're all saving ourselves, and cheerful about it. As I look around the room, I can't shake the thought that I have no power over some very basic things. It feels like ankle-deep mud sucking at my sneakers. I'd probably agree I'm not ready to have sex yet, but it sure would be nice to be asked if I was.

After we're done eating in the cafeteria, Jason and I check movie times and drive to a theater across town from the Bible college. There's a mall with a theater nearby, but we skip it. Jason isn't supposed to go to movies, either, during the semester, and we don't want to risk running into anybody we know headed to Banana Republic while we're at the ticket window.

Jason and I went to at least one movie every weekend last summer, and sometimes we'd see two or three. I've seen several more with him since we've been back from camp. I tell Mom and Dad we're "going to the mall" or "hanging out at the college," and then we go to the theater. Each time I sneak around to see a movie, I feel less guilty about it. Mom would say this is because I've seared my conscience.

"Aaron, once you quench God's Holy Spirit by ignoring his still, small voice in your heart, it becomes easier and easier to ignore him and to sin in the future," she told me once. "It's like the scar tissue from a burn forms around your heart. Once you build up that layer of dead skin with no nerve endings, you can't feel the heat, and you'll hurt yourself again and again and not feel a thing."

As we drive to the theater, I know there's no way we'll get caught tonight, but I'm still a little scared. It makes me think about a sermon Dad preaches called "Teaching Children the Fear of the Lord," where he quotes Proverbs 9:10: "The fear of the Lord is the beginning of wisdom." Dad says the word *fear* in the original Hebrew doesn't mean "respect." It means a healthy terror before an all-powerful God.

As we park at the theater, I look down at my gold ring. Do I have a healthy terror of an all-powerful God? Not so much. I think I have a healthy terror of what my parents will do if they find out I've been sneaking around. I've decided God doesn't care about my going to see a movie, but I know my parents do. I'm still nervous they'll find out somehow, but the pull of Julia Roberts is no match for the knot of nerves in my stomach. She's been my favorite actress since I saw her in *Pretty Woman* last summer. The movie tonight is a thriller. She plays the wife of an abusive husband and fakes her own death to escape him.

Jason and I speed back to the Bible college dorm and make it right on time for curfew. He does push-ups every night before he gets into bed, and tonight he insists that I join him.

"Drop and give me fifty, Hartzler," he barks with a grin. He's wearing only his boxers, and his chest and arms are flushed from the set he's just done.

"Fifty? I'll be lucky if I can do ten."

"Well, you gotta start somewhere," he says. "C'mon." He shoves a pile of laundry out of the way and watches my form. I surprise us both and crank out twenty before I collapse.

"Nice job, man! Let's see." Jason jerks his head toward the mirror where he's flexing. I hesitate, then pull my shirt over my head. The very faintest of lines has appeared down the middle of my chest between my pecs. I'm still pretty skinny, but I can see the promise of some definition there, and smile.

"Attaboy," says Jason. "We'll have you all ripped up in no time. The ladies won't be able to keep their hands off you."

"That's exactly what my dad is afraid of."

Jason laughs and starts taking out his contacts. I stand at the mirror and try to imagine a girl sliding her hands across my chest and gripping my arms. What would that feel like? Would girls really want to touch me? I glance at Jason's back reflected in the mirror. He's bent over the sink brushing his teeth. I can see why girls would want to touch Jason's muscles. I steal one more glance at myself. I'm no He-Man, but I look okay, I decide. I should do push-ups more often.

I slip my T-shirt back on and climb up onto the top bunk while Jason settles on the bottom. We talk for a long time about this girl Jason is going to ask out, and my parents, and how they'd freak if they knew we'd gone to a movie tonight.

"Don't worry, man. There's no way they'll find out," he says. "Besides, what they don't know won't hurt 'em."

The trouble is, they believe it *will* hurt *me*. Jason drifts off to sleep, but I'm wide awake thinking about how a Julia Roberts movie could be bad for me. It isn't that Mom and Dad are being strict for the sake of being strict. They're afraid I'll see people do things in movies and I'll decide it's okay for me to do those things, too. To them, it's simple: black and white. They've made these rules to protect me.

As I lie on Jason's top bunk, I wish it felt that simple to me. I wish I could protect Mom and Dad from who I've become. Ever since that day with the radio in the laundry room, I've been careful to show them the son they want me to be. I'm good at teaching kids, and singing songs, and playing the piano—I even enjoy all those things. But I also like Whitney Houston, and movies with Julia Roberts.

And that's what troubles me. I'm very good at pretending. Dad taught me how to act and I learned well. What they don't know won't hurt them, but how long can I keep hiding it from them? Mom and Dad might not ever find out I went to a movie tonight, but I know I won't be able to protect my parents from who I am forever. Eventually, they will find out, no matter how careful I am.

It could happen today.

It could happen tomorrow.

It's only a matter of time.

EXODUS

noun \ˈek-sə-dəs\: a mass departure

CHAPTER 8

A few seconds after the bell rings, I spot Daphne in her cheerleading uniform and slide into the desk she's saved for me. Not that it matters. Mr. Gregg is late to history class again.

"Welcome to the jungle," Daphne says, raising her voice over the din of our unsupervised classroom. This is the period following lunch. Near-lethal doses of Hostess snack cakes and Coca-Cola are flowing through the veins of our classmates.

"Thrilled to be here," I say.

Daphne is one of the few African American students in grades seven through twelve at Blue Ridge Christian School. We met on the first day of seventh grade, and over time she's become my best friend. From my short-lived, four-game appearance as the first male on the junior high cheerleading squad in eighth grade, to her house burning down during our freshman year, Daphne and I have weathered a number of ordeals, which have run the physical and emotional gamut from ridiculous to life-threatening.

"Where were you?" she asks.

"Going over my scenes one last time." Miss Tyler is holding auditions for the high school play this afternoon.

"Are you nervous?" Daphne asks.

"Butterflies." I point at my stomach. "I could barely eat."

A shriek pierces the air from the far side of the room. Daphne jerks, whipping around in her seat as if stunned by a jolt of high voltage.

"Is that *really* necessary?" she asks in the general direction of the tumult. Her question is ignored, and she turns back to me with a sigh.

"Aaron, let's describe the class."

Without hesitation I turn toward the mob scene in front of us and assume the dulcet tones of a pro-golf color commentator:

"Welcome to Mr. Gregg's fifth-period U.S. history class, ladies and gentlemen. I'm Aaron Hartzler and this is Daphne Walker. If you're just joining us now, we'll try to catch you up on the action already in progress. Dan Krantz seems to be experiencing a full demonic possession as he stands on his chair singing Jerry Lee Lewis's 'Great Balls of Fire' in a special vocal style that can best be described as Helen Keller with a kidney stone."

Daphne laughs and continues narrating where I leave off.

"Rick Street is passing a copy of his father's *Playboy* magazine around the room in a Trapper Keeper folder as Stephanie Gutierrez practices a new cheer she's just made up with the words of the Preamble to the United States Constitution."

We continue to crack each other up by quietly summarizing what is going on around us until our teacher arrives. Later, when Mr. Gregg asks Stephanie to name the country he is pointing to on the map, she responds, "Texas." Daphne turns to me and raises her eyebrows while I gently knock my forehead against my notebook.

This is why we're best friends. There is an understanding between us. We *get it*. There's a strange comfort in knowing another person bears witness to the absurd moments going on around you—the ones no one else seems to question. Every time Daphne catches my eye, a silent acknowledgment passes between us, and I know I'm not alone.

When the bell rings, we gather our books.

"Staying for the game tonight?" she asks.

I nod. "I'm not sure the clarinet is really necessary in a pep band, but for a game against Tri-City, it's the best seat in the house."

I don't really care about basketball that much, but the Crusaders of Tri-City Christian School are our biggest rivals. Last season we lost to them on our home court when our best player was ejected from the game for goosing the ref over a bad call.

"Yes, who knows what drama may erupt on the court tonight?" Daphne says. "Meet me in the gym after school and we'll go get some food before the game."

"I'll be there right after I get the lead in the play."

"Break a leg," she says.

This is why I love Daphne. She's never been in a play, but she knows you don't say "good luck" before a theater performance. She *gets it*. I smile all the way down the hall to the drama room door.

"How'd your audition go?"

Daphne and I are sitting in the bleachers watching Tri-City's basketball team and cheerleaders warm up.

"It went well," I say, but Daphne's not buying it.

"*Well?*" she asks. "It went '*well*'?"

I can't contain my smile. "I nailed it," I whisper.

"That's more like it. Which role do you want?"

"It's the supporting male lead," I say. "He's got all the funny lines. Miss Tyler was laughing out loud every time I read."

"Of course she was." Daphne smiles. "When does the cast list go up?"

"Monday morning."

A stray basketball flies toward where we're sitting. I catch it on a bounce and toss it back to a Tri-City player who has bounded over to fetch it. He is tall and muscular, with curly brown hair.

"Nice pass," says Daphne. "You know, you really could've been a basketball star. How tall are you now?"

"Six two," I say. "And no, I could not have been a basketball star. You remember why I quit."

"Oh, right." She laughs. "Didn't you make a layup for the wrong team?"

"Worse. I *missed* a layup for the wrong team." I am laughing, too. "And that was *after* I went to basketball camp that summer and won the Hustle Award."

Daphne can barely talk, gasping with her special brand of quiet laughter. "Wait. The *Hustle Award*? Is that like Most Improved Player or something?"

"No, Daphne. It is *not* like Most Improved Player. Most Improved Player is a separate award, an entirely different thing. The handsome plaque *I* received was for the player who tried the hardest *without* improving."

It feels good to laugh with Daphne about this. Two years ago it was no laughing matter. I hated basketball because I wasn't good at it. Dad started for his college team and has coached at the college off and on. I certainly inherited his genes, but his knack for and love of the game are sorely missing from my makeup. We've always had a hoop in the driveway, and Josh and Miriam are naturals.

They *love* it.

They *get it*.

I don't.

I have never liked the game enough to practice. I like playing the piano in the family room more than I do one-on-one in the driveway, and after I didn't make the junior high team that fall in eighth grade, I was relegated to the intramural B team. In our first intramural game someone passed me the ball, and I went for a layup at the A team's basket. Luckily—or embarrassingly—I missed. I was mortified.

That night I told my dad, "I don't understand why millions of people do this for fun."

He laughed and said, "You know I don't care if you play basketball."

"Really?" I asked. "Because I'd so much rather play the piano."

"Aaron," he said, "I'm so proud of you. You have so many talents. If you don't want to play basketball, you don't have to. Besides, music is the only thing that the Bible says for sure will be in heaven. Spend your time practicing the piano. You'll be good at that for all eternity."

I watch the guy from Tri-City with the curly hair go up for a three-point jump shot. His form is perfect. *Swish.* Nothin' but net.

"*That's* what a star basketball player looks like," I tell Daphne, but she is watching the Tri-City cheerleaders rehearse their halftime routine and pyramid.

"Their skirts are so *long.*..." Her voice trails off.

"Nearly tea-length," I say.

Tri-City Christian is run by a big independent Baptist church and is well known for superconservative rules and a strict dress code. The mascot is the Crusader, a knight with plumes coming out of his helmet. Even when the Tri-City cheerleaders jump, their knees stay covered. It fits somehow, these long skirts on the Crusader women. It seems almost chivalrous, as if when they leave the basketball court, they'll return to a royal court waiting for them somewhere in Blue Springs, a suburb to the east of the Kingdom of Kansas City.

"How can they even jump in those things?" Daphne asks. "I'd get my foot hung in the hem and break my neck."

"It's baffling," I agree. "Like they're cheerleaders from *Little House on the Prairie*."

"Whatever. It's nice that they have a couple of black guys on their basketball team. At least it adds some color to the contest."

"Red and gold isn't enough for you?" I ask, nodding at the Native American warrior painted on the floor of our gym.

"No, Aaron, it's not," she says with a smile. "And frankly, I think our mascot may be a little bit racist."

"It could be worse," I say. "At least we're not the Redskins."

"I suppose you're right." She checks her watch. "Well, I should go greet the Tri-City squad."

"Don't you mean 'Tri-*Pity*'?" I ask with a smirk. Everyone has been referring to our rivals with this nickname all week in anticipation of the game.

Daphne rolls her eyes. "Be nice," she says. Then she winks at me and walks toward the corner of the gym to say hello to the girls whose knees are covered by purple and gold.

Every so often a family from Tri-City will migrate to Blue Ridge. They come bearing horror stories: Girls have to wear culottes during PE class and bring their junior/senior banquet dresses in to have them approved by a female teacher for "modesty" before the big night. The guys tell stories about getting into serious trouble for going to see movies or listening to the wrong music—they've been benched from their sports games, kicked out of the musical groups and other extracurricular activities.

I only know a couple of people who go to school there, acquaintances from a church camp I've attended; but because Dad trains lots of Christian schoolteachers at the Bible college, he knows a lot of people on staff at Tri-City. He's friends with the principal and even speaks in their chapel services every now and then. Dad tends to defend the rules and the administration at Tri-City.

"They are a little strict about some things," he says, "but their kids sure have an excellent testimony for Christ. They know how to train students who have a sweet spirit about the things of the Lord."

Maybe they do, but the students who transfer to Blue Ridge all have a special bond: the camaraderie of people who have survived something together. You never hear about a family pulling their kids out of Blue Ridge and sending them to Tri-City. It's always the other way around, and we're proud to keep it that way.

A game against Tri-City sets everyone here at Blue Ridge on edge—even a lot of the parents who attend. None of the adults say it out loud, but it feels like there's this attitude in the air—that because Tri-City has stricter rules and longer skirts, they must think they're better than we are somehow.

It's almost as if they're the Crusaders of old, storming Jerusalem to bring truth to the infidels by force.

The rivalry is fierce, and tonight is no exception. The metal bleachers lining both sides of the gymnasium seem to hum with an electric current, and the fans on both sides are on their feet most of the time.

Tri-City has twin guards, and the guy I tossed the ball to before the game is their starting center. I find myself watching him as he sinks shot after shot. He never seems to lose his cool, no matter how physical the fouls get. He nails a final jumper at halftime to tie the game, and as I play "Louie Louie" on my clarinet with the pep band, he looks over at us on the stage that stretches across one end of the gymnasium.

A slow smirk spreads across his face. He shakes his head, then turns and jogs into the visitors' locker room with the rest of his team. He is so calm and collected it's almost unnerving—like he has prior knowledge of a secret weapon that will ensure their success. In that moment, I know somehow that we will lose, and I am correct. At the final buzzer, Blue Ridge is down by two.

While I am putting away my clarinet and Dan Krantz is packing up his trumpet, Dan sees the tall, curly-haired center zipping his warm-up jacket and heading toward the door and the Tri-City team's bus in the parking lot. As the player passes us, Dan slams his trumpet case and speaks loudly enough so the guy will hear him.

"These Tri-*Pity* kids," he says in disgust. "They think they're so much better than us."

The guy from the other team stops and slowly turns around. He looks at Dan, then at me.

I glance up at the scoreboard. "Tonight, they *were* better than us."

Dan huffs and jumps off the stage into the throng in the gym as the Tri-City center catches my eye and nods. It's a simple *thank you*, a nod of respect. A silent understanding passes between us. This is the camaraderie of acknowledgment—of surviving an awkward moment, of bearing witness.

I didn't get to choose the school I attend. My parents prayed for guidance, then announced God had given them peace about where to enroll all of us the fall of my seventh-grade year. I'll bet this guy from Tri-City didn't choose his school, either. He turns to leave, and I watch him push through the door into the parking lot. As he slips out of sight, I feel genuinely sorry for him and very fortunate, all at once.

CHAPTER 9

On Monday morning, during second period, Miss Tyler posts the cast list on her classroom door. There's a crowd of upperclassmen in front of us by the time Daphne and I get all the way down the hall. Luckily, I'm tall enough to peer over the heads of everyone in front of me, and I see my name: It's fourth on the list, right next to the character I want to play.

"Congratulations." Daphne's a head shorter than I am. There's no way she can see the paper hanging on Miss Tyler's door.

"How did you know?" I ask her.

"The subtlety of your gigantic smile." Daphne has mastered the art of the perfectly timed, comically droll understatement.

"That big, huh?"

"From space, Aaron. You could see it from space."

"Well, darlin', that's just *wonderful*."

Nanny is the first person I call when I get home from school. It's a slow night in the cardiology department in Memphis, so she has time to talk. "I was telling the nurses up in the unit about you the other day: 'That Aaron has it all. He's the most talented kid I got.'"

I smile when she says this. I know she shouldn't have favorites, but I'm secretly glad she does.

"Now, when do y'all practice?" she asks.

"Mostly during drama class and after school," I say. "Sometimes we rehearse during study hall."

"Well, you be careful. All sorts of things can happen in study hall. Just ask your mama."

I don't have to ask, but I love hearing the story the way Nanny tells it.

When Mom was a junior in high school, Papa was transferred from his job in Memphis to Kansas City. Mom enrolled at the school where my dad had recently started teaching junior high classes part-time while he worked on his master's degree. It was a small school, and the junior and senior high students attended class in the same buildings. One day, Dad poked his head into the door of Mom's senior high study hall and asked the teacher if a couple of the girls could help him grade history papers. When a friend of Mom's volunteered, Mom came along to help, and apparently Dad was hooked.

They claim nothing ever happened until they were married. Nanny says nothing would've happened at all if it hadn't been for a random bout of histoplasmosis.

"That winter your papa was traveling a lot for work, and some birds built a nest in the chimney. I was allergic to their droppings, which I wound up breathing in through the flue over the fireplace. Got sick as a dog and didn't know why. Your papa was away, and I couldn't get outta the bed."

"And that's when Dad showed up?" I smile into the phone.

"Oh, yes, sir. Here comes your daddy stopping by every other day: 'Oh, Mrs. Davis, can I do this? Oh, Mrs. Davis, let me help you with that.' I knew he was sweet on your mama, and I told him we had it under control, but I was finally so sick I couldn't move—thought I might go home to be with Jesus. Next thing I know, there's your daddy shovelin' the walk."

Nanny's laugh makes me grin. "Well, Dad *is* persistent," I say.

"And so handsome," Nanny says. "Couple months before your mama graduated, Papa got transferred back to Memphis, but we let your mom stay with a friend in Kansas City until she graduated. She got her diploma, then moved back down here to start college. Your daddy started flying down to see her, and it wasn't long before they were engaged."

There's something so romantic about the way my parents met. Dad is still every student's favorite teacher at the Bible college. He's got news-anchor good looks and a folksy Midwestern charm that belies his PhD. It doesn't surprise me that Mom fell in love with him.

"Your mama could've had any boy she wanted," Nanny says.

"She probably still could," I say, and Nanny laughs.

Mom is a pint-size Southern beauty who looks like Sally Field in *Steel Magnolias*, only she has freckles across her nose like I do. (Kiss marks, she insists. Left behind by angels.) She's only five feet tall and looks miniature next to Dad.

Sometimes Dad comes home from the Bible college with a fistful of flowers, and picks Mom up in the kitchen, and twirls her around in his arms while she giggles and shouts for Dad to put her down *this instant*, before she breaks his back.

When I was a little boy, watching this made me feel a special giddiness in my stomach—the same way I felt when I lay by the pool looking up at puffy white clouds in a wide Missouri sky, wondering if Jesus might appear in one of them right that second.

Dad was sort of like Jesus in those moments, showing up unannounced from work and sweeping Mom into the air. There was joy and excitement—a certain breathlessness about the whole affair. It seemed to stir up those feelings in all of us. Joshua, Miriam, and Caleb would race into the kitchen to be a part of it, too. When Dad finally put Mom down, she would stand on her tiptoes on top of his shoes, and they'd kiss while we giggled and squirmed between them, squealing and trying to pry them apart.

Now that we're older, none of us try to stop Mom and Dad when they make out in the kitchen. Josh and Miriam are usually outside making basketball a blood sport in the driveway, and Caleb just rolls his eyes at me, then diplomatically suggests Mom and Dad might be more comfortable in the privacy of their bedroom.

But I like it.

There's something great about knowing my parents are still into each other.

Nanny has to get off the phone. She's been called to the ER to do an EKG.

"Now, Aaron, your papa and I are coming to see this play of yours," she says. "Gonna buy the plane tickets tomorrow."

I can't believe it. They rarely come to Kansas City to see us. We always go to Memphis to see them. I tell her the dates, and she writes them down.

"Nanny, are you sure?" I ask.

"Of course I am, darlin'. Wouldn't miss it for all the tea in China."

She tells me that she loves me and how proud she is of me, and makes me promise to be careful in study hall.

"You'd be surprised how one thing leads to another," she says. "Bird poop, sugar. It's the reason y'all are all here."

I am shopping in Water Tower Place on Michigan Avenue in Chicago with my church youth group. Our youth pastor, Jack, drove us up for a quick weekend trip to see the sights. We've visited the whales at Shedd Aquarium and been to the top of Sears Tower, and now we're shopping until dinner at Ed Debevic's. Since I got that part in the play on Monday, my week has gotten better and better.

The only bad part is that my sort-of girlfriend, Erin (yes,

we have the same name), couldn't come, due to a scheduling conflict. She is my "sort-of" girlfriend because we really only see each other at church events and talk on the phone. I did take her to homecoming at Blue Ridge last fall, and once last month we kissed in an empty Sunday school room in the church basement next to the choir rehearsal room.

All morning I've been looking for the perfect souvenir to take back to her, but I don't want it to be anything Chicago-themed. I want to get her something I know she'll really like. Flipping through CDs at a music store with my friends, I see the *perfect* gift. As I am taking the *Pretty Woman* sound track to the cash register, I hear Pastor Jack behind me.

"Are you sure your parents will be okay with you buying that?"

An arrow of anger shoots up my spine. He's not asking any of my friends about whether or not their parents will like the music they're buying. He's supposed to be cool. He lets us listen to Amy Grant in the van, and my parents wouldn't like that, either.

"Oh, it's not for me," I say nonchalantly. "It's for Erin."

"Isn't *Pretty Woman* an R-rated movie?" he presses.

"I guess. I've never seen it," I lie, "but the music is *so great*. You've heard the Roy Orbison song, right?"

"Sure," he says.

I can tell he wants to say more, so before he can, I head to the checkout line and hand the CD to the clerk. I'm so angry that my hands shake as I take the cash out of my wallet to pay. This is my own money. I earned it working at my part-time job at the ice rink. I can spend it on whatever I want. Jack only asked about my parents because he knows them. He knows how conservative they are. I hate this situation. I hate that he's *right*. Of course my parents wouldn't want me to buy this CD.

I don't want to think about them right now. I don't want to feel guilty. I don't want to worry that I'm disappointing them or disobeying God's command to obey them. I don't think God really cares what CD I buy for my sort-of girlfriend.

I take a deep breath and smile as the clerk hands me a bag with the CD in it. I don't understand why it seems I have to go through this over every choice I make. I try not to think about my parents for the rest of the trip.

On the way back home in the van, I memorize lines for the play, and when I see Erin the next Wednesday night, I give her the CD.

She *loves* it.

See? I made the right choice.

It's no big deal. Mom and Dad will never know.

"Hey, Aaron."

It's Dad. He's stuck his head in my bedroom door. I casually close the purple paperback I'm reading, and deftly slide it under the bed. It's a copy of *To Kill a Mockingbird*. My cousin Sadie slipped it to me at Christmastime along with *One Flew*

Over the Cuckoo's Nest and *The Silence of the Lambs*. She's taking AP English at her public school in Memphis, and there are all these books on her reading list that I've never even heard of before. I know Dad and Mom wouldn't want me reading *To Kill a Mockingbird* because it deals with a rape. I can see Dad has something on his mind. Probably best not to complicate the issue with a book I shouldn't be reading.

"What's up?" I ask him.

"When you went to Chicago with the youth group last month, you said that Erin didn't go, right?"

Instantly, my stomach is in knots. *What does he know?*

"No, she had midterms that week."

"You said you bought her a souvenir—a CD, right?" he asks.

"Yes."

Dad looks down at the carpet in the room I share with my brother. I stand up and grab my backpack. I have homework to do and lines to review before tomorrow's rehearsal.

"Aaron, I talked to Pastor Jack today."

Crap.

Dad is looking at me with his "grieved" eyes. I hate this look. It's the look that says "I'm disappointed" without a single word. I don't want to disappoint Dad, but it's getting harder not to. So much normal stuff disappoints him.

"When I asked you if you bought Erin a souvenir on the trip, you told me that you got her a classical CD," Dad says. "Is that the truth?"

"I said I bought her a *classic* CD," I hedge.

"Was it classical music?"

"It was oldies. Roy Orbison."

Even as the words tumble out of my mouth, they sound lame. I'm smarter than this, and Dad knows it. It's insulting. Why do excuses like this always work so much better in my head? When Jack asked me if my parents would be cool with my buying this CD, why did I justify it by being able to say Roy Orbison is "classic rock"? What made me think Dad would consider this a reasonable excuse if it came up? My stomach is doing backflips right now. *Why do I have to lie about buying this CD in the first place?*

"Jack told me that it was the sound track to an R-rated movie you bought," Dad says quietly. "Is that true, son?"

"Yes, it was a sound track, but—"

"Have you seen the movie *Pretty Woman*, Aaron?"

I roll my eyes like this very idea is a personal affront, like he's being utterly ridiculous. "Dad, when would I have seen that movie? Even if I were allowed to go to the theater, I can't get into an R-rated movie yet. I'm only sixteen."

He seems satisfied by this, but I know he isn't stopping here.

"Last weekend, your mom came with me when I spoke at that little church out in Kansas," he says softly. "We were in our hotel room Sunday night and, flipping through the TV channels, we came across part of *Pretty Woman*. Aaron, that movie is about a man who hires..." He pauses, barely able to continue. "... a prostitute."

The word swings from Dad's lips toward the ceiling like a trapeze artist, somersaulting through the air in slow motion, high above the net.

Pros-ti-tute.

"We turned it off right away," Dad says.

Of course they did. So they didn't see the funny and touching and sweet parts. They only saw the sexy parts.

Dad looks down at the carpet again, and when he looks back up at me, his eyes are filled with tears. "Why would you buy your girlfriend the music to a movie about a man paying money to use a woman sexually?"

I feel split down the middle. Part of me wants to run to my dad and wipe his eyes and beg him not to cry. I want to tell him that it's okay, that I'm sorry I lied, that I'm sorry I am lying now. I want to bury my face in his neck the way I used to when I was little and we hauled firewood in his old '57 Chevy pickup truck—the light blue one with freckles of rust and no seat belts. Long before laws requiring children to be strapped down, I'd stand on the seat next to him, pinned in by his right elbow, my left arm around his neck. I'd lay my head on his shoulder against his soft flannel work shirt and watch the landscape fly by.

The other part of me knows that there's no way to make this better for Dad, and hot tears of frustration well up in my eyes. I don't see anything wrong with this movie, or movies in general. I don't think God does, either. This movie made me feel good when I watched it. If it was so sinful, why would God allow me to like it so much?

I'm angry I have to lie about the music I listen to, and the CDs I buy, and the movies I see. I want to make my own decisions about these things and not be questioned, or have to sneak around. Why does Dad have to make this a big deal? I'm not a bad kid. After all, I didn't hire a prostitute. I only bought a CD.

I can barely breathe as I struggle not to throw my backpack against the floor. But I don't. My fear tempers my anger with practicality. Time to cut my losses, minimize the damage, and brace for what comes next—probably the belt. I haven't been spanked in a while, but no matter how I cut it, this is deceit, pure and simple; there's no getting around it. I've been caught. I can argue the semantics of "classic rock" versus "classical music" all night long, but it's not going to do any good.

"Why, Aaron?" Dad repeats himself, waiting for an answer.

This is not a rhetorical question. He really wants to know, and stares directly into my eyes, trying to find the answer.

"I don't know," I say quietly.

For the first time tonight, I'm telling the truth. I don't know why I like this music and this movie so much. My brain goes all mushy when Dad asks these kinds of questions—it's like slush. I can't marshal the words that so rarely fail me.

How do I tell Dad that of all the movies I saw last summer with Jason, *Pretty Woman* was my favorite? That one day I want to live in Los Angeles and climb up a fire escape with flowers in my hand for somebody I'm not supposed to love?

There's a crazy guy on the street at the beginning and end of the movie who walks around saying, "Everybody's got a dream. What's your dream?"

My dream is to be an actor and live in that sunny city and ride around in a limousine and make movies like *Pretty Woman* and have my dad see me in them—really see me—and not mutter "sick" and change the channel. I dream that one day my dad will watch the whole story and see that the man who searches everywhere for love finds it in the place he least expects it. I don't know if my dream pleases God or not, but it pleases me. And doesn't God love me? Doesn't he want me to be happy? It feels like everything I like is always wrong.

I don't know how to say any of that. Instead, I whisper, "I'm sorry."

Dad looks at me, perplexed. "Didn't you know that if you asked me if you could buy that CD for Erin, I'd say no?" Dad asks.

"Yes." I speak softly, trying not to let too much slip out.

"And yet you did it anyway. Then when I asked you about it, you lied to me because you wanted to have your way. You wanted to make your own decisions, instead of honoring your father and mother. God's word calls that rebellion."

I take a deep breath and close my eyes. *Here comes the snake.*

"Satan was an angel before he was a serpent, Aaron. Lucifer—the angel of light—the most powerful angel in heaven. What does the Bible say was Lucifer's sin?"

"Rebellion," I say.

As Dad works his way through the rebellion speech one

more time, I feel the scorn clawing its way up the back of my throat. I know all of this. I've heard it so many times I could give the speech myself.

"Satan wants to murder you, to take your soul to hell for all eternity. You've trusted Jesus as your savior, so he can't do that, but he'd love nothing more than to murder your testimony for Jesus Christ by tempting you with all the things that this sinful world has to offer: the movies, and the rock music, the sex…"

"Dad, I don't go to movies," I lie, "or have sex." This is true, but Dad doesn't seem to hear me.

"This is more than a lie about a CD," Dad says. "This is about you choosing whether or not you are going to serve the Lord Jesus Christ."

I can't stand it any longer. "So, are you going to give me a whipping?"

Dad looks past me and rubs a hand over his thick auburn hair. When he focuses on me again, there's a faraway look in his eyes, as if he's seeing a stranger.

"Son, I don't think a whipping is going to fix this. You're too old to spank."

Something about this news should be comforting. Instead, it's chilling. If he's not going to spank me…

"I am so grieved about this that I don't know exactly what to do. Your mom and I have been praying about how to discipline you. She is as heartbroken about your rebellion as I am."

They've known about it for days. This was an ambush. I walked right into it. Dad gave me enough rope to hang myself. As I swing from the gallows of my own deceit, tears fill his eyes again.

"Do you remember when you were little and you asked me who spanked me when I did something wrong? Do you remember what I told you?"

Dad waits. I don't want to be having this conversation. There's a desperate panic in the pit of my stomach.

"You said God spanked you, but not with a belt; that there are some things that God allows to happen as the consequences of our actions that are worse than a spanking."

Dad crosses his arms and leans against the wall in my room. His gaze wanders past me toward the ceiling.

"I've been praying about this, Aaron, searching for the answer. How do I handle my own son lying to me?"

He pauses. The silence is horrible.

"I've talked to your mom about it, and I feel like you need to lose something that's so important to you that you'll never forget this lesson."

I can't swallow. I can't blink. I stare at Dad, waiting.

"I've made an appointment to talk to Miss Tyler up at Blue Ridge on Monday. I think as a consequence for lying to me about this CD, you're not going to be able to be in the play at school."

When Dad says these words, there's a roar in my ears like the sound of the jets flying over the air force base down the road from our house. It rockets into my chest, then full throttle out of my mouth.

"Dad, you can't do this!"

Mom appears at the door of my bedroom. I am crying and yelling and I don't care. "That punishes the *entire cast*, not just me. I'm one of the *leads*. I'm in almost every scene. Monday is the beginning of spring break, and we have rehearsals every day until we open."

"I realize that, son. Which is why I'm going to talk to Miss Tyler about it. I don't want to put her in a bind if I can help it."

"A *bind*? Put her in *a bind*? We open the show in *two weeks!*" I am so angry that I can see spit and tears flying as I speak.

"I understand that, but if Miss Tyler feels that she can recast your role and still open the show as scheduled, I'm going to pull you out of the production."

"Dad, please don't do this," I say quietly. I hate myself for begging. I hate that he can win like this.

"Aaron, I love you so much, and I know how much this means to you. Jesus Christ, the Son of God, came to earth and suffered and bled and died for your sin of lying. He knew while he was hanging on that cross that one day Aaron Hartzler would lie to his dad about buying a CD for his girlfriend, but he loved you so much that he let those Roman soldiers crucify him anyway."

"I'm sorry, Dad!" I am hysterical, but I can't stop the explosion. "You can spank me if you want, or don't let me drive. Why do you have to take me out of the play?"

Even as I say the words, I know that I've just sealed my own fate by bargaining. I can see it in his eyes: He knows he's hit me where it hurts.

Game over. He wins.

"Aaron, this play is more important to you than anything else. I feel like being an actor has become more of a priority to you than your commitment to Christ, and nothing should be more important than that."

I can't argue with this, because he's right. Being in this play *is* more important to me than Jesus.

"Dad, I can still love God and be an actor."

"I know that, son, but not if you're lying and being deceitful. Jesus Christ is coming back to the earth very soon. We need strong young men like you who stand up and say, 'I'm living for Jesus Christ.' If God has called you to be an actor, you can do quality biblical plays that you tour around to churches, or direct Christian school kids in plays that lead people to the Lord."

I don't want to tour churches or teach at a Christian school. I can't imagine myself doing that as an adult. My head hurts from crying and yelling, and I don't want to be in the same room with him anymore.

"When do you talk to her?" I ask.

"Monday morning."

"And if she says that she can't do the show without me, you won't pull me out?" I ask. There's no way that Miss Tyler will let him do this. I'm the best thing in the show and she knows it.

"Yes," Dad says, "in that case, we'll figure out some other form of discipline."

"I have lines to review," I say, and start digging my script out of my backpack.

Dad stands in my room, Mom at the door, watching as I wipe at my face and sit down on the floor with my back against the bottom bunk of the stacked beds that I share with Josh. I stare at the yellow highlighted lines without reading them. I can't even see the words.

"We love you, son."

When Dad says these words, I want to throw the script at the wall.

Instead, I do nothing. I stare at the page, and I wait in the silence until he moves into the hall with my mother, and I hear the creak in the hallway floor that lets me know they've made it to the kitchen.

CHAPTER 10

"Let's pray before we get there, and ask God to really use our ministry tonight," Dad says.

We're driving to church on Sunday night through a Kansas City thunderstorm. Our pastor asked Dad to preach tonight, and I'll be playing the piano for the whole family to sing. Dad likes for us to do the special music when he preaches, especially when he gives a sermon for parents about raising godly children. We're sort of like a modern-day von Trapp family, only instead of tunes about tiny white flowers and going to bed, we sing songs about Jesus. We're the example of the family you can have if you follow the instructions Dad gives on the overhead transparency.

"Honey, you want to start us off?" Dad asks. Mom closes her eyes and bows her head in the front seat.

"Dear Heavenly Father, we want to thank you for this opportunity to be used by you in the lives of others. We pray that as Hubert speaks, and Aaron plays the piano, and the children and I sing, this will not be a performance for our glory but a ministry for your glory...."

As Mom prays, I stare at the rain-slicked streets in the dark and think about the song I'll be playing. We practiced this afternoon in the family room. It's a beautiful tune by a composer who lost an eye to cancer and now writes Christian musicals under the name Patch the Pirate. The song is all about giving your heart to Jesus while it's still tender, and surrendering all your talents for God to use them as he sees fit. The problem is, I don't *want* to surrender my talents to God. What if he makes me use them as a missionary or a Christian schoolteacher? That isn't the life I want for myself.

Mom wraps up her prayer. When she says "amen," Dad encourages each of us to search our hearts and make sure that we're "right with God."

"If there's any unconfessed sin in your life, God can't hear your prayers," he says. "Each of you take a few minutes and make sure that you're a vessel of service that is fit for use by the Lord tonight."

The car is quiet except for the *swish-swoosh* of the windshield wipers. Dad goes to talk to Miss Tyler tomorrow. I think of the lies Mom and Dad know about now, and the ones they don't know about yet, and my stomach turns. I always get a little nervous about playing the piano in church, but this feels worse. I don't want to mess up. Will God help my fingers hit the correct keys if I confess my sin? Will he keep Dad from taking me out of the play?

Silently, I try to pray. *God, I'm sorry for lying to Dad. Tonight, I dedicate my talents to you. Please help me to hit all the right notes, and please, please let Miss Tyler convince Dad not to take me out of the play.*

Dad pulls into a spot in the church parking lot, and we make a dash through the rain to the front door.

During the service the storm outside lets up, but the butterflies in my stomach do not. It is not uncommon for preachers to speak a great deal about God's plan for you, but tonight Dad's sermon has a catchy title: "Satan's Plan for Your Life."

"If you're already a Christian, the devil can't murder your soul and bring you to hell with him for all of eternity," Dad explains, "but he *can* murder your Christian testimony so that you can't be of use by God here on earth."

Dad illustrates this point with a story about a friend of Mom's when she was in high school. The young man's name was Chris, and he had turned his back on God and taken to a wild life of drugs, rock and roll, and hitchhiking. One evening, Chris had hitched a ride and tried to rob the driver, who shot him.

"The emergency room doctor told Chris's mother that the bullet only grazed him and that he shouldn't have died from the wound," Dad says. But Chris's mother knew what had *really* happened. Two days later, Dad says, she stood in front of a congregation of sobbing high school students at Chris's funeral and explained that Chris had strayed so far from God's plan for his life that God allowed him to be killed. The Good Shepherd, she said, had called home his wayward lamb.

"Surrender your will and your talents to the master's plan for your life," Dad says, quoting a verse from Philippians, "and you, too, will know 'the peace of God that passes all understanding.'"

This story isn't helping the butterflies in my stomach. I've heard it before, but now I wonder if it applies to me. Will God allow me to be killed in a freak accident if I keep lying to my parents about music and movies?

As Dad wraps up his sermon, he says, "I'd like to call my family up to the front to sing a song about dedicating your heart and soul to the lordship of Jesus Christ. As Belinda and the children come to sing, I trust that if you haven't already, you'll consider telling the creator of heaven and earth that every part of you is dedicated to serving him."

When I reach the piano bench, I wipe my hands across my slacks and wait for Mom's nod to begin the introduction to the song. I love playing the piano, because as soon as I start, everything else drops away—the butterflies vanish, the staccato fears pinging around my head quiet down, and I become lost in the notes and the rhythms. Mom's light soprano wraps a beautiful obbligato harmony over the clear voices of Josh, Miriam, and Caleb, who sing the melody.

As I play the final notes of the song, stillness settles over the congregation, a sort of holy hush, finally broken after several seconds by a chorus of hearty "amens"—what we do in church instead of clapping. My fingers found every note perfectly. Maybe God heard my prayer in the car. Maybe he's not upset with me after all.

After church, Erin finds me in the foyer and tells me I did a great job.

"Thanks," I say, and smile.

We're not dating anymore. When I told her what happened because of the CD, she decided we should go back to being friends.

"You doing okay?" she asks. "When do you find out if you still get to do the play?"

"Tomorrow." I can't stop staring at the sheen of pink gloss on her lips. I wish I'd tried to kiss her more when she was my girlfriend. *Why didn't I?*

"I'll say a prayer," she says.

"Great. And just so we have all the bases covered, I'm going to cut myself and worship Baal." I'm joking, but she doesn't get it.

"What?" She frowns, confused.

"Never mind." I smile and shake my head. "A little Old Testament humor."

"Oh!" She laughs, but it's awkward. "Let me know how it goes."

"I will."

She turns to leave, then looks back over her shoulder. "I really like that CD," she says. Then she pushes through the double doors and into the parking lot.

"I talked to Miss Tyler, Aaron."

I am standing in my parents' bedroom, waiting for the

next sentence to come out of Dad's mouth. The verdict. He and Mom have been here with the door closed since he returned a half hour ago. I could hear hushed voices from the hallway, but I couldn't make out what they were saying.

My stomach is in knots, and my shoulder blades are pulling into each other like penguins huddled together for warmth on an ice floe.

C'mon, Miss Tyler, please…

I've been quietly chanting this all morning, sending a silent message to the drama classroom at my high school, hoping against hope that Miss Tyler will somehow be able to talk my father into an alternative—any alternative—to pulling me out of the play.

I am somehow startled by the stuff that hangs on the walls of Mom and Dad's bedroom, as if I am seeing it for the first time: lace doilies crocheted by Papa, a leaning goose I made from stained pine in sixth grade, groupings of plaques and needlepoint samplers of inspirational sayings and Bible verses, a sheaf of wheat tied with a ribbon, and, over Mom's antique nightstand, a mirror framed inside an actual horse collar—the kind of black, rubbery harness with big metal rings on the sides that might have been slipped over a Clydesdale's head and then hitched to a buggy a hundred years ago. It's a very country, very homespun decorating style, very Early Baptist Bookstore.

I hate it.

I hate the way my stomach feels as I'm looking at it.

I wonder where the horse collar came from. I think about

how I saddled up the horses with Jason last summer at camp in Nebraska, and how exhilarating it was to ride at full gallop. I felt the same sense of sheer glee and power I did with the wind whipping through my hair as Jason and I raced along the rain-slicked Nebraska highway in his little red sports car, speeding back to camp with the music cranked up after we saw that first movie—high volume at a high speed.

Dad's voice snaps me back to this moment, my fate rushing toward me like a brick wall.

"We talked for quite a while up at the school."

High speeds. High volumes. My heart is pounding, the blood racing through my ears with a roar only I can hear. I want to feel rain on my face, a ticket stub between my fingers, wind through my hair. I want to be anywhere but here.

"So, am I still in the play?"

Even as I ask the question, I want to take the words back, pluck them out of the air, stuff them down my own throat. I don't want to know the answer, because I know the answer.

"No, son, you're not going to do the play."

Mom looks up at me, startled, and only then do I realize that I'm yelling the word "no" at the top of my lungs. I've always read in books about how people can't breathe when something dreadful is happening—like they're drowning and their lungs won't work. Apparently, I don't have that problem.

"Dad, you can't! You can't do this."

"Son, I know you're upset—"

"You can't punish the rest of the cast like this," I cut him off. I'm desperate, and I don't care about being disrespectful.

"Aaron, lower your voice," Mom says, her tone a flashing red light of warning.

"How can you do this to me?" I yell, pressing the accelerator, gathering speed. "Nanny and Papa have already bought plane tickets. They're coming for opening night!"

"Aaron, I want you to realize that there are some consequences to sin that are worse than a spanking," Dad says.

"And you think this is going to make me want to *obey* you?" I floor it.

"Aaron Hubert." Mom uses my middle name, a full-on squad-car siren.

"I know this hurts," Dad says, "but you have to learn that you cannot lie and get away with it."

"It was a *CD*, Dad! If you weren't so uptight about the music that we listen to, I wouldn't have had to lie about it."

"Aaron, I have to cause a crisis in your life now so that you learn this lesson before it's too late." Dad's voice is quiet, steady, grieved. "We don't want to lose you to the world, son."

"*Lose* me? You don't want to *lose me?*" I am blind with rage, plowing full speed ahead.

"Aaron, we love you." Dad's quiet, slow voice. The freckled blue pickup truck is square in my headlights.

"I HATE YOU."

The impact is deafening. The part of me so desperate for Dad's approval is dead on arrival.

"I HATE YOU. I HATE YOU. I HATE YOU."

No one has ever dared to say these words to my parents in our home before, much less shout them at a volume that surely the neighbors can hear. Yet in this moment, I'm unafraid. I don't care. I'm not worried about the consequence. Shouting these words has changed me on the inside.

I'm sobbing, and all I want to do is get away from this. I turn on my heel and walk down the hall to my bedroom, away from their disappointment, their rules, their restrictions— away from *them*. I hear Mom and Dad calling after me, pleading, telling, begging, warning.

I ignore them.

What could they possibly take away now?

Dad decided to take me out of the play the first day of spring break. Rehearsals were already scheduled for each of the five days off from school, and now he drives me to the first one that afternoon. He wants me to explain to the cast, to ask their forgiveness. "The only way to turn away from sin is to stand up and admit what you've done wrong," he says, and then he prays with me in the parking lot and asks God to give me strength.

Miss Tyler gathers everyone to the bleachers by the stage in the gym, and Dad calls the cast to attention. "Aaron has something he'd like to say to all of you."

My friend Dawn has a quizzical expression on her face. She sits in front of me in typing class and has big, beautiful eyes like a Disney princess. I can tell she knows something is up. As I stand there facing her and all my other friends, I still can't believe this is happening.

"I need to apologize to all of you," I begin. Trying to force these words off my tongue is like trying to push a cat into a bathtub. I might be able to do it, but I will be torn and bleeding by the end. I soldier on. I explain about the CD and lying to my dad about it, and how I can't do the play as a result.

Miss Tyler hugs me when I finish, and as I walk toward the door of the gym with my dad, Dawn catches my eye with a small wave of her hand. She and everyone else sit wide-eyed and uncomfortable on the bleachers, unsure of what has just happened, uncertain how the *Pretty Woman* sound track and my lie to my dad is any of their concern.

As I follow Dad to the car, tears fill my eyes once more, but I am tired of crying and angrily blink them away. How had I let him convince me this was about asking forgiveness of the cast? I don't feel absolved; I feel ashamed and ridiculous. It's bad enough I don't get to be in the play. Did he have to embarrass me in front of everyone, too?

Daphne has tried her best to cheer me up, but it's been hard to think about anything else for the past two weeks, and even harder to talk about. Not even Daphne has been able to make me laugh about this, and as the student body files into the gym to see the final dress rehearsal during sixth period, she sits down next to me at the end of a row of bleachers in the back.

"Are you okay?" she asks.

I try to smile, but I can't. Even before the curtain opens, I know I won't be able to watch what is about to occur.

And I'm correct: The play is a disaster.

Miss Tyler recast my role with a soft-spoken junior who is a nice guy, but not particularly great at comedy. He has no presence in the hallway between classes, let alone onstage. After he butchers the funniest line of the first scene, I slip off the bleachers and leave the gym. I walk down the hall to the music wing, close the door of a practice room, sit down at a glossy black lacquer piano, and cry.

I have heard the words *broken heart* before, and I suppose I have been sad in the past, but I realize I have never understood what that phrase means until now. I have never cried like this before. I want what I'm feeling to end, but it will not.

I'm not even sure what the feelings are; it seems there are so many at once, roiling and rolling over one another. Anger, hurt, and the numbing boredom of sadness have paralyzed me during the past two weeks since Dad told me I wouldn't be doing the play. I can't laugh with Daphne. I can barely smile.

I am exhausted from crying and worn out from these feelings—the gnawing anxiety of knowing this day would come, that I'd have to watch this dress rehearsal with the entire high school and feel my humiliation and heartbreak all over again.

My tears are splashing down onto the shiny white keys of the piano, and I lift my hands to wipe away the wet spots. As I do, my fingers find the keys, and the notes of a hymn arrangement I've known for years fill the practice room. Over the past few weeks, I've been practicing the piano a lot. When I'm at the keyboard, I drop into the music and everything else falls away. This is one of those songs I don't have to think about; my fingers know it from memory, so I can put my hands on autopilot and be alone with my thoughts. It's a beautiful, majestic arrangement, and I play it well. As my fingers float over the keys, the lyrics run through my head:

> *When peace like a river attendeth my way*
> *When sorrows like sea billows roll*
> *Whatever my lot Thou has taught me to say*
> *"It is well, it is well with my soul."*

Horatio Spafford wrote these words on the back of an envelope in 1873 while sailing to meet his wife in Europe after she had been rescued from a shipwreck that had claimed the lives of his four daughters. No one has died in my family, so why is the sadness I feel so profound? Why does my grief feel like I've lost more than a part in a play?

Dad did more than teach me to act when I was a little boy; he entrusted me with his *love* of something. Acting is the thing he and I share, just like he shares basketball with Josh and Miriam. When I am up in front of a crowd at church or at school singing in a musical or acting in a play, I feel his endless encouragement and approval. I see the pride that shines in his eyes. Dad knew this was the one thing he could do that would hurt me the most. He thinks this pain will somehow bring us closer together, but he's taken away the thing I feel makes us a team. How can he not see this?

This isn't discipline. It's betrayal.

As I play the final arpeggio of the song, fresh tears begin to fall. I am so angry, and so hurt, and so tired of being angry and hurt. I want the pain to go away. I want all to be well with my soul. I've prayed a hundred times in the past few weeks, but I don't know if God can hear me. I've begged for forgiveness, I've bargained and pleaded, but nothing changed the outcome. I'm still sitting in this practice room while someone else mangles my jokes onstage. In one last-ditch effort, I raise my eyes toward the ceiling.

"Please," I whisper. "Please, help."

It's the only prayer I can manage.

Then I practice the Brahms étude I'm supposed to have memorized for my lesson next week. Maybe God answers my prayer. Or maybe I don't have any tears left to cry. At some point, I realize my eyes are dry, and I look at the clock. I head to my locker before the curtain call and make my way to the car before the whole student body floods the hallway. The fewer people I have to see, the better.

Nanny is waiting for me in the garage when I pull in. Mom called her three weeks ago to tell her I wasn't going to be in the play after all, but she insisted on coming for the weekend anyway.

"You better put down that backpack and give your Nanny a hug."

I obey, and suddenly I am crying again. Nanny kisses my cheek and holds me for what feels like a very long time.

"Darlin', what's wrong?" she whispers.

"You came all this way to see me in this stupid play." I sob into her shoulder. "I disappointed everybody."

"Hey. Hey, you look at me, young man." She steps back and takes my face in both her hands. "Nothing you could do would *ever* disappoint me. Do you hear me? *Nothing*."

I raise my eyes to meet hers shining back at me, bright even in the dim light of the garage. "I'm sorry you can't be in this play," she says, "but that's a decision your daddy made. I'm here to celebrate *you*."

She hugs me tight once more, and I remember the night she carried me into McLemore's market, wrapped up in Papa's crocheted afghan. Nanny always makes me feel safe.

"Now then," she says, heading over to the trunk of Dad's car, "will you be a gentleman, please, and help me carry up another tank of oxygen for Papa?"

Papa's breathing has grown steadily worse. He wheels a little green tank of oxygen around with him wherever he goes now.

"How is he doing?" I ask.

"As well as you can do with emphysema," Nanny says. "Your uncle Edward won't quit smoking, and I've informed him he'd better have other plans for long-term care. Your papa is my last emphysema patient."

I lift a green tank out of the trunk.

"'Course Papa is a stubborn man, darlin'. He may outlast us all," she says. "I sat him down the other day and said if he didn't stop being so ornery, we weren't gonna have a funeral for him."

"Nanny!"

She laughs and winks at me as she closes the trunk. "Told him he best start being sweet, or I'm gonna use his insurance money to put a swimming pool in the backyard. We'll bury him under the diving board."

The next night after dinner, instead of heading up to school so I can get into costume and perform, I sit at the table and wait as Dad takes out his Bible and leads family devotions. He reads a passage of scripture, then Josh reads from a little devotional book called *The Daily Bread*. Mom has Miriam pull a postcard out of the Missionary Prayer Box, and we all take turns praying for the missionary family whose picture is on the card.

This is supposed to be my big opening night. Instead, it's like every other night—only Nanny is here with her coffee cup, Papa is here with his oxygen tank, and Dad has an announcement:

"I know we thought we were going to see a play at Blue Ridge tonight," he says, "but because that didn't work out, I thought we'd go see the musical at Tri-City tomorrow."

"Tri-City?" I ask. The alarms are ringing in my head. I feel like I've been punched in the stomach. "How'd you hear about the musical at Tri-City?" Something about this feels wrong. *Very* wrong.

"I went to speak in their chapel service last week, and the principal, Mr. Friesen, invited us all to come and see the show tomorrow night."

"You spoke in chapel at Tri-City last week?" I ask.

"You know they've got this big new church auditorium, where they're doing the play," Dad says, "and they're building a brand-new high school wing."

"Aren't they sort of crazy conservative?" I ask.

"Yeah," says Josh. "I hear they don't let boys and girls talk to each other between classes."

"Don't be ridiculous." Dad laughs. "Besides, your friend Erica from camp goes to school there."

It hits me like a ton of bricks out of the clear blue sky— right there in the kitchen while Nanny pours more coffee, and Mom loads the dishwasher, and Papa breathes air through a tube in his nose. A horrible certainty settles in the pit of my stomach:

Dad is going to make us go to Tri-City next year.

I can see how the whole weekend will unfold with perfect clarity before I even leave the dinner table. I can see us watching the musical, and Dad introducing me to the director. I can already hear his sales pitch about how great the music and theater and sports programs are. I can see right now how I will argue and bargain and beg, and ultimately it will not matter. God already knows who will get into heaven, and Dad already knows we'll be changing schools.

Dad has decided, and that settles it. His decision started two summers ago when I bought a ticket to a movie he doesn't know I saw—a movie that led to a sound track I loved, a lie I can never un-tell, and three words I can never take back.

Across the table, Nanny smiles and winks at me, unaware of what has just transpired.

You'd be surprised how one thing leads to another.

CHAPTER 11

A short, stout woman in her fifties with an enthusiastic wave and no waist swings open the door of the school office when she sees Dad and me striding down the empty corridor of lockers and classrooms. She's the same size from her shoulders to her ankles, and I imagine her welcoming Santa Claus home on Christmas morning from a night dodging angels and delivering gifts.

"Oooooooooooh, Dr. Hartzler," she squeals in a thick Southern drawl, "we are so excited that y'all are joinin' us here at Tri-City this year."

Dad smiles. "We're glad to be here, Lynne. This is Aaron."

I am instantly engulfed in a bear hug. Lynne is wearing denim from head to toe, and her straight skirt clings to her thighs like a sausage casing. This woman is a blue-jean hot dog.

"I'm Principal Friesen's wife, Lynne, but you can call me Mama Friesen." She turns to Dad. "Larry is in a meeting, but he'll be done in a sec, so let's get Aaron down to play practice."

I cringe. Everyone who knows *anything* about theater

knows the word is *rehearsal*, but I keep my best smile plastered firmly in place as I follow her and Dad down the hallway. I've been here for roughly fifty-seven seconds, and I already know I have zero intention of referring to this woman as "Mama."

After weeks of pleading with Dad to not make us change schools, the deed is done. Classes start at the end of the month, and we'll be driving thirty minutes across town to attend until we find a house closer to the school. Dad has worked a deal with Principal Friesen and the drama teacher, and somehow I've been assigned a part in the school play, which was cast last spring. I got a call from a Mrs. Hastings two weeks ago informing me I'd been given a small but memorable role—no audition required.

Dad has been trying really hard to reach out to me over the past few weeks especially. There were surprise tickets to a Royals game, a trip to Worlds of Fun, and a hundred hopeful glances in the hallway. He's been very vocal about how beautiful my piano playing is when I'm practicing, and the other night he turned on the lamp next to the chair where I was reading in the living room, and stood there waiting until I looked up at him.

"What?" I asked.

"Nothing," he said. "I just love you so much, Aaron."

When the part in the play came through, his relief was palpable, like this would fix everything. "See?" Dad said with a hopeful smile when I hung up the phone. "The Lord is working everything out for you, son. 'God delights to give his best to those who leave the choice with him.'"

Of course, I have had no choice about this at all. If it were my choice, I wouldn't be here for the first day of rehearsal for the play at Tri-City. For weeks Dad has been trying to make this better somehow—brokering a role in the play, telling me over and over again how this is what he and Mom "have peace about," explaining how much they prayed about making this decision.

They spent a lot of time asking God if they should put us in a new school. I wish they'd spent time asking me about it. I'm the one who has to go to class here every day. They care more about what God thinks of where they send me to school than they do about what I think, that's for certain. Dad said it best the other day:

"Aaron, I have to answer to God one day for the decisions I make as a parent. I want to send you to a school where the students are going to exert positive peer pressure on you to serve the Lord."

As we walk down the hall toward the rehearsal, I feel my stomach turn. At least if I have to go to school here, I'll get to be in the play, but even this makes me nervous. I'm simply being given a role. How does that look? *Did someone else lose this part because I got it?*

Dad and Mrs. Friesen are chatting like old friends. "Larry was so happy this all worked out," she says. "And, Aaron, you'll just *love* Mrs. Hastings, the drama teacher. She's done such a wonderful thing with our plays and musicals. I know she's looking forward to having you here."

I see Dad's eyes glance over at me, watching for my reaction. He wants so badly for this to work.

"Yes, we saw the musical this past spring," I say cheerfully. "It was terrific." My face already hurts from smiling, but I can tell Lynne Friesen thinks I'm the bee's knees.

"Aaron's the best actor I've ever directed," Dad says. "I directed him in a play when he was four years old. He stole the show then, and he's been a natural ever since." I realize he's right. Even now, Mrs. Friesen has no idea how much I don't want to be here. Maybe this is going to be easier than I thought.

We reach the door of a large multipurpose room. Through a thin window I can see the backs of two other students holding scripts and reading lines while a woman with red hair scribbles notes on a clipboard. The rest of the cast watches the rehearsal from large round tables off to the side.

"This is where y'all will practice until school starts," Mrs. Friesen says. "Then we move into the church auditorium. Ready?"

Without waiting for an answer, she turns the handle and swings the door wide, plowing a course for center stage directly through the scene, already in progress.

The drama teacher looks up, startled, as Mrs. Friesen marches into the room, but when Mrs. Hastings sees me standing next to my dad, she lets loose a warm smile, her lips a hypnotizing shade of pink.

"Aaron!" She floats over and extends one hand to me,

the other folded across her chest as she turns her head to the side in the sort of demure curtsy one might expect of a lady-in-waiting to Queen Victoria.

This is it. It's up to me how this goes from here. I make a split-second decision and turn on the charm.

"Mrs. *Hastings*." I take her extended hand in both of mine and grasp it as if being welcomed by royalty. She pulls herself close to me in a cloud of gardenia perfume and whispers, "We're so pleased to have a true thespian of your caliber in our midst."

"Good to see you again, Margaret." Dad is smiling at Mrs. Hastings, who smiles at Mrs. Friesen, who is smiling at me as I smile back at all three of them. Smiles all around. We're a smiley bunch of Baptists.

"We really enjoyed the musical this spring," says Dad. "Thank you for making room for Aaron in your new production."

"Oh, Dr. Hartzler, that's so kind of you. I am thrilled that Aaron will be joining us here at Tri-City this year. He's simply perfect for this role."

Although he is firm about making me change schools my junior year, Dad also knows how upset I am about it. He wants me to want this. He wants me to be happy here. "Have a good rehearsal, son." Dad's smile is full of hope. "I'm going to go talk with Mr. Friesen, and then I'll be back in a couple hours to pick you up."

Something in his eyes pleads with me as he heads off to the principal's office. Suddenly, I feel sorry for him. He's the expert on teaching kids how to be Christ-like, and he's had to move his kids to a new school because I wasn't doing the right thing. It must be embarrassing. Even though I don't like it, I realize I can't change this anymore. I'm here now. This is real.

I want to make this work for him.

Being charming to the drama teacher is one thing, but I know I'll have to really sell it if I'm going to reassure Dad and the principal's wife I'm on board. Lynne stands at Dad's elbow, and as they turn to leave, I fix her with a smile that threatens the structural integrity of my skull. "See you soon, Mama Friesen."

"Oh, sugar! Welcome *home*!" This was the right answer. She flies back toward me, throwing her arms around me. Her hug is crushing and spins me toward the two students who were running a scene when we stormed in. I can't avoid looking at them any longer.

I instantly recognize the girl as the captain of the Crusader cheerleading squad. She has her head down, flipping through her script, but the guy stares straight into my eyes with a sort of bewildered disbelief. He's the starting center with the curly hair from the basketball game last year. The right side of his mouth curls into the same half smile I saw in the gym at Blue Ridge. Before he turns away, I can tell from his expression he hasn't forgotten that night.

Christy! is a new musical based on the novel *Christy* by Catherine Marshall, adapted for the stage by Mrs. Hastings. The story is about a young schoolteacher who leaves a life of wealth and privilege to become a missionary teacher in the Appalachian Mountains, fighting the ignorance and backwoods superstitions of the local populace she came to educate and serve.

I have been cast as Christy's chief hillbilly nemesis, Bird's Eye Taylor. It isn't a large role, but I know it will be memorable, mainly because the script calls for me to shoot a double-barreled shotgun at the character of David, the young, single preacher who is one of Christy's two love interests.

Mrs. Hastings hands me a script as the door of the rehearsal room closes behind Dad and Mrs. Friesen. I can feel the heat of every gaze in the room on my face as I flip through the pages, looking for my character's name but seeing nothing. I imagine what the rest of the cast must be thinking:

So, this is the new kid who didn't audition but somehow has a great role.

My stomach is a tile bathroom and it feels like someone has teed off a new golf ball inside me. I think I might throw up, and the permanent burrito funk that hangs in the air of the room isn't helping.

Mrs. Hastings turns to address the rest of the cast. "Everyone, may I have your attention, please?" This is only an odd request because no one is talking. Everyone is silently looking at me.

"This is Aaron Hartzler, and he's the newest addition to our cast. He'll be playing the role of Bird's Eye Taylor. Let's take five and you can introduce yourselves. Then we'll start right in."

"Aaron!" I recognize the voice before I see her. Erica Norton, my friend from camp, generally sounds as cheerful and fresh-scrubbed as she looks. Her straight blonde hair is held perfectly in place by a headband and flips up right at her shoulders. As she approaches, I open my arms for a hug.

"Whoa!" she says, leaning away from me, then glancing side to side, embarrassed.

"What—?" I ask.

"Watch the random hugging around here," she whispers earnestly. "It's not camp."

"Really?" I ask.

"Really," she says. "They're pretty strict about PC."

"PC?"

"Physical contact," she whispers. "C'mon, let me introduce you to some people."

As I follow her across the room, I notice Erica is wearing a pair of culottes. In fact, all the girls seem to be wearing culottes for rehearsal, and I remember Erica telling me about the dress code. Girls aren't ever allowed to wear shorts or pants to school. If there's a casual event, culottes are the only alternative to a skirt or a dress. I've seen older women in split skirts before, but I've never noticed how weird they look on girls my own age.

Erica introduces me to the girl playing Christy—the

captain of the cheerleading squad. "Heather, this is Aaron Hartzler."

"Welcome to Tri-City," she says brightly. "I feel like I've met you before."

"I've seen you at basketball games at Blue Ridge."

"Right!" she says, turning to her friend. "Megan, have you met Aaron yet?"

"I thought you'd never ask." Megan fixes me with a clandestine smile, as if we share a dangerous, delicious secret. There's something different about her, and I realize she's the only girl in the room who isn't wearing culottes. Megan is wearing a long, slim skirt and a crisp, expensive-looking blouse.

She extends her hand. "Hi. I'm Megan." Her voice is warm and full, like a thick sweater sliding over my shoulders, so textured it feels like I'm sinking into it—almost raspy but somehow soft, not rough.

"Nice to meet you," I say.

"We've heard a lot about you." She glances at Erica with an eyebrow raised. Is this a challenge? An invitation? Both?

"All bad, I assume?" I smile.

Megan drops her blue eyes to my toes, then draws them up to my chin. "Yes," she says grimly. "Reports have been *dreadful*."

For a moment, she looks at me with a dark stare, and then she laughs. Head back, chestnut spirals spilling over her shoulders and down her back like Julia Roberts in *Pretty Woman*. Her laughter makes everyone smile.

Everyone but Erica.

"I'm going to run to the ladies' room before we get started

again," Erica says, then spins toward the door in a swirl of blonde hair and heads into the hallway.

An awkward silence settles over Megan and Heather as I watch Erica leave. I turn back and see them both looking at me, waiting, curious to see what my reaction will be.

"I'm going to look over my script," I say. "It was nice to meet you both."

I walk across the room to a row of chairs against the wall and open my script.

"Wow. You've been here for, like, thirty seconds, and they're already fighting over you."

I look up and see the basketball player smirking down at me. This is the moment I've been dreading all day. *Is he putting me down or joking?* I can't tell, until he smiles.

"Bradley," he says. "I play David, the preacher."

"Aaron," I say, shaking his hand and smiling with relief. "I play the hillbilly who shoots at you."

Bradley sits down in the chair next to mine. "So. Blue Ridge, huh?"

"Yeah," I say, scrunching my eyes closed and wrinkling my forehead. "Hope you won't hold that against me?"

"Hold it against you? Just sorry that you wound up here," he says. "I love playing Blue Ridge. You guys always look like you're having so much fun. I wish they'd let us have a pep band. Or see our cheerleaders' knees."

"You know the seductive power of the kneecap," I say.

"Are you...joking?" Bradley asks.

"No," I whisper earnestly. "All these girls in culottes are giving me a boner."

Bradley laughs a little too loudly, and once again every eye in the room turns my way. "Thank God for some fresh blood around here."

"Is it that bad?" I ask.

"You have no idea."

When Mrs. Hastings calls us back, we block my first scene, then run it. I go all out with an accent like the one Nanny's sister from Virginia has—Southern, but with a hard *R* that makes me sound like a hick from the mountains. Bradley and Heather crack up when I start talking, and we have to hold for a second so they can compose themselves. By the time we're finished rehearsing the scene, I'm a star.

Megan is still laughing when I sit down at the table next to her. Apparently unconcerned about the PC issue, she reaches over and squeezes my leg. "You're hilarious," she says. "You're going to steal the show."

"Thanks." I smile. "Can I ask you a question?"

"Sure."

"Why aren't you wearing culottes?"

She arches an eyebrow. "Besides the fact that they're hideous?" she whispers.

"Thought it was just me."

"If the choice is between a skirt and looking like a moron, I'll go with the skirt, thank you very much."

Megan grabs her script when the next scene is announced, and walks across the room. As she waits for Mrs. Hastings to give blocking, she turns back to the table, catches me watching, and winks.

Erica sighs, and I realize she has seen this entire exchange. She looks at me as if she can't remember who I am, then rolls her eyes and opens her script.

A careful reading of the dress code in the Tri-City *Student Handbook* proves enlightening. No jeans for boys, only chinos and slacks. No pants for girls, only dresses or skirts that cover the knee. Only shirts with collars are allowed, and no shirts with writing. When I finish familiarizing myself with the rules, I go downstairs to the laundry room, plug in the iron, and turn the dial all the way to the cotton/linen setting.

As I wait for the iron to heat up, I wander over to Dad's desk in the family room and dial Daphne's number.

"What are you doing?" she asks.

"Planning my outfit for tomorrow."

"Your decision?"

"Going with something classic," I say. "Blue-and-white-striped oxford. Navy chinos. Penny loafers."

"The Polo oxford?"

"Yeah." Daphne and I have a penchant for discount name brands, but Dad's Bible college professor salary doesn't really allow for brand-new Ralph Lauren shirts. However, thanks to a few shopping trips with Nanny in Memphis, excursions to the outlets and consignment shops with Mom, and selected hand-me-downs from church friends and cousins, I've been able to put together several looks from a *GQ* magazine spread I saw in the fall fashion issue Jason had in his dorm room. He gave me a few of his old issues, and I keep a secret stash under some bins in the back of my closet.

"Very preppy," says Daphne. "Good way to start."

"Well, I'm not allowed to wear jeans of any kind, so it's going to be pretty preppy all the time."

"Nervous?"

"Yeah." The butterflies in my stomach had kicked into high gear on the way home from church this morning.

"No one ever knows when you're nervous, Aaron."

"I do."

"At least you know some people from the play already, right?"

I smile. This is what Daphne does; she looks for the good in everything, every time. Usually, she finds it.

"Yeah, I guess."

"Are your parents still talking about moving closer to Tri-City?" she asks. Daphne lives only a few minutes from my new school.

"House goes on the market next week. They're looking not far from where you live."

"Well, at least we'll live closer together," says Daphne. "That'll make it easier to hang out on the weekend."

We're both silent for a moment. In the stillness, I try to look for the good in this—the *plan*. Mom keeps quoting this Bible verse to me, as if it will magically erase the sadness from my eyes and put a smile back on my face: "All things work together for good...." I can't see it. This doesn't feel like the loving hand of a divine master plan. It feels like Dad is getting even.

After a minute, I remember the iron. "Guess I should go press my shirt before I burn down the laundry room."

"Call me tomorrow and let me know how it goes?" Daphne says.

"Of course."

CHAPTER 12

You can see the Tri-City Baptist Church and Christian School for miles. A white ski slope of roof races up four stories toward the three crosses that comprise the towering steeple, a massive edifice of smooth white plaster, glass, and chrome—like the temple of an alien god from a *Star Trek* episode. You can see it for miles down Interstate 70, a sparkly spaceship for Jesus.

The first time I climbed the stairs to a school building was the day I started kindergarten. Mom waited in the station wagon by the curb to make sure I got into the building. As I reached the door at the top of the stairs, Josh called out to me through the open car window: "Aaron, be a good soldier for Jesus!"

As we walk up the front steps at Tri-City Christian, I can tell Josh is nervous. I can see it in the way his shoulders slump slightly under his book bag. This is his first day of ninth grade, and he's not in a hurry. He's got a small part in the play and has been to a few rehearsals in addition to his JV soccer practices, so he knows a few people, but this is the first time we've been tossed in with the entire student body, and suddenly I feel protective of him. We're starting a new school today because of my actions—not his. He has to go through this upheaval because of me.

I want to make this better for him, easier somehow. I want us to be friends again. I want him not to be upset with me for lying about the CD, for buying it in the first place, for screaming "I hate you" at Mom and Dad. I want him to smile at me with the grin he used to have when we were kids building bike ramps in the driveway. I want to take his hand and tell him I'm sorry.

We reach the top of the stairs and I hold the door open for him. "Be a good soldier for Jesus," I say.

He rolls his eyes. "Here goes nothin'."

As we walk through the front door, I stop for a moment and stare. I feel like I'm four years old again, standing in the wings, covered in blood. I'm about to make my big entrance, only this time there's no muscular guy to carry me on. I have to walk out into the light and make up my own lines.

No playing dead this time.

"Aaron! Josh!" I spot Erica's blonde hair coming toward us down the hall. She is waving and smiling in a navy dress with a lacy collar and mauve roses swirling down the front. She looks like she's been ambushed by a Laura Ashley bed-in-a-bag. Still, I am relieved to see a familiar face.

"Hey, guys!" She rushes up breathlessly. "C'mon! We all wait in the gym for classes to start."

The gym smells like sweat and new varnish. The floors have been refinished, and the gloss of the hardwood catches the sun streaming through the high windows above the bleachers. Erica is engulfed in a circle of hugs by a group of giggling girls wearing bows, or flowers, or both. I spot Bradley sitting on the top bleacher. He sees me and Josh and waves us over.

"Hartzler!" he says. "And younger Hartzler." He jerks his chin up at Josh. He does this thing with his chin where he flips it up at you, and it feels like you're getting a hello from a movie star. It's the coolest thing ever. I couldn't pull it off if I practiced in the mirror for hours.

"So...you boys ready for your first discipleship group?" Bradley teases. "You're going to *love* it."

Discipleship groups are little student-run prayer meetings that take place once a week between second and third periods. Bradley is a senior, so he's in charge of one.

"You're both in my group," he informs us, grinning.

"Really?" I ask. "How'd you make that happen?"

"I have my ways," he says.

"I'll bet." Josh laughs, and when I see his smile, I know it's going to be okay. It's our very first day, and we're already talking to one of the most popular seniors in school.

"So, I guess we owe you now?" I ask.

"Only Josh owes me." Bradley winks at me and grabs at the collar of his shirt, pulling it down to reveal his clavicle while quoting Madonna. "Hey, Josh. Justify my love."

147

"Get away from me." Josh laughs and moves down a row on the bleachers.

"Don't leave me, Josh," Bradley pleads, faking a desperate grasp.

A bell rings and we all grab our stuff. "Our discipleship group meets in here on the stage," Bradley says. "See you then."

"If you're lucky," Josh says, smirking. My brother slings his backpack over his shoulder and disappears down the hall toward his first class. I watch him go and smile to myself. His shoulders aren't slumped anymore.

Bradley and I walk toward our lockers.

"Thanks," I say.

"For what?" he asks.

"Being nice to Josh."

"No worries. I came here from a public school last year. It was a crazy change. I can't imagine what it would be like transferring here from the biggest rival school."

"Why did you switch from the public school?"

"The academics are a lot better here than at Lee's Summit or Blue Springs."

"So your parents don't care where you go?"

Bradley sort of half laughs and then looks at me. "My parents don't care about anything."

When Bradley says this, a bell goes off, but not in the hallway—in my head. I suddenly feel hopeful. "What do you mean?"

"Let's just say that they aren't really into the rules and the religion of all this," Bradley explains. "They think it's fine, but when my dad moved back in, he agreed to pay tuition here so I can get better test scores."

"Your dad was living somewhere else?"

"Yeah. He and Mom got divorced a couple years ago, but then the fling he was having didn't work out, so they got back together."

"What was it like when they got remarried?" I ask.

"Oh, they didn't get remarried," says Bradley. "He just moved back in. They're gonna see how it goes. So far, it's been pretty cool. You should come meet 'em. They're fun."

"Sounds great," I say. I am trying not to seem too excited.

"Cool," Bradley says. "Let's figure out a time this weekend."

My mind floods with questions: What is it like when your parents don't live together? What does it mean that your parents are *divorced* and living together? How are they "fun"? My parents can be fun, but for some reason, I think the way Bradley is using the word is not the same way I would use the word. I feel certain our lexicons differ.

We close our lockers and walk toward the stairs.

"Buckle up," Bradley says.

Then he tosses me a chin and heads down the hall.

Josh has JV soccer practice after school, and since I'm his ride, I'm going to practice the piano until he's finished. I load up an armful of music: Brahms, Hanon and Czerny, Khachaturian, and Bach.

As I swing my locker door closed, Megan appears, like magic. She must've been standing behind it. She is wearing her cheerleading uniform and a smirk. "Did I scare you?"

"No—yes—I mean—" What is it about this girl that catches me off guard?

"Whatcha doing?"

I hold up the music. "I have some ivories to tickle."

"Walk me to cheerleading practice first?" There's something in the way she arches her eyebrow. It's not so much a question as a dare.

"Sure."

She smiles. I smile. We walk.

The athletic fields are across the street from the church and school, a rolling expanse of well-manicured green. A baseball diamond is sandwiched by two soccer fields. The cheerleaders practice outside while it's still warm. A light breeze catches Megan's curls and whips them into her face. When she tosses her head, I can smell her perfume.

"You smell good," I say. *Wow, that was lame.*

She laughs. "Thanks. It's called Trésor by Lancôme. My favorite."

The other girls haven't arrived yet, so Megan drops to the grass and starts stretching. We watch the soccer team running lines and drills on the field.

"Why didn't you go out for soccer?" she asks.

"Not my thing," I say. "More of a music-and-acting guy. I like to run, but you guys don't have a track team."

"Yeah, we're big on the sports you can cheer for."

"Not so wild for the team sports," I say.

She cocks her chin and eyes me with a smirk. "More into one-on-one?"

I'm blushing. Girls at Blue Ridge never talked to me this way. Why am I having trouble with a snappy comeback?

"Are you already harassing the new guy?" It's Heather, aka "Christy"—the captain of the squad.

"Trying," says Megan.

"Run while you can, Aaron," says Heather. "This one is dangerous."

I smile at Heather. "I can hold my own."

Bradley's light blue Geo Storm is so new and shiny it catches the late-afternoon sun and almost blinds me as it zooms up next to the soccer field. He pulls up near where we are sitting. A short, blonde senior named Angela jumps out, and when she does, Bradley calls to me across the seat. "Hey, Hartzler—what are you doing?"

I stand up and dust the grass off my chinos. "Headed back to the choir room to practice the piano."

"Nuts. I was gonna see if you wanted to run lines."

"Can't tonight, but you can give me a ride back to the parking lot if you want," I say.

The rest of the cheerleading squad is arriving. Heather is going over names on a clipboard and sorting through a big box of uniforms. Megan waves at Bradley.

"Hey, Bradley." She smiles at him, then turns to me. "See you tomorrow?"

"If I survive this ride to the parking lot."

She laughs. "I'll say a prayer."

When I get into his car, Bradley turns up the stereo, and tight vocal harmonies cascade over a beat that pours out under a lyric I've never heard before: *Baby, you send me...*

"Who is this?" I ask.

Bradley blinks at me like I've lost my mind. "P.M. Dawn? The most incredible hip-hop single of the year?"

"Yeah... I don't get to listen to secular music at my house." It feels like a confession.

Bradley frowns. "Dang. That's harsh. No music at all?"

"Only the beautiful, sacred music of KLJC," I say, parroting the station's tagline.

"Wait—isn't that the Christian radio station at that Bible college in Belton?"

"Yeah. My dad teaches there." I look down at my hands. This is where he realizes I'm too weird to hang out with.

Bradley laughs. "There's a lot of great music in the world, and as far as I can tell, there is not a high percentage of it on KLJC. We've got to get you to my house soon so I can give you an education."

I exhale with relief. "Name the day."

"You should crash at my place Friday night. You can meet my parents. I'll play you the Bradley Westman Essential Collection, and we can run lines before we go to rehearsal Saturday morning."

My palms are sweaty against the seat. "Sounds good."

I try to keep my voice level. Don't want to act like I'm too excited. Bradley puts the car in gear and eases back toward my little brown Toyota Tercel in the parking lot.

I glance at the cheerleaders as we drive away. "What about Angela? Do you guys have plans that night?"

"Not really," he says. "She'll probably stop by and hang out for a little while. You should see if Megan wants to come by, too."

"What?"

"Don't play stupid. She can't wait to jump all over you."

"I dunno," I say. "She's friends with Erica Norton."

"Oh, yeah." Bradley nods. "I heard about that. You guys know each other from camp or something, right?"

"Yeah. And I took her to the Valentine's banquet at Blue Ridge in ninth grade."

"How was that?" he asks.

"I don't think Erica and I are ... a match."

"No kidding," he says, laughing. "She's as buttoned up as they come."

"She's really sweet and my parents love her, but I don't think she'd ever sneak out to a movie with me."

"Wait," Bradley says. "You have to sneak out to *movies*? Like, you're not *allowed* to go to movies?"

"Yeah, movies are right up there with P.M. Dawn."

"What do you do for *fun*?" he asks.

"Hopefully, hang out with you."

"Done," he says.

Bradley parks next to my car. "Well, congrats." He sticks out his hand.

I shake it. "For what?"

"You survived your first day at Tri-City," he says.

I smile, and nod. "Praise the Lord."

Bradley laughs as I climb out of his car and close the door.

CHAPTER 13

"Do Bradley and his parents go to church at Tri-City?" Mom asks. She's all smiles this afternoon, very excited that I'm making friends so soon.

"I don't think so," I say, biting into one of Mom's first-day-of-school chocolate chip cookies at the kitchen table. Mom is a diabetic and a label reader. She believes in healthy after-school snacks like carrot sticks and apple slices, except for the first day of school: homemade chocolate chip cookies, fresh from the oven.

"Did you hear Bradley say where they go to church in discipleship group?" I ask Josh as Dad walks into the kitchen, loosening his tie and kissing Mom.

"No," he says. "I didn't."

I am dangling the discipleship group in front of Dad in hopes of distracting him from where Bradley goes to church. Here's the deal: I know Mom and Dad will never let me go to Bradley's house if they hear that his parents are divorced and living together, or that rock music is on the agenda. I'm sure

Bradley's parents don't go to church anywhere, and I'm sure if my mom and dad know all this, Bradley and I will not get to hang out. There will be no TV, no movies, and no music.

I hate lying to my parents, but if I want to hang out with Bradley, I don't have a choice. I try to make the lies as small as possible. I try not to actually lie, but I don't go into extended detail about the whole story. I try to mix as much truth as I can with some things that are *probably* true and only a few things that are probably *not* true, in order to get the answer I want from Mom and Dad. My goal is to keep the actual lie-to-truth ratio as low as possible.

It's my first day at a new school, and I'm already back to my old tricks.

"Bradley is in your discipleship group?" Dad takes the bait.

"He's actually the leader of the group."

"It's so great that he's reaching out to you guys already," Dad says. "He's in the play with you, isn't he?"

I nod. "Bradley wanted me to spend the night on Friday so we can run lines before rehearsal on Saturday."

"Are his parents going to be there?" Mom asks.

"Yes, ma'am."

"Where did you say they go to church?" asks Dad.

"I'm not sure. I'll ask him tomorrow."

"Okay," Dad says.

I can tell he wants to say yes. He wants to know that I don't hate him anymore. He wants me to have friends. This is the tricky part—the part where I have to make it seem certain that Mom and Dad can trust me, that I've had a fresh start at this new school—a spiritual awakening. I have to make it appear as authentic as possible, because the truth is, I don't care what they think about Bradley. I just want them to let me go.

I can feel the nervousness inching up at the back of my throat. This is delicate work, like defusing a bomb. I can't go too fast, or it'll get sloppy. I've seen Dad deal with people I know he thinks are a little wacky at churches or at the Bible college, and he has this way of speaking to them very sincerely. It's not an act. It's an incredible skill he has that makes every person he comes into contact with feel cared for, seen, and heard. I try to effect his people skills now as I attempt to persuade him that Bradley is the kind of friend he'd want me to have.

"How long has Bradley attended Tri-City?" Dad asks.

Bingo. This is my "in."

"He actually came over from Lee's Summit last year." (The true part.) "He didn't have very many Christian friends, and they were teaching lots of evolution in his science classes." (The might-be-true part.) Bradley probably *didn't* have a lot of Christian friends at his public school, and they probably *did* teach evolution in his science classes. He hadn't actually told me that, but it was very probable, and it was exactly what I needed.

Dad nods thoughtfully. "That's quite a sacrifice for parents to make. Tuition is expensive at Tri-City. The only reason we can afford to have you kids there is because they give me a discount for being employed in a full-time Christian ministry."

"Bradley really likes Tri-City," I tell Dad. "He says it's a lot easier without all the peer pressure." (The not-true-at-all part.) I cringe a little on the inside, but I know I'm speaking Dad's language. I know what he wants to hear.

"Sounds like Bradley really has a heart for the Lord. I think it'd be okay." Dad turns to Mom. "Honey, what do you think?"

Mom is starting dinner. "I think it sounds fine," she says. "Can you bring your brothers home from play practice on Saturday if I drop them off?"

"Yes, ma'am."

"I'm really glad you've made a friend already," Dad says, and smiles.

Relief floods over me, followed by a torrent of guilt. I got what I wanted: the buy-in on Bradley. Something else hits me: Mom and Dad don't know *anyone* at this new school. They don't know who the "good" kids are—the ones my dad would say "have a heart for the Lord." They don't know which families go to church where. They have to trust me to tell them the truth.

But they shouldn't.

After dinner, I practice the piano for an hour and then call Daphne.

"You survived," she says. "How was it?"

"Weird. I missed you."

"Likewise. I'm not sure who is going to plan the junior/

senior banquet now that you're gone. When the committee met today to select themes for the evening, Dan Krantz suggested 'A Night at the Bean Dip Ballroom.' Any new-friend prospects?" she asks.

"Well, Erica was there, of course."

"From the Valentine's Day banquet two years ago?"

"That's the one." I sigh. We'd double-dated with Daphne that night. It was weird. Daphne's date was the son of her mother's friend, and he didn't speak to her the entire night. "The night of Silent Joe."

"Eighteen months, and I still wake up screaming," says Daphne.

"The only thing more strange was Erica's dress."

Daphne laughs. "Well, it matched your cummerbund perfectly."

"Yes," I say. "All seventy yards of fabric."

"It was certainly a full-coverage banquet gown," Daphne agrees. "Where do you think she bought it?"

"Her mom made it."

"I remember I was glad you didn't get her a wrist corsage," says Daphne.

"Yeah, because you couldn't see her wrists."

"Or her ankles."

"I'm surprised it didn't come with a hood."

"Still, Erica was very sweet," she says.

"Yes, at least she could talk," I agree.

"Her mouth was the only thing on her body the dress didn't cover."

Daphne and I have to stop talking for a minute because we are laughing so hard. Finally, she takes a deep breath. "Okay. Other potential friends?"

"There's this senior named Bradley. He asked me to come over and hang out this weekend."

"See? I knew it'd be no problem for you."

"Well, the jury is still out. We'll see if Dad and Mom let me go."

"How are they doing with all of this?"

"Happy as clams," I say. "It's weird. I realized today that they don't know who the good kids are, so they sort of have to..."

"Trust you?" Daphne asks. I can hear her smile over the phone.

"Yeah."

"I smell trouble." Daphne knows me better than anyone.

"I will not stand for these wild allegations."

Daphne sighs. "I have to start reading *Silas Marner*."

"I have to start reading *A Tale of Two Cities*."

"Keep me posted," she says.

"I will. I have some ideas for the Bean Dip Ballroom."

She laughs and tells me good-bye.

"The person with the dirtiest towel wins."

Coach Hauser is speaking in our Friday chapel service. Between second and third periods each week, we all walk down the hall to the giant church auditorium, sing a few hymns, and listen to a sermon. It's like a mini church service, in addition to our daily Bible class. Coach Hauser is the PE teacher and basketball coach. He's been speaking about John 13, where Jesus washes his disciples' feet at the Last Supper.

"I want to see the most popular kids in our school being the biggest servants to others. That's what Jesus taught us by his example: Humility is not weakness. It's using your power to serve others. Jesus was the Son of God, the creator of heaven and earth. But the night before he died, he grabbed a cloth and a basin and washed the dirty feet of the men who followed him. As we start a new school year, let's see who can be the biggest servant among us. How dirty is your towel? Whose feet will you wash today?"

Walking out of the church auditorium, I head back toward my locker to grab my chemistry notes. Bradley intercepts me and pulls me over toward the bulletin board outside the office. The list is tacked directly in the center:

SENIOR HIGH SELECT VOCAL ENSEMBLE

Twelve names are listed, including Erica's, Bradley's, and mine.

"So glad you'll be there," Bradley says. "See you eighth period."

When we meet back up in the choir room that afternoon, Erica is about to explode. "I *knew* you'd make the ensemble. This is *so great!*"

"Yeah, wait'll you see the outfits Mrs. Friesen picked out." Bradley sighs.

"Outfits?" I ask.

"Just saw her squealing over them in the office. This year it's mauve polyester blazers to match the flowers on the girls' dresses."

"Mauve?" I whisper, blinking, horrified.

"We're going to look like a country craft."

Mr. Green, the music teacher, walks in and starts class as the bell rings. "Welcome to senior high ensemble," he says, adjusting his glasses. "I hold auditions for this group so we can sing music more challenging than 'Mr. Whole Note Takes a Walk.'" He tells us to start thinking now about duets, trios, and quartets. "We'll need some song selections of your own for the tour in the spring, and anyone who plays an instrument should be working on a solo of some kind as well," he says.

I nudge Erica. "Hey," I whisper. "Maybe we can do that song we sang at camp this summer?"

Erica frowns. "I don't know about that," she says slowly.

"What song is it?" Tyler Gullem, a senior, pipes up from behind us as Mr. Green passes out sheet music and folders.

"It's this great song that—"

"That you'll have to wait until next week to hear!" Erica cuts me off.

"You sang it at camp last summer?" Tyler asks.

I open my mouth to say something, but Erica leaps in

again. "Yep. We did—right before Aaron's dad preached at the evening service."

She turns to me with a grin even larger than her standard smile, and her eyes go a little bit wider than usual. Without moving her mouth, she whispers through her teeth at me, "We'll talk about it later."

After we sing for an hour, the bell rings, and Erica follows me to my locker.

"Aaron, you have to be careful," she says.

"About what?" I ask, loading up my backpack. I'm headed to Bradley's tonight, and I want to get out of here.

"Nobody can know that song we sang at camp was a Sandi Patty song, or else they won't let us sing it in chapel," she whispers conspiratorially.

Sandi Patty is a contemporary Christian singer whose recordings are sometimes a little jazzy even for my parents, but as long as I sang them accompanied by a piano, there wasn't a problem. "Sandi Patty is off-limits...completely?" I ask in disbelief. "That's ridiculous."

"It's just the way they are here," she says.

"Fine. I'll Wite-Out her name on the music and photocopy it before I bring it in."

"I don't know," Erica says. "Isn't that...lying?"

I heave a sigh as I stuff books into my backpack. "My parents are the most conservative people I know, and if *they* like this song, why is it a problem?"

"Okay," she says. "I don't want to be deceitful."

I shake my head. "So tell them the truth."

"They'll never let us do the song."

I sigh again. "Feels like a lot of hassle to sing a song. Let's just pick something else, then."

"Hartzler!" Bradley pops around the corner, making Erica jump at least a foot in the air. "What's up? You ready to head out?"

"Sure," I say. "Give me a second."

"Cool—meet me down in the parking lot. We can leave your car here tonight, and I'll bring you back for rehearsal tomorrow."

"You're going to Bradley's house?" Erica asks, frowning.

"Yeah, we're going to run lines tonight."

"Oh…well…have fun," she says. "Is anybody else going over there?"

Her question irks me for some reason. "I don't really know what he's got planned."

Erica stands there, staring at me.

"What?" I ask, zipping my choir folder into my backpack. "I'm just getting to know Bradley."

"But his parents aren't…*married*…and they're *living together*."

"So?" I snap. I am annoyed with this conversation. I already have to finesse everything I want to do with my parents. I don't need this from my friends, too.

"Well…I guess I didn't think you'd be hanging out with people who…"

"Who *what*? Who asked me to come hang out my first

164

week at my new school?" Crap. That came out wrong. I feel guilty instantly. Erica's been nothing but nice to me. She blushes and looks at her shoes.

"I'm sorry," I say quickly. "I didn't mean it like that."

She turns to leave.

"Erica...wait."

She stops as I close my locker and sling my backpack over my shoulder.

"You aren't going to be my only friend here," I say quietly. "But you were my *first* friend here. And that's important."

She looks at the floor, then down the hall past my shoulder and sighs, tucking her hair behind her ear. "Don't forget to bring the music Monday," she says. Then she turns around and walks down the hall.

"You in a hurry?" Megan has materialized at my locker again. It's strange how I never see her coming.

"Headed down to meet up with Bradley."

"Bradley?" she asks. "That's trouble."

"Don't worry, I already got the lecture from Erica."

"Oh, jeez." She laughs, and I can't help joining her. She laughs with no reservations, daring anyone to hear her. "Do you have any idea how into you she is?"

I look up at her, a little surprised. I thought I was the only one who noticed.

"I don't wanna know."

"Let's just say that the picture of you two at the Valentine's banquet at Blue Ridge is still in her locker. From two years ago."

"Please tell me it's the wallet-size shot."

"Five-by-seven, handsome." Megan is enjoying this. "So, I'll see you at rehearsal tomorrow?" she asks.

"Yeah. Bradley and I are running lines tonight."

"That's what I hear," she says, breezily sweeping her curls behind her shoulder.

"From whom?" I ask. News travels fast around here.

"Angela was telling me at practice. One of the JV girls wanted all the details when your name came up. Ashley? She's a sophomore—in your geometry class." Megan says this like an indictment.

"Oh, yeah...Ashley." I pretend I haven't really given her much thought. She's as curvy as Megan is lean and athletic. They couldn't be more different. "She seems nice."

"She *seems* about ten pounds too heavy for a basket toss." Megan laughs. "Sturdy, that one. She's a base until further notice."

"She said she was the captain of the squad at her public school last year."

"She says lots of things," Megan replies a little too sweetly.

We walk down the stairs and out the back door to the parking lot. The late August sun shimmers off the sweltering blacktop like an unholy ghost. Angela is sitting in the front seat of Bradley's car and jumps out as she sees us coming.

"Hi, Angela." Megan smiles, then waves at Bradley. "You two going to cause some trouble tonight?" she asks.

"Gonna try," Bradley says. "Maybe we'll cruise Nolan. See what the public-school girls are up to."

Megan laughs. "Angela, you better keep these two on a short leash."

"Don't worry," says Angela, her hands on her hips. "The public-school girls will be up to nothing at all tonight," she says pointedly. Then she smiles and says, "At least not for Bradley. Aaron, on the other hand..."

"Public-school girls terrify me," I say. "Don't they eat Christian-school guys for dinner?"

"Why do you think we're gonna cruise Nolan?" Bradley laughs.

I get into the passenger seat and buckle up.

"Have fun tonight," Megan says.

Bradley backs out slowly as Megan and Angela head inside to change for cheerleading practice.

"Shouldn't you be peeling out or something?" I tease him. "There are girls to impress."

"Probably," he says, "but that sort of shit makes me crazy. I always want to roll down my window at the guys who do that and shout, 'Sorry about your tiny penis.'"

I laugh, and Bradley cranks the stereo. The car almost shakes with the sounds of a hip-hop beat. A voice blasts the words "You're unbelievable" over a syncopated bass line.

"This is EMF, my friend," Bradley shouts over the speakers, smiling as he answers my unspoken question and pulls out of his parking space.

"It's great!" I yell back, but I see Bradley's eyes go wide, and he quickly reaches down and turns off the music.

"Shit," he says, and I follow his gaze to Coach Hauser,

167

holding up his hand at Bradley, signaling him to stop the car and roll down the window. "You've got to be kidding me...."

He presses the button, and his window drops to reveal Coach Hauser in aviator sunglasses, looking like a cop in a polo shirt. To my surprise, Coach smiles.

"Hello, gentlemen."

"Hey, Coach," says Bradley.

"Have a good first week, Mr. Hartzler?" he asks me.

"Yes, sir, I have," I reply, church smile firmly in place.

"Great to hear." He smiles back. "What's not so great to hear, Mr. Westman, is your stereo blasting music that I can only describe as 'questionable' while you are still in the parking lot."

My heart is racing, but I keep smiling into Coach Hauser's black lenses.

"That's truly puzzling, Coach," says Bradley. I shift my focus to his face as the words come out of his mouth. Bradley is totally cool. "Are you sure it was this car?"

"I'm in a great first-week-of-school mood today, Bradley." Coach's smile is still present, but no longer pleasant. "You know, after you leave this parking lot, I can't hear what is coming through your speakers anymore, but God can."

"Yes, sir," says Bradley.

"I hope you're having a good influence on our new student from Blue Ridge?" Coach says.

"Sure trying to," says Bradley.

"We're clear, then?" he asks both of us.

"Crystal," I say.

"See you next week," says Coach. He stands, pushes his glasses back up on his nose, and walks toward the building without looking back.

Bradley rolls up the window.

"Welcome to Tri-City," he says, shaking his head.

"No worries. I'm used to it," I say. "My dad would've made me turn it up and tell him what I was listening to."

As we drive away from the school, Bradley starts laughing.

"What," I ask.

"Did you quote *The Breakfast Club* to Coach Hauser?" he asks.

I smile. "Maybe," I say sheepishly. "Did it come through loud and clear?"

"Crystal," Bradley says.

He cranks up the music and merges onto the highway. A few minutes later, we ease down a long exit ramp. The tall, blond summer grass whips around in the landscaping of the freeway median, and I catch a glimpse of a subdivision down the road: large lots, sprawling houses, perfect lawns.

"Wow. Is the grass in your yard always that green?" I ask.

"All summer long," Bradley says. "Big trucks spray fertilizer every week from March to September. Dad is convinced we'll all die of brain tumors, but it's pretty."

Before I can stop myself, I'm imitating Mom: "Green reminds us of new life in Christ."

Bradley laughs. "Yeah, something like that."

He stops at the QuikTrip convenience store near the entrance of his neighborhood and pulls up to a gas pump.

"What do you want to drink? Dad's gas card is buying."

We get fountain drinks and Twix bars, then drive through the streets of Bradley's neighborhood. I feel like a blank slate—and it feels hopeful. Everything is new and at the beginning. Every impression is a first. I have no history here. I can be anyone I want.

As we turn into Bradley's driveway, I realize that I don't have to put on an act or pretend to be anyone I'm not. I can be exactly who I really am around Bradley. I don't have to hide anything or put on a show. The thought is exhilarating. It's the same feeling in my chest that I had when I went to the movies in Nebraska.

It's the feeling of freedom.

CHAPTER 14

Bradley's dad is in the garage unloading cases of Budweiser from the trunk of his Cadillac. "Hey, guys." He smiles and runs a hand through his longish hair.

"Hey, Dad," says Bradley, eyeing the stack of Budweiser cases. "We having a party?"

"Stocking up. You guys help yourselves. Who's your friend here?"

"I'm Aaron," I say, extending my hand. *Did Bradley's dad offer me a beer before he asked my name?*

"You keeping this joker in line?" He nods at Bradley as he shakes my hand.

"Gave up," I say without smiling. "It's hard work, and I need a break."

Mr. Westman sizes me up, and then he cracks a smile and chuckles. "Got a live one here, Brad. He's gonna give you a run for your money with the public-school girls."

"Why do you think we're hanging out?" says Bradley. "I've got overflow. Need a wingman."

I smile. *Wingman*. The word conjures up someone cool and close and...then I see an angel in my mind's eye—Bradley with wings—and that makes me feel ridiculous. Why does almost everything make me think of something Bible-related?

"Will you two help me get these into the kitchen?" Bradley's dad points to the cases of beer left in the trunk. "I'm gonna fire up the grill."

"Sure," Bradley says, and grabs a couple of cases. He heads up the stairs as Mr. Westman gets the charcoal and lighter fluid and walks out of the garage and toward the back deck.

I stand there, staring at the beer. Mom and Dad would not want me to do this. Is it *wrong* for me to haul them upstairs? *Is this where it starts?*

"You get lost?" Bradley is back. He grabs the last two cases out of the trunk and hands one to me.

"Sorry." I take the case of cans and follow him up the stairs to the kitchen.

I feel like I've time traveled to a different country—maybe a different planet. I've never held a case of beer before. I've never been in a home where there are cases of beer to be held. The cardboard feels alive with energy, somehow pulsing in my hands.

Bradley slides one case into the fridge, then opens a tall cabinet and stacks the others on the lowest shelf. The upper shelves are stocked with bottles of liquor. I stare at green bottles of gin and clear bottles of amber whiskey and scotch. One shelf holds Absolut vodka in glossy bottles with shiny silver caps, and I wonder why they've left the *e* off the end of the brand name. There is something incredibly cool and modern about Absolut bottles—something that makes me feel like an adult simply by looking at them. Above the Absolut, on the very top shelf, is a collection of glasses and stemware.

The stemware stored with Mom's wedding china at home in our dining room buffet is etched with a capital *H* for *Hartzler*, but I've never seen those glasses filled with anything other than iced tea during Thanksgiving dinner.

At my house, nobody drinks alcohol at Thanksgiving.

Or at Christmas.

Or any other time.

I've seen people drink beer and wine in restaurants and from plastic cups when Dad takes us to Royals games, but we all stick with Diet Coke and creamy chocolate malts. Trying to picture my mother sipping a glass of chardonnay is like trying to imagine her wearing a bikini: It's something that will never happen.

When drinking has come up at home, Dad always quotes Ephesians 5:18: "Be not drunk with wine…but be filled with the Spirit." Dad says it's not necessarily a sin to drink, but it's something that can ruin your Christian testimony, so it's something we shouldn't do. "If you're under the influence of alcohol, you're not allowing the Holy Spirit to control your actions," he explains. He also tells us the wine Jesus drank in the Bible was more like grape juice, not fermented like wine is today.

Drinking has always been something we consider dangerous, a fact clearly underlined on my first day of sixth grade. It was a half day of school, and Mom was driving us to the neighborhood pool we belonged to at the time for one last afternoon in the sun, when a drunk driver ran a red light and slammed into our station wagon. Mom's jaw was dislocated by the impact, and five years later, she still can't chew solid food without pain.

Stay away. A neon warning sign flashes in my head, and my heart beats a little faster as I close the Westmans' liquor cabinet. I guess I've always known there are people who mix cocktails at home. I just didn't realize I'd meet some tonight.

Bradley's dad finishes lighting the grill on the deck and comes through the sliding door to wash the charcoal off his hands at the kitchen sink. "Hey, Wingman," he says with a jerk of his chin that looks exactly like Bradley's, "grab me a Bud? And Bradley, get the burgers and some tongs, will ya?"

"Sure thing, Mr. Westman," I hear myself say. *Are you actually going to* touch *a beer?*

"Mr. Westman is my father," he growls. "Call me Drake."

"Sure thing, Drake," says Bradley.

"Smartass." Drake snaps a dish towel at Bradley, who yelps as he pulls a tray of ground beef patties out of the fridge and heads toward the grill. I'm up next at the refrigerator and see the Budweiser cans lined up in perfect rows on the third shelf down. I grab one and notice it's taller and more slender than a Diet Coke can.

Beer cans are cooler than regular cans.

My hands shake a little as I pop the tab, and a bit of fizz bubbles up at the top of the can.

Calm down. You're just opening it. You're not going to drink it. You're not doing anything wrong. This is how normal people live.

I pass the can across the island to Drake, who is gathering a plate and utensils for the burgers.

"Thanks, Aaron." I watch as Mr. Westman downs a long swallow of beer, then juggles the plate, the burgers, and the beer can out the back door toward the grill. Drinking is so *casual* for them. Bradley didn't even blink twice, but my heart is racing. *You were just holding a cold beer.* I try not to imagine what Mom and Dad would say about this.

Bradley is laughing at something his dad says on the deck. He comes over and pokes his head in the door.

"Whatcha doing, man? C'mon—I wanna show you the hot tub."

I follow Bradley outside and up the steps to the Jacuzzi.

"You say Tyler is coming over tonight?" Drake asks.

"Dad, be nice."

"Why? That kid is such a putz."

"Dad! He was one of my best friends."

"Wait—Tyler Gullem?" I ask.

"Yeah," says Bradley.

"Oh, God." Drake grimaces. "You have the misfortune of knowing him, too, huh?"

"He's in our vocal ensemble," I say. "You don't like him?"

Drake takes a swig from his beer. "Think he's a little uppity is all."

Bradley rolls his eyes. "Tyler used to be over here all the

time—especially in the summer. He and Dad used to watch golf together."

"Golf?" I ask.

"I don't get it, either," Bradley says. "We have the biggest TV screen in the Western Hemisphere, and you still can't see the ball. It's like watching a camera pan around a landscape painting."

"We used to watch golf and have a few beers is all." Drake flips the burgers with short, jerky movements. "Then he went and got brainwashed."

"He's not brainwashed, Dad—he's really into Janice." Bradley turns and fills me in. "Tyler 'rededicated his life to Christ' last year, so he doesn't hang out much anymore."

Drake scoffs and finishes his beer. "He's really into Jesus, to hear him tell it."

All at once, I'm worried: Does Drake think Tyler is brainwashed because he's into Jesus or because he doesn't drink anymore? I wonder if Drake will think I'm brainwashed, too, if I don't drink.

The kitchen door slides open and a woman with a sweet smile and designer jeans steps out onto the deck, holding a glass of white wine. "Hey, boys. How goes the hunting and gathering?"

"Hi, Mom." Bradley scrambles down the stairs from the Jacuzzi and kisses her on the cheek. "This is Aaron."

"You're one tall drink of water, young man." She winks, and I feel myself blush.

"Nice to meet you."

Drake hands me the tongs and gives an empty platter to Bradley. "Two more minutes, gentlemen, then pull off the burgers. I'm going inside with this hot mama to mix up some margaritas."

Mrs. Westman giggles as Drake pinches her on the behind and pulls her into the kitchen.

"Get a room, you two!" Bradley calls after them. "Jeez," he says, laughing. "They've been horny as hell since he moved back in."

"When was that?"

"After Christmas last year."

"How long had he been gone?"

"About two years." Bradley opens the grill and squints down at the burgers. "Yeah, I was in ninth grade when he moved out."

"Where'd he go?"

"I dunno, exactly. Stayed with some girl from his office, I think."

"Wow. So they got a divorce?"

"Yep. They got a divorce, and then this chick turned out to be a nightmare. Coke fiend, the whole thing."

"So...he came back?"

"Well, not quite that easily. Mom was done with him."

"How'd he convince her?" I ask.

"He changed," Bradley says, with a quiet smile. "Let's pull these off."

I grab the tongs and put the burgers on the platter Bradley is holding.

"He wooed her," Bradley explains. "Sent flowers, bought jewelry, made promises he actually kept. Came to every one of my basketball games, even though he hates the school."

"Think they'll get married again?"

"Oh, no." Bradley smiles. "Mom's smarter than that. She missed him. I knew she did. But that was something she's never giving up again."

I close the grill as Bradley covers the platter with a piece of aluminum foil, and we walk toward the kitchen door. As Bradley reaches for the door, he pauses and smiles.

"It's weird, but they're happier now than they ever were when they were married, I think. At least from what I remember."

As we walk into the kitchen, Bradley's parents are locked at the lips, pressed up against the sink going at it.

"God! Would you two stop it already?" Bradley cries out in mock horror, but he's smiling as he places the burgers on the counter and grabs a handful of the potato chips Mrs. Westman has put out. The smile stays on his face the entire time we eat.

I'm amazed at how Bradley's parents treat him like an adult. It's like they're old friends who get together for dinner at night. It's bizarre. No one prays before we eat; no one reads the Bible afterward. When we're through eating, Drake lights a cigarette out on the deck and refills their margarita glasses. There's something about it that makes me feel excited—like I'm doing something dangerous.

Maybe I am.

Mom and Dad believe that people who engage in worldly behaviors like drinking, swearing, smoking, and dancing aren't exhibiting the "fruit of the Spirit" in their lives. I've never thought of Mom and Dad as judgmental, but they would definitely question whether the Westmans are Christians.

If Jesus came back right now, would the Westmans be left behind? If they died, would they go to hell?

It feels strange to even think that, because the Westmans are so loving: to each other, to Bradley, to me. They're kind, and funny, and downright sweet. They may not be married anymore, but they obviously love each other.

Dad says God's plan for romance is marriage: "One man with one woman for life." The Westmans have followed a different plan, but it seems to suit them. It doesn't seem they love each other any less because they aren't married.

After we finish eating, Bradley and I run lines for an hour, then start watching the episodes of *Beverly Hills, 90210* Bradley has recorded. In one, the whole gang goes on a camping trip, and Dylan storms out after a fight with Brenda. Brandon goes after him and right as they head off on a hike by themselves, there is a knock on Bradley's front door.

Bradley hits Pause and opens the door for Tyler and Janice.

"Hey, man!" says Bradley. "Good to see you." He and Tyler do an awkward handshake.

"Hi, Janice." I wave from the couch as she walks down the three stairs from the front door and peers at the screen. "Have you seen this episode?" I hit Play, and Brandon and Dylan jump to life again.

"Oh, yes!" Janice runs around the couch and plops down next to me. "This is the one where they go camping, right? We watched this one together, Tyler."

"Yeah, I don't watch that anymore." Tyler doesn't smile when he says this.

"Really?" Bradley asks.

"Yeah, the kids on that show are always drinking and talking about premarital sex. It's not what we should be thinking about."

"It's only a TV show," says Bradley.

"Yeah, but it's a TV show about kids being immoral. It's not pleasing to the Lord."

There's an awkward silence. Janice looks at the floor. This is exactly what my dad would want me to do in this situation. He'd want me to hang out with Tyler, not with Bradley. As we all wait for whatever will happen next, I realize I've never been good at doing the unpopular thing in front of a crowd. When I was a kid, it was my brother Josh who used to tell older neighborhood boys not to use bad words, never me. It wasn't that I didn't love God; I just wanted them to think I was cool.

Is Dad right about me? Maybe I am *too worried about what other people think of me.*

Finally, Tyler clears his throat. "Well, we just wanted to come by and say hi."

"Are you sure you can't stay for a second?" Bradley asks.

On the screen, Brandon's foot slips on a rock during the

hike, and suddenly he's hanging on for dear life with one hand. Dylan rushes to help him and grabs his wrist. Their friendship hangs in the balance: life or death.

"Yeah, I have to get Janice home," says Tyler.

Janice stands up again and gives me a small wave good-bye. Bradley walks them up the stairs to the front door again. "Don't do anything I wouldn't do," he jokes.

"I won't," Tyler says firmly. "I won't do most of the things you would do." He's not joking, and when the door closes, Bradley just stands there for a second.

"Jeez. What was that all about?" I ask.

"I don't know. He's changed." Bradley walks back down the stairs to the couch. He tries to shrug it off with a smile, but there's something sad in his eyes. "I think Tyler's a really good guy, but I don't get this holier-than-thou thing. He used to be so cool—like you."

I can't help but smile. *Bradley thinks I'm cool.* As Dylan pulls Brandon to safety on the screen, I feel a surge of relief— not for Brandon Walsh but for myself. I'm glad I'm not as uncool as Tyler, and I don't think it's wrong to be happy that Bradley likes me. Just because I'm watching a TV show about teenagers drinking and having sex doesn't mean I am going to drink or have sex. Besides, this show is really about the importance of being there for your friends—your best friends—and right at this moment, that's all I want.

Bradley settles onto the couch and turns the volume back up. We hang out on the couch, surfing back and forth between MTV and VH1. Pop Up Video is running a marathon and it's addictive. After a while, we are both yawning and head to bed.

When we get into Bradley's room, he grabs at the neck of his T-shirt and pulls it off forward over his head. He's still tan from the summer, and I can't help but notice how muscular his chest is. *No wonder the girls love him.* I make a mental note to do more push-ups.

Mrs. Westman appears at the door. "You boys have everything you need?" she asks with a yawn.

"Mom!" exclaims Bradley, staring at his calves in the mirror. "Look how big my legs are getting."

She laughs and joins me behind Bradley at the mirror. He does have muscular calves.

"Bradley!" says his mother in mock horror. "You're so conceited!"

"What? No!" Bradley protests. "I've been doing calf raises. They're looking killer, right?"

Mrs. Westman rolls her eyes, then reaches up and runs her hand through Bradley's hair. "Yes, darling. You're a real He-Man. Aaron, good luck fitting into the bed with this one. His head is liable to take up the whole room."

Bradley laughs and blows his mom a kiss good night, then reaches over and pulls back the comforter and crawls into bed. "You need extra pillows or anything?"

"Nope. I'm good."

I'm nervous in this weird way, like when I opened Mr. Westman's beer earlier, but I don't understand why. I notice the sheets on Bradley's bed. The pattern is a light gray grid with red, blue, and yellow geometric shapes scattered sparingly. No floral prints here. Bradley's room is cool and contemporary, like the rest of his house. I lift the corner of these stylish sheets and gingerly slide in next to him.

The queen-size bed feels huge, so different from my twin bunk bed at home. There's no danger of me brushing against Bradley, but I stay as close as I can to my edge of the bed. I don't want him to think I'm trying to snuggle up or anything. He clicks off the lamp, then flips over on his stomach and hugs the pillow under his head.

"Thanks for having me over," I say.

"Sure, man. I'm glad you came."

"Your parents are awesome."

"Yeah." He laughs. "And they like you. You'll have to come back next weekend."

I smile to myself in the darkness. "Sounds great."

Bradley's breathing seems to even out, and after a moment, I'm pretty sure he's fallen asleep. It startles me a little when he says one more thing.

"And next week: girls."

CHAPTER 15

Oh be careful, little eyes, what you see,
Oh be careful, little eyes, what you see.
For the Father up above is looking down in love,
So be careful, little eyes, what you see.

Mom has never been shy about singing Bible club songs in public venues, and the checkout line at the Hy-Vee grocery store is no exception. As she sings, she reaches up to flip over the *Vanity Fair* magazine she thinks I am looking at. This action, coupled with the song, produces the desired effect. I quickly drop my gaze and swivel to face the candy display as if I've been caught.

"Guard your eyes, sugar," she whispers to me.

Mom has told me to "guard my eyes" every time she sees a billboard or a TV commercial or a rack of magazines since I was four years old. The stars on the magazine covers have changed, but her sweet Southern drawl and her admonition to guard my eyes has not. She smiles at me, and I smile back at her, relieved to pretend that I was indeed looking at the *Vanity Fair* she flipped over.

Barbra Streisand was splayed across the cover in a knit beret, and while she was wearing a baggy cashmere sweater and fishnets the color of sin, she was not wearing pants. Nothing was seen, but everything was suggested.

"She's got such a beautiful voice." Mom sighs. "It's a shame they have to take pictures of her that are so immodest."

Mom and I came to get groceries for our new house while Dad directs unpacking efforts with Josh, Miriam, and Caleb. Our new place is on an acre of grassy property: a corner lot with a stream along the back in a subdivision across the street from a state park. It's bigger than our old place, and I finally have my own bedroom.

As Mom begins to unload the cart, I cautiously glance up at the magazine rack again. It's hard not to look at the black-and-white photo of Jason Priestley, who is grinning down at me from the cover of *Entertainment Weekly* like the happiest guy in the world. He and I both know I wasn't looking at Barbra Streisand's fishnets. Shannen Doherty is giving him a little peck on the left side of his forehead. Luke Perry's arms are draped around both of their shoulders. I wonder if this has something to do with why Jason is smiling more broadly than Brandon Walsh ever does on *90210*. It feels good to have a friend you're really close to. I'm starting to feel that close to Bradley.

When I bend down to heft several two-liter bottles of Diet Coke onto the black conveyor belt, Mom snags my left hand and taps at the gold signet ring on my fourth finger.

"Remember, sweetheart," she whispers, "it's temptation to see it. It's only sin if you keep looking. When you see a picture that doesn't please the savior, you can always choose to look down at this ring instead."

As Mom pays for the groceries, I spin my virginity ring around my finger with my thumb and study the cover of *Entertainment Weekly*. Yesterday, after ensemble practice, Bradley saw me tossing *The Scarlet Letter* into my backpack, and now he keeps telling me that the *A* on my ring stands for *adultery*.

"You should have Bradley come over for dinner," Mom says as she takes the receipt from the clerk and puts her wallet back into her purse.

"Okay," I say. "I'll ask him tomorrow."

I try to imagine Bradley sitting at our kitchen table holding hands and praying with everybody. It's a terrifying thought. He'll think it's totally lame. Nobody will offer him a beer or a margarita, that's for sure.

"What are you guys going to do tomorrow night?" Mom asks.

"I'm not sure," I tell her, pulling my eyes from the magazines and pushing the cart toward the car. "Probably hang out at his place and work on our lines for the play some more."

It's another lie of the not-the-whole-truth variety. We're going to watch a marathon of *90210* episodes Bradley has recorded, and he's invited a couple of girls over. I feel guilty about lying to Mom, but if she knew what we had planned, she wouldn't let me go.

What she doesn't know won't hurt her.

I am standing in Bradley's driveway, leaning against his car. Actually, I'm leaning against Ashley, the sophomore from geometry, who is leaning against Bradley's car. The car is freshly waxed, making Ashley sort of slide around as I lean into her. Her lips are slick like the car, and I realize that her light pink lip gloss is probably all over my face.

"You're such a good kisser," she says softly.

"You are, too." I whisper this into her ear and feel her twist away from my breath involuntarily. She pulls me closer to her.

Note to self: Breath on the ear seems to have a generally positive effect.

"Mmmmm…" Ashley's tongue is all the way in my mouth, and I kiss her back, strongly, almost forcefully. I've never French kissed anyone before. I feel relieved it's finally happening. I know Mom and Dad would say what I'm doing is sin, but I try not to think about it. I'm already nervous about whether I'm doing this right or not. No need to bring my eternal soul into the mix.

Ashley slides her arms around my neck and lays her head back against the roof of the car. I know Bradley is inside the house with Angela, and my mind wanders to what he's doing with her on the couch in front of his parents' big-screen television.

I imagine Bradley wrapping an arm around Angela's lower back and pulling her into him. I imagine what his face looks like while he kisses her. I imagine what his breath feels like as it breezes against her neck. I try to do exactly what I see him doing in my mind and, suddenly, I'm not nervous anymore. In fact, I am very *noticeably* not nervous. Ashley notices, too, and presses more closely against me.

"Hey, big guy." She giggles. "You feel good."

I don't know what to say. My heart is racing, and my mind is barely keeping pace.

"There's more to me than my lips, you know," she says softly. She grabs my hand and slips it under her sweater and onto her stomach.

Her skin is soft and warm, and I can feel her body rise and fall with each breath. She slides her arms around my neck, then slowly weaves her legs around mine. I've never been pressed up against a girl this close before. I open my eyes and look down at her as our mouths melt into each other. She is lost in our kiss, holding on to me like I might float away.

All at once, it feels like I've lost my place. A knot of panic forms in my stomach and rolls up my spine: *I'm not sure what to do next.*

I clamp my eyes closed again and try to imagine what Bradley would do now. I picture his legs tangled up with

Angela's on the couch, his hand under her shirt, resting on her stomach. I see him press into her gently, so I do that, too. Ashley moans softly.

So far, so good.

I pretend that I'm Bradley, and suddenly there is life in my hand. It's not simply resting on Ashley's stomach; it's softly caressing the skin under her sweater. There's a movie screen in my mind, and I can see Bradley calmly, surely moving his hand up, up, up toward Angela's chest. I do the same with Ashley, and as I do, my fingertips brush the cool satin of her bra.

Ashley pulls her lips from mine, and her head rolls back, her eyes closed, and I kiss her chin, then her neck, as I watch Bradley do the same in my head. Ashley arches her back as my hand slides over her bra and I gently caress her breast, and I hear a soft, low moan escape her lips.

Something about that sound is like a record scratch that cuts into the movie in my mind. I lose the picture of what Bradley would do next, like static blurring out the picture on an old TV set. All at once, I feel what is actually happening in the body beneath my brain. My face feels wet, almost sloppy, and my back is hot. My knees are weak, and I realize that my hand is touching Ashley's right breast.

I feel us breathing together as her body rises to meet me, but it's like someone has thrown a switch. Suddenly, my hand is frozen on the cup of her bra, just sitting there. Hanging out, like an accessory—a breast-cessory: *Hey, I'm Aaron's hand, and I'm hanging out on your breast. We'll see if he's got any more moves.... Hmm. Nope. Nope, he doesn't. So... I guess I'll just sit here for a second.*

I realize that I am imagining my hand talking to me, and this feels ridiculous. I hear laughter, and to my horror, I realize it's my own.

Ashley's head pops up. "What? What's wrong? Did I tickle you?"

"No! No...you're...fine," I say. *Quick. Think of something.* "I'm thinking this is not a very easy...position...for all of this. You can't be comfortable pressed up against this car."

"Oh!" Ashley starts laughing. "Yeah, totally," she says, and giggles. She lays her head against my chest. "God, you feel so good. I could kiss you all night."

"Well, if you stay leaned up against this car all night, you're going to need a chiropractor," I joke.

"Or a condom," she whispers.

The words fall from her lips as if she's said them a hundred times. She wraps both arms around my waist, then gently spins us so that my back is leaning against the car. She's short enough that her head fits snugly beneath my chin.

A condom? Is Ashley saying that she wants to have sex with me?

None of the girls at Blue Ridge had ever hinted at having sex with me, but I didn't really have a girlfriend at Blue Ridge. Erin from church decided she wanted to be "just friends" not long after the CD incident. Daphne was the girl I'd spent the most time with at school, but our relationship had never been romantic.

Of course, just because no one had ever tried to have

sex with me personally didn't mean sex wasn't happening at Blue Ridge. There were definitely rumors about people having sex—rumors that had been confirmed last spring when George and Ginny Karaft had come to the school for Spiritual Emphasis Week. We'd had chapel every day for a week, led by my dad's friend George, a tall guy with a mustache from the seventies, and his wife, Ginny, a petite woman with a pointy nose and poodle-tight curls, who strummed an Autoharp as she sang scripture songs she'd written from verses in Proverbs.

George and Ginny ran a camp for teenagers in Oregon during the summer. At the end of the week, there was a bonfire ceremony to induct campers into the "Council of the Rising Son"—*Son* referring to Jesus, the Son of God. During this ceremony, you could take a symbolic stick off the pile and throw it on the fire. The stick represented your life, being burned up in the service of Jesus. George and Ginny traveled the country as evangelists the rest of the year, challenging teenagers to "sell out to Jesus Christ."

George's energy was infectious, and on the last day of Spiritual Emphasis Week, he finished his message and then encouraged students to come and share what God had done in their lives that week.

"I know that we don't have a bonfire here in the auditorium," he said, "but we don't need sticks and fire to talk about how the Lord Jesus has set your heart ablaze for him!"

A line formed at the side of the auditorium, and student after student got up and talked about what they had learned that week. George had encouraged us not to hold anything back from the light of God's love.

"What part of yourself have you been unwilling to give God?" he asked us. "Give it to him now, in the quietness of your heart, then stand up and be counted in front of your friends."

Some students said that they had never really committed their lives to Jesus, and that they had prayed for salvation. A junior named Jimmy apologized for being disrespectful to our study hall supervisor in front of everyone, and promised to let the Lord control his heart and his actions in study hall from now on.

Then Marjorie Shackley stepped to the front of the line. Marjorie was gorgeous—one of the prettiest girls in the school. She had perfect auburn hair that blazed red in the sun when she ran track. She was petite and energetic, with a perfect figure and fiery blue eyes. When she reached the microphone, there were already tears running down her cheeks.

"I have to be honest," she said, and sobbed. "I haven't lived for Jesus."

She covered her face with her hands for a moment, then leaned forward into the mic. "I lost my virginity," she cried. "No! No, I didn't *lose* it. I gave it away," she said, choking. "I gave it away on the hood of a car."

The silence that descended over us was complete. No one moved. No one breathed. Finally, Marjorie choked out a few more sentences asking for our forgiveness and God's, then stumbled back to her seat.

I turned to Daphne and whispered, "Did that just happen?" She responded by digging her fingers into my leg and shaking her head in disbelief.

Making out now with Ashley leaning up against this car makes me think of Marjorie Shackley losing her virginity on the hood of another. My hand on Ashley's breast, and thinking about what Bradley would do, and sex in general suddenly seem *very* important. It feels like any decision at all could be fatal—like the next move I make could be my last.

I try to calm down. *Maybe it's not that big a deal.*

If I'm really honest with myself, having sex with a girl has never seemed like a huge temptation. After all the sermons and instructions about how having premarital sex will ruin my testimony for Christ and my ability to have a healthy marriage, I'm sort of fine with not doing it. I understand that having sex as a teenager does come with more high-risk consequences than, say, listening to rock music or sneaking out to movies. Where sex is concerned, I've been told I should stay as far away from girls as possible. It's all about saving, and waiting, and not putting yourself in a position where you can't stop yourself.

"If you don't want the truck to go over the cliff, you don't park it right on the edge," Dad likes to say. "You keep a healthy distance." And Dad practices what he preaches. He has a window cut in the door of any new office he moves to at the Bible college. That way, if he's alone in a meeting with a female student or professor, others can't accuse him of questionable behavior. They can see what's going on for themselves, right through the door.

This was my first big make-out session, and while I was definitely turned on, making out with Ashley certainly didn't feel like something I couldn't control. I wonder if I'm doing it right. What I felt was exciting, sure, but it didn't seem like an unstoppable lust worthy of putting windows in doors.

What does Bradley feel when he's making out with Angela? Is it different?

Ashley shivers in my arms. The temperature is starting to drop, and the car feels cool against my back.

"C'mon. Let's go kick those two jerks off the couch," she says. "If we don't get to make out, nobody does."

I kiss the top of her head. Her hair smells clean and fruity, a scent I recognize but can't quite place until she pulls me past the half bath in the Westmans' family room, and I realize we use the same conditioner.

After the girls leave, Bradley and I head into the kitchen to grab some leftover pizza. As we pass through the living room, Mrs. Westman peers over the edge of her reading glasses and smiles at us.

"Who are these handsome men coming up my stairs?"

"Shh! Mom, quiet! The paparazzi will hear. We gave 'em the slip." Bradley speaks in a loud whisper, then grabs the pizza box and a couple of Cokes out of the fridge.

Bradley's mom seems sleepy but happy, not unlike Benny, the long-haired Persian cat curled on her lap. She is reading a thick hardcover novel and holds a large wineglass with a small amount of red in the bottom. Soft piano jazz plays over speakers I can't see. Bradley plops down on the floor next to the overstuffed chair where she is sitting, takes a bite of pizza, then puts his nose against Benny's and scratches the cat gently behind the ears.

I join him on the floor and watch Benny open his eyes. He regards Bradley with mild disdain before shaking his ears and issuing an expansive yawn. His pink tongue unrolls slowly, and I notice a blank space in his mouth.

"Is Benny missing a tooth?" I ask.

Bradley immediately begins to laugh, and his mom reaches out and playfully bats him on the head. "Bradley, you stop that this instant. It's not funny."

Bradley snaps into a false composure. "You're right, Mom. It's not. It's not funny at all. Go ahead. Tell Aaron what happened to Benny's tooth."

Mrs. Westman takes the last swallow of wine from her glass and flips her book closed, then gingerly places both on the marble-topped end table at her elbow and buries her nose in Benny's fur.

"Oh, my poor little prince," she says to the cat. "It was an accident. Benny was a show cat—he'd been winning awards and everything."

"He's too sexy for his tail," Bradley says, giggling.

"He was doing *very well* regionally," Mrs. Westman says.

"Doing so well he got worn out and decided to take a nap in the dryer," Bradley says.

Bradley's mom reaches down to smooth Benny's tail. "I was in a hurry, and I didn't see him there when I tossed in a load of sheets."

Bradley bursts into another fit of giggles, and laughs until there are tears in his eyes.

Mrs. Westman is shaking her head, and she starts laughing, too. "Poor Benny," she says. "I heard the *thumpity-thump* right away and ran back down the stairs, but he'd already snagged an ear and lost a tooth."

Bradley is gasping with laughter. "You've never lived until you've seen...a cat come out of the dryer...and try to walk...."

I'm laughing now, in spite of myself.

"My poor little Benny. It's not funny." Mrs. Westman kisses Benny between the ears. "Okay," she admits. "Maybe it's a *little bit* funny."

"At least he doesn't have to do those damn cat pageants anymore." Bradley wipes his eyes. "I'm glad he's okay, but God, those cat shows were boring. Besides—he looks tougher now."

"Did the girls go home?" Mrs. Westman asks, brushing her white bangs out of her eyes. Her hair is a beautiful silver color, the cut short and stylish—it gleams in the soft lamplight.

"Yeah, Angela had to be home by midnight," says Bradley.

"And who was the other girl...Ashley?" Mrs. Westman asks, a question in her smile.

"She's in Aaron's math class," Bradley says.

"I took Algebra One and Two back-to-back at Blue Ridge, so I'm taking geometry with the sophomores this year," I explain.

"A younger woman." Mrs. Westman arches a playful eyebrow. "And you only just met her? You don't waste any time."

"Well...Bradley sort of...arranged for her to come over," I admit. "I wasn't sure if she was really into me."

"Oh, please!" Bradley rolls his eyes. "She's done nothing but follow you around. And she's not the only one, Mom. Aaron's the new stud on the block. Megan Swift is about to throw herself under a bus for him, and Erica Norton almost cries every time he talks to her."

"Erica Norton. She's the blonde girl in the vocal ensemble, right?"

"Yes, ma'am." I nod, and Bradley looks at me like I've suddenly sprouted antennae.

"What did you say?" he asks.

"Bradley, he said 'yes, ma'am' because he is being genteel, something *you* wouldn't know anything about."

Mrs. Westman tousles Bradley's curls playfully, then moves Benny off her lap. She grabs the big round bowl of her empty wineglass and pads toward the kitchen. "Aaron, that's a lovely habit. Your mother obviously has good breeding."

Bradley and I follow and sit on the stools at the large island while she pours another glass of wine from the bottle on the counter. She swirls the crimson liquid, holding her nose over the glass.

"Mmm…this merlot your father brought back from his trip is fantastic," she says, sighing in Bradley's general direction.

"Lemme try it." Bradley reaches across the island.

"Oh, all right, but only a little sip."

Bradley takes the glass and downs the contents in a single swallow.

"Fantastic," he says, smacking his lips with an evil smirk.

"Bradley!" Mrs. Westman shakes her head. "You didn't even ask Aaron if he wanted to try it." She turns to me. "Shall I pour you a little sip?"

I am trying not to fall off the stool. I've never been offered even a sip of alcohol in my life. At our church even the communion cups are filled with grape juice.

"Try some!" says Bradley.

"I'm okay." I smile at him. "Thanks, though, Mrs. Westman."

"Have you ever had a drink?" Bradley asks.

"Actually, no," I admit.

"That's a good plan." Mrs. Westman rinses the glass in the sink. "You paying attention, son?"

Bradley moans.

"I'll bet you have straight As, don't you, Aaron?"

"I do, too," Bradley protests. "Well, As and Bs."

"It's no wonder the ladies like you," Mrs. Westman says to me.

"Yeah! How'd it go with Ashley tonight, anyway?" Bradley fixes me with the kind of grin associated with devious schemes. "You guys were out in the driveway for a long time."

"It went... well."

"Are you blushing?" Mrs. Westman laughs and reaches over the island to pinch my cheek. "Oh, my God, I could just eat you up."

"Mom! Gross!" Bradley is protesting, but I can tell he loves this. "Besides, Aaron can't go too far with the girls. He's got that ring."

I am leaning on the island, and spread out the fingers on my left hand. "Oh, *my*, that's a *lovely* ring. Let me see that."

I stretch my arm across the island and she takes my hand in hers. Her fingers are slender and warm. She peers at the ring in the soft light of the pin spots mounted on the vaulted ceiling in the kitchen. *I wish we had lights like this in our kitchen.*

"Oh, there's an *A* on it. That's beautiful. Was it a gift?"

"Tell her what it means," Bradley urges. I shake my head and laugh at him. He's truly fascinated by this ring, but I hesitate. I know my parents meant well when they gave it to me, but it seems sort of embarrassing and old-fashioned now—especially in light of the Westmans' living situation.

"You don't have to tell me, Aaron," Mrs. Westman says gently. "It's good to have a few things that are only for you."

Something about her smile makes me want to tell her the whole story about the ring. So I do. I tell her how it makes me feel a little silly. How I wasn't really asked if I wanted to pledge to save myself until marriage. How Mom and Dad assumed I was going to. It doesn't feel like I am talking to a parent. It feels like I am talking to a wise older friend with lots of experience—someone who is interested in how I feel about all of this. It's a lot like talking to Nanny when I was a little boy.

Later, Bradley and I stay up for a long time talking about Ashley and the pros and cons between her and Megan and reading a pile of Drake's *Penthouse* magazines. Well, I am reading. Bradley is definitely a pictures guy, but I find stories in the "Forum" section way more interesting. There are these letters that guys write in about these girls they have sex with. Sometimes it's sex in a crazy place, like a van in the mall parking lot, or sex with more than one girl.

Bradley's dad keeps this stack of *Penthouse*s on his desk in the office downstairs—in plain sight. Not hidden, but neatly stacked on the corner next to the printer. It's like he doesn't think pornography is wrong—something else that would not fly with Dad and Mom. I can't really tell what's making my heart race faster—the stories I'm reading or the fact that I'm holding a *Penthouse* in the first place.

Later, when I crawl into bed next to Bradley, he turns off the light and then props himself up on his elbow.

"Spill it, Romeo."

"What…?"

"Don't play dumb with me. How'd it go?"

"With Ashley?" I ask.

"No, with Mariah Carey," he scoffs. "Yes. With Ashley."

I am blushing and smiling, and glad it's a little dark.

I've never really talked about girls with a best friend before except with Jason at camp a couple of summers ago—and he was the one with all the experience. This time I have something to say.

"We kissed a lot," I begin.

"Have you ever kissed a girl before tonight?" Bradley isn't making fun of me; he's really curious. Something about the way he asks lets me tell the truth.

"Not really," I admit. "There were never tongues involved."

"I mean, I'm guessing your parents wouldn't be so happy about you getting to second base with Ashley."

"How'd you know I got to second base?" I ask him.

"I didn't, but I do now." I can hear his smirk in the dark, and I laugh. I sort of feel embarrassed, but mainly I feel good—like I'm finally one of the cool guys.

"Mom and Dad wouldn't be too thrilled with *Penthouse*, either," I say. "They don't like me even reading *GQ*. I have to hide the ones my friend Jason gave me."

"Wait. What's wrong with *GQ*?" Bradley is amazed.

"They say the women in the cologne ads are dressed immodestly, and that I put too much emphasis on my outward appearance."

Bradley laughs. "Oh, my *God*, man. Your parents are hard-core."

"You're lucky," I say. "Sometimes I feel really guilty."

"For *what*?" Bradley asks.

"For…everything," I say. "Going to movies, listening to music, reading your dad's *Penthouse*, even being around your parents while they're drinking. I really like your parents. They treat you like an adult. I wish my family were that way. It feels…easy."

"It's not always a cake walk," says Bradley. "But they're pretty cool for the most part."

We lie there quietly for a minute. I feel so close to Bradley, lying here, talking about stuff that's so private, so personal.

"Do you believe in all that ring stuff your parents do?" he asks. "I mean, are you saving yourself for marriage?"

"I've never had anybody ask me if I believe it or not," I tell him. "They assume I am on board because it's the right thing to do."

"The right thing for who?"

"I've never really thought about it that way," I say. "It's weird. My dad would say Satan is using you and your house of booze and porno to lure me away from the One True God."

Bradley laughs into his pillow. "Do you think I'm corrupting you, Hartzler?"

"I hope so." I say it as a joke, but maybe I mean it. "It's really nice not to have to put on an act around you."

"That's what I hate most about Tri-City," says Bradley. "I mean, why would a God create all of us and put us here if we were supposed to go around feeling bad about ourselves and pretending to be somebody we're not? How is hiding who you are telling the truth?"

"But what happens when the truth inside me feels different from what my parents say is the truth?" I wonder aloud. I don't expect Bradley to have an answer to this question, but he does.

"I think that's called growing up," he says.

I'm still considering these words when I hear a light snore from Bradley's side of the bed and realize he has drifted off to sleep.

CHAPTER 16

The next morning at rehearsal, while Bradley is onstage rehearsing with Heather in the church auditorium, I join Megan and Angela in the back pews under the balcony. Everyone is trying to catch up on homework between scenes.

"A certain sophomore I know had a really fun time with you last night." Angela's smile is a homing beacon, and I instantly realize I'm sunk.

Megan narrows her eyes and shoots lasers in my direction. "Oh, really?" she says. "Do tell."

Angela is breathless with details. "All I know is that while Bradley and I were on the couch watching TV, Aaron and Ashley took a *very long walk* outside."

"Where'd you guys go?" Erica whispers as she plops down on the pew in front of us and leans over the back to get in on the conversation. My misery is complete.

Hell. I'm in a church auditorium and hell at the same time.

"Nowhere," I say, desperate to change the subject.

"That's not what Ashley told me when we walked to our cars," says Angela.

Shut up. Please. Shut. Up.

"Ashley who?" asks Erica.

"Ashley Steele," says Megan, with a too-kind smile. "The sophomore? She's in Aaron's geometry class."

"Oh, yeah," says Erica, still not catching on.

"Apparently, while we're in Algebra Two, Aaron is working all kinds of angles down the hall," Megan says, gathering her bag, her purse, and her chemistry book.

"Where are you going?" Angela asks.

"I've got homework to finish. I have a date tonight." Megan smiles fiercely in my direction, then turns and walks down to the end of the next row.

Erica tucks her hair behind her ear. "Are you...*dating* Ashley?" she asks.

"What? No. No—we hung out for the first time last night at Bradley's."

Angela opens her mouth to say something. I shoot her the look my mother used to give me when I was a kid and talked during the sermon in church. *You're about to cross the line.* Angela closes her mouth.

"Don't forget the music on Monday," Erica says quietly, and then she grabs her script and heads back down to the front rows to watch rehearsal.

"Sorry," says Angela. "I didn't mean to cause a problem. I just..."

"It's okay," I say, rubbing my eyes. "I didn't realize I was capable of making two girls mad at the same time."

"Ashley is really into you."

"How?" I ask. "We hung out for the first time last night."

Angela levels her gaze at me. "C'mon, Aaron. You didn't just hang out. Not according to Ashley, anyway. Besides, haven't you ever been into somebody right away?"

"I'm barely getting to know people," I say, grabbing my stuff. "I don't want to upset anybody. I'm not 'into' anyone yet."

"Well, maybe you should have told Ashley that before you felt her up in the driveway."

My mouth drops open when she says it, and for the third time in thirty-two seconds, a girl gathers her things and stalks to a different pew, leaving me alone in the back row.

My scenes are done for today. Bradley is still onstage rehearsing. I want to be riding shotgun in his crazy little sports car, with the windows rolled down and the music turned up, headed away from this place and these girls. In the meantime, my car will do.

I walk out to my used Toyota Tercel in the parking lot, worried that Megan, Erica, and Ashley are all upset with me; that Angela will tell Bradley I'm a jerk; that Bradley will stop inviting me over. I'm worried about the questions Mom will ask me when I get home: "Did you have a good time? What did you have for dinner? Did you find out where they go to church?"

She won't think to ask me: "Did you read Mr. Westman's

Penthouse collection? Did you feel up a girl from your geometry class? Did Mrs. Westman offer you a glass of merlot?"

Deep down, what I worry about is that despite the straight As and awards for playing the piano and singing and acting; despite working hard, and looking good; despite my ability to be kind and charming; despite the fact that other adults really seem to like me; despite all of that, I'm afraid I really am a bad kid. I feel a wave of guilt that I know my mom would say is the "still, small voice" of God's Holy Spirit convicting me of my sin.

Do I really believe that?

As I pull out of the school parking lot, I stare up at the crosses at the top of the church building. There are big, white cumulus clouds behind the steeple—the kind that led Moses and the "children of Israel" into the Promised Land; the kind in which Jesus will appear.

Or at least that's what they say.

It makes my stomach hurt to think about it. I need some music. This car was born in the eighties, so it only has a cassette tape player. I reach under the seat for the case that holds my contraband tape collection. My tastes are eclectic, and my fingers flip through my favorites—Amy Grant, Bette Midler, Phil Collins, Michael Bolton, Wilson Phillips, Roxette, Suzy Bogguss, Trisha Yearwood, and several singles—Linda Ronstadt and Aaron Neville singing "Don't Know Much" and Bon Jovi's "Blaze of Glory" from the *Young Guns II* sound track. I pop in "Blaze of Glory" and crank up the volume.

I'll have to hide the tapes again before I pull into the driveway, and that makes me angry.

Why can't my mom and dad be like Bradley's?

I think about Mrs. Westman last night, standing in the kitchen. Her eyes were so warm and kind. I think about how upset my mom and dad would be that she offered me a drink—not angry upset; they'd be sad. There'd be tears. Mom would cry. Dad would tell me that he was "grieved" that I'd misled them about Bradley's parents and the kind of people they are. They'd tell me that Mrs. Westman isn't "living for the Lord," that she not only broke the state law but was leading me down the broad path toward destruction.

How could my experience of Mrs. Westman be so different? When I looked into her eyes, I saw someone kind and loving—someone who understands her relationship with Bradley and his friends differently than my parents think about their relationship with me.

She loves Bradley, but she's not afraid for him. Or of him. She knows it's going to be all right. She knows he's a good kid. She knows I am, too.

And that's why even though Mrs. Westman is really a perfect stranger, I told her all about my ring, and how silly I felt when I got it, and how I think the whole thing is kind of embarrassing. Those are all things that I've never told my parents. Not because I don't love them, but because I know that it would hurt them. It would disappoint them. It would prove to them that I'm not the son they want me to be—that they *need* me to be. I could tell Mrs. Westman those things because she doesn't want me to be anyone I'm not. She accepts me exactly as I am.

I can see it in her eyes.

When I walk into the kitchen to hang my car keys on the hook by the phone, Mom looks at me across the kitchen, and I see something in her eyes, too: tears.

There's a stack of *GQ* magazines sitting on the island by the sink.

"I found these in your room today when I was putting away some laundry."

I have nothing to say. There's no way to make an excuse. I hear Josh and Miriam shooting hoops outside. Caleb is practicing the piano. I wish I could be anywhere but here.

When I don't answer, Mom stares at me, then looks down at the magazines. "Aaron, these magazines are full of pornography."

"Mom, these magazines are not pornographic."

Her eyes blaze. "Then what do you call this?" she snaps, pulling open the issue on the top of the stack and flipping to a cologne ad. There's a scantily clad female model lying across a bed, staring out at me, her hands tossed over her head. Everything is covered. Just barely.

"Can you honestly tell me you're a red-blooded American male and this doesn't do anything for you?"

I am stunned that my mother has said these words. I feel my cheeks burn. My nervousness turns to anger. What was she really asking me?

Was that a put-down?

"Mom! I don't read *GQ* to get turned on. I read it because I like knowing what's in fashion. I like seeing the clothes and the hairstyles."

"Of course," she says. "Your hair looks like his. And his." She points to different models as she flips through the pages. "I can't get you out of the mirror in the bathroom. You're more concerned with looking good than you are about doing what's right."

"There's nothing wrong with *GQ*, Mom."

"Oh, there isn't?" She flips to another page in the magazine. "Look at how immodestly this woman is dressed."

She holds up a fashion editorial spread: "New Suits for Fall." The woman on the model's arm wears a strapless minidress. "Would you want Miriam to walk around in a dress like this?"

"No, Mom. She's far too tall for that dress. It would look awful on her."

"Aaron! I am not joking."

"I'm not, either," I say quietly.

"I thought after the whole thing with the CD and the play, and putting you in a new school, you'd have learned your lesson."

I shrug and walk toward the living room. This is an argument I cannot win.

"Don't walk away from me, young man. We're not done here."

I stop in the kitchen door, suddenly exhausted. "Throw

them away, Mom. Do whatever you want. It's not worth fighting about."

"It breaks my heart that you don't see how wrong this is, my son."

There are tears in her voice, and when I look into her eyes, I see the disappointment once more. I feel it leap out of her and land on my chest in a crushing weight. I'm on a balance beam, shakily walking the line between who I am and who she wants me to be. The force of her need makes me wobble; it makes me want to give up, to spread my arms and let myself fall backward into the nothingness.

I know I'll always think about fashion and want to look good. I'll always read *GQ*. I'll never be the guy who thinks cologne ads are sinful. *I'll never be the son you want.*

"I'm sorry, Mom," I say quietly. She thinks I'm apologizing for the magazines. She sighs and shakes her head.

"Don't you *want* to please the Lord, Aaron?"

Please the Lord. I realize I don't know what those words mean. I only wish I pleased *her*. Right now, I do not.

"Of course," I say. This is the dutiful answer, the answer Mom wants to hear. The one I know will honor her, even if it isn't the truth.

"From now on, for every minute you spend in the mirror fixing your hair and getting ready for school, I want you to spend at least one minute reading God's word."

"Yes, ma'am." This is always the answer: more God.

"'Draw nigh unto God, and he will draw nigh unto you.'"

Mom quotes the book of James, but I don't know how I could get any closer to God. We pray at every meal and before each class at school. I have Bible class five times a week, not counting chapel services, or devotions after dinner. If reading the Bible made me closer to God, one might think I am already as close as I am ever going to get.

And still, in this moment, God seems very far away.

CHAPTER 17

"If you search for God, you will find God."

Dr. Spicer, the pastor of Tri-City Baptist Church, is speaking in chapel today. He is very adamant that God is close. Very close. But must be searched for. There's a code to it—a combination that unlocks the mystery. You have to seek God with "your whole heart" in order to find him.

"The prophet Jeremiah tells us in chapter twenty-nine, verse thirteen, that God says, 'And ye shall seek me, and find me, when ye shall search for me with all your heart.'"

Then he leans into the microphone. His voice is dramatic and filled with urgency. "Young men and young women, are you *searching for God*?"

With that question, he begins his closing prayer, but instead of bowing our heads and closing our eyes, Erica and I get up and make our way to the front. We're closing today's chapel service with the duet we've been practicing. I see the pianist take her place at the grand piano stage right with the photocopy of the sheet music where we Wited-Out Sandi Patty's name.

As Dr. Spicer prays, I see Coach Hauser get up from his seat at the end of a pew near the stage and station himself at one of the auditorium doors for hair check. Miss Foster stands at the other doors in the back. Today, the boys will file out past Coach Hauser, who will check to make sure our hair is short enough, and the girls will file out past Miss Foster, who will check to make sure that their skirts are long enough.

We don't search for God here at Tri-City. It seems he's already been found and written into law. Our God here believes in long skirts and short hair. I realize I don't have to look very far for this version of God—he's everywhere, and he can hear my thoughts right now. That doesn't feel comforting, because once again I'm afraid he doesn't like what he's hearing.

Not only is there no search for God, there's no escape from him.

As Erica and I are singing the second chorus, I see Janice sitting six rows back on the right, smiling and mouthing the lyrics along with us, and realize we've made a terrible mistake. Erica and I assumed that no one would know who sings this song, because most of the families at Tri-City don't listen to contemporary Christian recording artists. We were wrong. Janice knows.

This wouldn't be a cause for alarm in and of itself, except that Janice is sitting next to Tyler. Tyler is not smiling. He looks very serious—as serious as I suddenly feel. Erica and I finish singing and take our seats. I walk back and sit down next to Megan as Principal Friesen reminds the student body that today is hair-and-skirt-check day, then dismisses us.

"That was great," Megan says. She's talking to me again. My make-out session with Ashley seems to have been forgotten since Ashley told the cheerleading squad about the football player from Lee's Summit she made out with the next night.

I smile back at Megan and notice Janice a few pews down, rushing over and hugging Erica. Tyler is right behind her, and he stares directly at me. No smile. No nod. He simply catches my eye and stares.

As Megan walks toward skirt check and I fall into line for hair check, I watch Erica chatting with Janice, and I know one thing for certain: We've been caught.

"Ready for the big dance-off this afternoon?"

Bradley punches me in the shoulder. We have a special "choreography" rehearsal this afternoon. Mrs. Hastings insists that Baptists don't "dance."

"Um, I'll be doing Acceptable Baptist Movement this afternoon," I say in mock seriousness.

"You do whatever you want," he says, and grins. "I'll be dancing."

"Don't look now, but Tyler Gullem is shooting daggers our way."

Bradley glances over at him and shakes his head. "Poor guy," he says. Then he raises his arms and swivels his hips like Elvis. "Just needs to shake his moneymaker."

After our haircuts have been approved with a nod from

Coach Hauser, we walk to my locker. I stop to grab my chemistry book. As Bradley continues down the hall toward his next class, he turns around and points at me. "See you in dance practice. And good singing, Hartzler. You make Jesus proud." Bradley doesn't see Tyler watching him as he struts down the hall "dancing."

But I do.

Tyler shakes his head as he gathers his books and closes his locker, then turns and walks away.

"If anyone asks, we are not *dancing*." Mrs. Hastings is standing at the front of the drama room by a television on a cart. "This is Acceptable Baptist Movement. There's a *difference*. Especially to most Baptists."

When I laugh, Mrs. Hastings smiles, her fuchsia lipstick framing perfect pearly whites. We're sharing this joke. There is no difference between dancing and choreography. It's all semantics.

Call it whatever you want....

The choreography we're learning for *Christy!* the musical is a jig, based on an Appalachian folk dance. There's a big scene at the end where my character, the drunken, angry hillbilly, finally makes peace with everybody after Christy almost dies of a mountain illness that has been ravaging the rural community. The original music composed by Mr. Green is great, especially this jig at the end—upbeat and peppy. Mrs. Hastings had a dance instructor friend choreograph an authentic jig after researching the time period and region, then record video of it at her studio.

We spend some time working through the steps. They're sort of tricky, but Angela, Megan, and Heather pick them up quickly. They're cheerleaders, after all, and used to moving their bodies in rhythm. Bradley and I are slower but get it down after about twenty minutes. Turns out jigging is really fun.

Mrs. Hastings clicks off the TV at the front of the classroom, and we move the whole rehearsal onto the stage in the auditorium so we can practice in the space where we'll be performing. It's a little harder on the stage without the instructor on the TV, and I hear Megan laughing on my right.

"What?" I ask.

"Nothing. You look like you're thinking."

"I *am*!" I say.

"You guys, shut up!" moans Bradley. "You're messing up my count."

"Well, at least try not to stick your tongue out and frown. It looks bad," teases Heather.

"Might I remind you that you're wearing *culottes*?" I ask her. Megan laughs when I say this. She's dancing in the skirt she wore to school today.

Heather laughs, too. "Pretty sexy, huh?" She holds out the fabric of her split skirt while continuing to jig.

"Why won't they let you wear shorts?" Bradley asks.

"The lower the hemline, the closer to God," I say, loudly

enough that even Mrs. Hastings laughs, and we all lose the step.

"Take five, everybody," Mrs. Hastings says. "We'll do this one more time, and I'll watch you guys."

I follow Megan down the hall to the water fountain. "How was your date last weekend?" I ask.

She slowly wipes a drop of water from her lip as she stands up. Her eyes narrow, and she flips her long curls over her shoulder. "If you want to know how a date with me goes, why don't you ask me out on one?"

She turns and strides back down the hall toward the auditorium.

"One condition," I call after her. She stops but doesn't turn around.

"What's that?"

"You have to wear culottes."

She turns around slowly and walks back toward me down the long hallway of coat hooks outside the auditorium, one hand languidly trailing along the wall, her head tilted to one side with a sweet smile.

Usually, this hallway is bursting with noise. Now I realize how quiet it is with only Megan and me and the spin in my brain. She stops in front of me and leans in very close.

Too close.

Against-the-rules close.

If Mrs. Hastings walks around the corner right now, we're dead.

Her lips are almost touching my ear. Her whisper is full-blast, and I can smell her Trésor by Lancôme. "If I say yes when you ask me, you'll be so incredibly lucky that you'll be *thrilled* if I show up wearing culottes."

She straightens the collar on my polo, pats my shoulder twice, and walks away.

After rehearsal, I head home to practice the piano. I start by warming up with scales: up four octaves, down two, contrary motion for two octaves out and back, then down two octaves. Up one half step. Repeat.

My fingers fly over the keys on autopilot. All I can think about is Megan's breath on my ear. It made me feel all sorts of things. I'm trying to figure out what, exactly. Sometimes it helps to distract myself with the piano. When I fall into the music, ideas come. I can drop into focus on a particularly hard passage and forget about something that's bothering me, or I can play easy stuff like scales and let my mind search out answers about something.

Or someone.

Someone like Megan.

It's true: I can tell Megan likes me. It's pretty clear she wants me to ask her out, but I don't know that I feel excited about it. It feels inevitable somehow, like these scales I'm playing. After years of practice, I know what the next move is; my fingers just know where to go. It feels like the next move everyone expects me to make is to ask Megan out on a date. I *want* to be more excited about it.

Bradley talks about girls with this confidence I don't have. He seems to think that I should have this same confidence, but I'm not sure I'm feeling the right thing. Maybe being excited about going out with Megan is like the piano: I'll get better at it with practice.

I finish my scales and open the sheet music I'm working on for competition in the spring. I'm drilling the *andante espressivo* section in the middle: "a walking pace, expressive." The notes in this section swirl around each other in competing rhythms. Sometimes they bump into one another or barely miss each other. It is a sweet, mournful cacophony. I work these twenty measures for an hour or so, until the notes pour out of my fingers like syrup, slowly, sweetly swelling to a place where the beautiful layers meld into a single note, repeated in triplets over and over. This repetition grows in volume and speed until tumbling back through the dissonant full-keyboard runs at the end of the piece, each driving to an explosion of four chords in the last measure. When played as written, these final fistfuls of notes sound violent and jarring, as if a barrel of bricks has been dropped onto the keyboard from a great height.

Dad walks through the door from work as I'm finishing, and listens, shaking his head as I bang out the final chords.

"The sound of war is in the camp," he teases me with a smile. I follow him upstairs to the kitchen, where Mom is getting dinner ready. He kisses her hello, then I help him set the table.

"Is that your new recital piece?" Dad asks.

"It's the piece I'm taking to state this year. The Khacha-turian Toccata in E-flat Minor."

"The catcha-who-what?" Dad asks with a grin, and I laugh.

I started taking piano lessons when I was four years old, and a couple of years later I begged to quit. Dad grew up on a farm, the middle son of five boys, and he told me that the way he saw it, I didn't have any cows to milk, or chickens to feed, or hogs to slop, so the least I could do was give him thirty minutes a day on the piano. Now I'm good enough to win competitions and accompany choirs at church and school. It's the one thing I'm grateful Dad forced me to do.

"He's a Russian composer," I explain, folding napkins to the left of each plate. "This is his toccata. A toccata has lots of fast-moving passages that emphasize the skill and dexter-ity of my nimble fingers."

"I dunno," Dad says. "Sounds like a big train wreck to me."

Mom comes to my rescue as she takes a homemade chicken potpie out of the oven. "Aaron has been very diligent with this piece. It sounds incredibly difficult. I'm not sure how you even tell when you're playing the right notes."

"It *is* pretty dissonant," I agree. "Twentieth-century com-posers use lots of clashing tones to build tension—along with lots of random emphasis on the two/four beat." I love teasing Dad about his rock music theories. I raise my eyebrows and smirk at him. "Aren't you glad you didn't let me quit taking lessons?"

Dad laughs. "What I didn't tell you back then is that when you turned seventeen, you'd have to start paying for your lessons yourself."

"Careful what you wish for, Dad. You wanted a son who played the piano in church. That's what you got."

"Glory," Dad exclaims. "Can't you practice some of those pretty hymn arrangements? I'm not sure how much more Russian tension I can take."

"I'm done for tonight." I smile. "No more Russian music torture until tomorrow."

Mom calls Josh, Miriam, and Caleb to join us at the table for dinner. After we eat, Dad reaches for his Bible as Mom grabs the Missionary Prayer Box and pulls out a prayer card for a missionary family.

I look around as Dad reads, and think about my family. As much homework as I have to do after dinner, something about this feels good. It's nice to sit down together like this every night. Not many other kids in my class at school do this.

My family is like the *andante espressivo* section in the middle of the toccata. Sometimes I feel like the melodies we play are always in conflict—that I'm constantly hitting the wrong notes. Often our rhythms are set against one another, and we clash. Then there are moments like this, moments where I hear it all come together, and realize if we keep at it— keep practicing, keep searching for the right combinations— we always make an accidental harmony. Our individual notes come together in ways we never knew were possible, ways that surprise me.

Maybe the searching *is* the music.

After I finish my chemistry homework, I call Daphne and tell her about Megan.

"Do you like Megan?" she asks.

"Well…yeah."

Daphne's soft chuckle is the response. "That wasn't a ringing endorsement."

"It seems like everyone expects me to ask Megan out, and I don't want to hurt Erica's feelings. I think Erica is really hoping I'll ask *her* out."

"What do *you* want to do?"

When Daphne says these words, I realize something: *No one ever asks me that.*

"I want to hang out with Bradley and talk to him. Get his advice," I say.

"Sounds like a plan. You really like this Bradley, don't you?"

For some reason, the way she says it makes me blush. "Yeah." I smile into the phone. "He's the best."

"Well, I trust you'll introduce me to Megan and Bradley this weekend. I'm coming to see your play on Saturday."

"Excellent. I'll be the hillbilly with the beard and the shotgun."

Daphne laughs. "Naturally."

CHAPTER 18

There's a serial killer in my Bible class.

Every day after geometry, seventh period is Bible class. Mr. Kroger teaches us evangelical theology, and we memorize entire passages of the Bible for a grade in our verse quiz each week. Bradley calls it "mandatory God."

Mr. Kroger also shows videos in class from time to time. Today's video features Dr. James Dobson, a Christian psychologist and author who founded a ministry based in Colorado Springs called Focus on the Family. My mom listens to his radio show every day.

On the video, Dr. Dobson is interviewing Ted Bundy, a serial killer who was executed several years ago after systematically kidnapping, raping, and killing many women over twenty years. No one really knows for sure how many. He confessed to around thirty killings, but experts estimate the true number may have been as high as one hundred. Dr. Dobson doesn't really talk to Ted about that. He's more focused on the big issue at hand: How does someone do this to so many people?

I expect the answer might be mental illness. Maybe Ted was off his meds?

But according to Dr. Dobson, it isn't. The reason Ted Bundy says he did all these things?

Pornography.

Dr. Dobson asks Ted if the pornography he looked at made him want to degrade women. Ted explains that it did. The message of the video is very clear: Pornography makes you want to hurt women and girls. If you look at enough porn, you might not be able to control your fantasies; you might start to act them out on unsuspecting women and girls. And then kill them.

There is a big ad campaign around town right now, which is funded by a church group, about the dangers of pornography. There are billboards all over Kansas City with famous sports stars, mainly major-league baseball players. They're all smiling and happy and very clean-cut looking, wearing spotless sports uniforms. The tagline reads REAL MEN DON'T USE PORN.

Not far from our house in Lee's Summit, there's an adult bookstore. The billboard above the bookstore is a spoof of the ads about not looking at porn. It's a picture of four guys in athletic uniforms from *behind*—presumably the same four guys in the billboards that read REAL MEN DON'T USE PORN. Only, in this picture, the point of view is the back of each of these guys, and we see each one has a *Hustler* or a *Playboy* rolled up in his back pocket. The tagline above their heads is in big, bold letters: REAL MEN DON'T NEED TO BE TOLD WHAT TO READ.

A knock on the classroom door jolts me back to reality. Mr. Kroger presses Pause on the remote, and one of the junior high girls who helps out in the office during study hall hands him a note.

"Aaron, Mr. Friesen needs to see you."

I knew it.

I can feel every single eye in the room burning into me. I grab my books and head to the door. I walk down to Mr. Friesen's office, my stomach flip-flopping the same way it does every time I'm "caught." This is about the song I sang in chapel with Erica.

When I reach his office, Mr. Friesen indicates a chair, and once I'm seated, he leans across his desk and confirms my hunch. "Aaron, we need to talk about the song that you and Erica sang last week in chapel."

"Sure." Open. Friendly. Warm. Not hiding anything. *Play dumb.*

"You know, we're really glad that your dad decided to bring you and your brothers and sister to Tri-City. One of the things he talked to me about when y'all came here was how he was concerned about your attitude and your commitment to Christ."

I am silent. There's no way to deny it. That's why I'm here.

"It's come to my attention that you have been bragging to other students that you got away with singing a song by Sandi Patty in chapel. Is this true, Aaron?"

I'm used to edging around the truth with my parents, but this is the first time I've done it with Mr. Friesen. My heart is pounding, and my palms get sweaty, but I maintain eye contact and try to speak casually so I don't sound defensive. *Stay cool.*

"The song came out of a book of duet arrangements. Erica and I sang it at camp last summer. Everybody loved the song so much we thought we'd sing it here, too."

Mr. Friesen peers at me through his bifocal glasses. He has salt-and-pepper hair and a tan. He probably used to be handsome when he was younger and thinner, back when he was in the military.

He is silent. Inscrutable. A real man. I wonder if he ever looked at porn magazines in the army.

"Aaron, Tyler Gullem told me that you were pretty proud of yourself for pulling one over on Mr. Green and singing a song that was recorded by a Christian singer we wouldn't normally allow here."

Tyler Gullem, you have met your match.

"I'm not sure where Tyler heard me saying that, Mr. Friesen. I think Janice asked me who sang the song, but I certainly wasn't bragging about it—or pretending to pull one over on Mr. Green. I really respect Mr. Green. He's one of my favorite teachers."

"You know, the song was a fine song, but it didn't have much good theology in it. I don't even think the song had the word *God* in it. It was . . ." He pauses, searching for a phrase.

"Beautiful," I say quietly. "The song was beautiful."

228

Mr. Friesen looks at me hard. We lock eyes. I keep my smile plastered firmly in place.

Real men don't need to be told what to sing.

"Mr. Friesen, the song is a song about God's love. It never uses the word *God*, but that's what the song is about. I'm sorry Tyler thought I was bragging about this. I wasn't. If you'd like to call him in here, we can talk about it."

Mr. Friesen looks down at his desk, then back up at me.

Home run.

"Be careful of how you're perceived here, Aaron. You seem to be a smart young man who can do great things for God. The other students here already look up to you. I'd hate to see you lose your testimony by being deceitful. I know that was one of the things your dad was concerned about when you came to school here."

Assure him there's nothing to worry about.

"I wanted to sing a beautiful song, Mr. Friesen. I'm sorry that all of this got misconstrued. I really love it here at Tri-City. I wouldn't want to do anything to jeopardize that."

My stomach feels better. Mr. Friesen doesn't know we used Wite-Out on the music. Tyler missed that part.

Mr. Friesen smiles and pats me on the back as he walks me to his office door. "Remember, Aaron, I'm not the only one watching. You might be able to fool me, but you'll never be able to fool Almighty God. Make sure you keep your attitude and your heart right before him."

I turn to him with a serious nod. "I will, Mr. Friesen."

Back down the hall in Bible class, Ted Bundy is telling

James Dobson about how pornography finally pushed him over the edge to murder.

"Would it be accurate to call that a sexual frenzy?" Dr. Dobson asks.

"That's one way to describe it," says Bundy. His eyes are clear. He has dark hair. There's something handsome about this serial killer. "Another fact I haven't mentioned is the use of alcohol. In conjunction with my exposure to pornography, alcohol reduced my inhibitions and pornography eroded them further."

I look around at the guys in my class. If *I've* been reading *Penthouse* at Bradley's house, I know somebody else has been reading it. Surely I'm not the only one.

Is this how Ted Bundy started?

About a week ago, I went to the adult bookstore with Bradley one night after rehearsal for the play. It was dark, and we parked behind the building in case anybody drove by who might recognize our cars.

My heart raced as we got to the door. I wasn't sure if they'd stop me and ask for my ID. I wasn't eighteen yet, but the guy behind the counter was watching a football game and barely glanced over at us. I followed Bradley, who headed straight for the magazines at the back.

"This place is wild," he whispered as we walked past a row of sex toys. One shelf held different devices demonstrated by a muscular, naked guy on the front of the box. He was handsome and his eyes were closed, his head back, and he was very noticeably aroused from using this device.

For some reason, that's the only image from the store I really remember.

It's weird.

I know we looked at other stuff. I know Bradley showed me some pictures in magazines and pointed out girls he thought were really hot, but I can't picture any of them now. All I can picture is the naked guy on that one box. That certainly doesn't seem to make me want to hurt any girls. I guess I'm not in danger of becoming a serial killer.

I don't want to hurt anyone at all.

Dr. Dobson wraps up his interview with Ted Bundy by talking about Jesus, and the Twenty-Third Psalm, and walking through the "valley of the shadow of death." Ted will be put to death in the electric chair for his crimes a few hours after this taping, but he's accepted the wondrous grace of God's forgiveness. He's accepted Jesus Christ as his savior, and there'll be a place for him in heaven when he is executed.

"Do you draw strength from that as you approach these final hours?" Dr. Dobson asks.

I can't even hear what Ted Bundy says in reply. A needle scratches across the record in my brain.

Ted Bundy is going to be in heaven?

Everything I've ever believed about the importance of mission work explodes in my brain. I teach Good News Club with Mom because kids who know the difference between right and wrong but don't believe in Jesus will die and go to hell for all eternity. But apparently, Ted Bundy will be in heaven because he asked Jesus into his heart after he raped and killed thirty women—at least.

I look around our Bible class. Does anyone else think this is weird? Is this the God my parents believe in?

Is this the God I believe in?

When the bell rings, Erica follows me to my locker. "What did Mr. Friesen want to talk to you about?"

"The evils of Sandi Patty," I say grimly. I toss my notebook into my locker and grab my brown paper lunch sack.

"I was afraid of that." She sighs. "Why didn't he call me in, too?"

"Tyler Gullem doesn't have it in for you."

"Are you mad at me?"

"Nope. Just tired of this game we're all playing."

"What game?" she asks, blinking, bewildered.

A slow sigh escapes me. "The game where kids in the jungle go to hell, and serial killers go to heaven," I say quietly.

Alarm wrinkles Erica's forehead. "I don't know what you're talking about, Aaron."

"Exactly."

I turn and head down the hall to the lunchroom, leaving Erica staring after me, clutching her notebook to her chest.

Megan appears at my elbow. "Principal's office by the fifth week of school. I knew you were trouble."

"Yep. Me and Satan-worshipping Sandi Patty. Wait until I sing an Amy Grant song in the cafeteria."

Megan shakes her head and laughs. "Good Lord. This place."

The general noise of the lunchroom is a welcome reprieve from the din in my head. We snag chairs in a back corner and eat in silence for a minute.

"You know, people are going to start talking if we keep having lunch together like this," Megan says.

I am tired of games. "So let's have dinner."

"I'm open to suggestions."

"You'll have to meet my parents first," I say. "It'll be easier to get a 'yes' to go out with you if they know you first."

"I'm great with parents."

Megan is telling the truth. I'm great with parents, too. Takes one to know one.

"They'll be at the play this weekend. I'll introduce you afterward. Then maybe we can do something next Saturday."

"What did you have in mind?" she asks.

"Let's start casual," I say. "Burgers? A movie?"

"Your parents will let you take me to a movie?"

"Of course not. We'll tell them we're going to watch something at your place."

Megan smirks at me, amused. "Christian rock. Sneaking out to movies. I'd better be careful. You're probably going to try to get to second base on our first date."

"I can assure you, I am a perfect gentleman."

She eyes me as she gathers up her lunch bag and purse, then flips her curls over her shoulder. "That's not what *I've* heard," she whispers.

She winks at me, then walks out of the lunchroom without looking back.

"Aaron, I can't get over how excellent you were in the play."

Christy! the musical closed last night, and on the way to church this morning Dad is still beaming about my performance as the jigging, rifle-toting hillbilly.

"Yes, honey!" Mom chimes in. "You stole the show, and it was so nice to meet Megan afterward. She seems like a real sweetheart. Did you say she's a cheerleader?"

"Yes, ma'am. I was thinking maybe I'd take Megan out for dinner next Saturday night. I have the afternoon shift at the ice rink. Would that be okay?"

"I don't see why not," says Dad. He looks over at Mom.

"Fine with me." Mom smiles. "She seems to have a really sweet spirit."

"Aaron's got a *girlfriend*," Caleb pipes up from the way back.

Dad laughs. "Let him go on a first date, will you? Who knows?" he jokes. "Maybe she won't like him at all."

"Oh, thanks a lot," I say, laughing.

"I can't believe it's already time for the ice rink to open again," says Mom.

I've worked for her friend Deena at a seasonal outdoor rink in Kansas City for the past two years. From October to March, the Carriage Club in Kansas City opens for figure skating, hockey leagues, and late-night broomball games. I'm a rink guard, and every now and then I help teach ice-skating basics to the toddler classes. Deena and the rink manager, Carla, came to the play last night, too.

Deena skated competitively and then in the Ice Capades. Now she and three former pro friends run the skating school at the Carriage Club.

"Deena says everyone is welcome next weekend if you want to come skate while I'm working."

"That'll be fun." Mom smiles. "I'll get details from her if I see her after the service."

Our pastor recently heard the call of God to go be the pastor of a different church, so Dad is filling in until they can find somebody else. Before he starts preaching, I play the piano for Mom to sing a song called "It Will Be Worth It All," about how all our trials and tribulations on earth will melt away in the bliss of seeing Jesus when he comes back, or when we die—whichever happens first.

Dad's sermon is about God's grace. He explains how God demonstrated grace by sending Jesus to pay the price for our sins. This was an elegant act of mercy that saves us from an eternity in hell if we allow it to.

"'For by grace are ye saved, through faith,'" Dad quotes from Ephesians. "It's God's grace that allows us the chance at eternal life through Jesus Christ."

All I have to do is believe.

The decorative cross over the choir loft in our Bible church is empty. "We don't keep Jesus hanging on the crucifix, like the Catholics do," Mom likes to say. "The empty cross is a reminder that Jesus is *risen!*"

While Dad talks about God's amazing grace, I try very hard to understand how letting your child die a horrible death for someone else is an act of mercy. It seems to me an all-knowing God could have headed this off in the first place. If he's truly omniscient, God *knew* long before he created Adam and Eve that they would sin. He made the snake, after all, and the fruit, and the rule that said Adam and Eve couldn't eat it. Why bother to make humans in your perfect, sinless image, then allow a temptation you *know* they will inevitably succumb to, and then blame them for their failure?

It doesn't seem very merciful to set a trap where millions of people will spend eternity burning in hell and the rest will only be saved by the grisly death of your own beloved Son. Why not start by committing to loving all of these imperfect people you're planning to create, without engineering the whole heaven-and-hell situation in the first place? The test seems unfair—rigged from the beginning—and I sit in the pew wondering just how amazing God's grace really is.

"Jesus is coming back," Dad says as he ends his sermon. "Accept God's gift of grace, and be ready." I glance around the auditorium. The whole thing seems preposterous, but these are the fundamentals of our faith. *Am I the only one bothered by this?*

As I bow my head for Dad's closing prayer, I wish that I

could accept God's grace without all these questions—or that maybe God would simply accept me, just as I am, questions and all.

A few weeks later, right before Thanksgiving, Dad walks through the door holding a brand-new TV just in time for the holiday weekend.

General mayhem ensues. Or, as I told Daphne later, "If there were a Bible story written about this moment, it would read, 'Great rejoicing was heard throughout the land.'"

The idea that a brand-new color television is now a permanent fixture in our home, that it will not disappear with the Christmas tree during the first week of January, is something both thrilling and unbelievable. The magic of the holiday season is truly at hand.

"Where is my father and what have you done to him?" I ask Dad. Josh and Miriam are already unpacking the set, plugging in the VCR, and setting up the antenna.

Dad explains he'll be keeping a tight rein on the remote, but he feels he can trust us. "You kids are all older now. You know the difference between what's acceptable and what isn't. We won't be watching anything unpleasing to the Lord. Besides, it costs almost as much to rent a TV these days as it does to buy one. It's a better use of money."

Holiday tradition at our house dictates that Dad's extended family comes over for Thanksgiving, and we spend Christmas in Memphis with Mom's family. Each year there's an unofficial contest to see whether Dad's turkey smoked on the grill or Mom's roasted in the oven is the prettiest.

Mom bakes all kinds of breads the night before Thanksgiving—banana, pumpkin, cranberry—and makes the creamiest chocolate fudge I've ever tasted. She can whip up a centerpiece from nothing more than a brown paper grocery bag, some Elmer's glue, and a series of clever folds. An authentic-looking horn o' plenty results, and spills tiny pumpkins and squash across the kitchen table beneath the festive Pilgrim and Native American mobile that hangs from the ceiling fan.

Mom insists it's a shame that the stores leap right from Halloween to Christmas.

"We have so much to be thankful for," she says.

As I look around this year, I can see so clearly that she is right. The Macy's Thanksgiving Day Parade has never appeared sharper or more brilliant, and after the whole family sits down at three different tables, Mom starts passing a little basket around and directs our attention to the three kernels of popcorn that have been preset on everyone's plate.

"When it's your turn, place each kernel in the basket and say one thing that you're thankful for!"

Once dinner is over and the bowl games have begun, I sneak downstairs to the family room to call Daphne.

"Wait. You're serious? A color television? Like a *full-size TV*?" She's as shocked as I am.

"I know. It's like aliens have landed and made off with his body, leaving an impostor in his place. If you don't hear from me tomorrow, call the police."

"What's happening now?" she asks.

"Well, it's halftime of the Cowboys game, and the cheerleaders are immodestly dressed, so Dad has turned off the new TV until the second half starts, and is leading a headstand contest with the cousins in honor of my late grandfather."

"Aaron, your family is so weird."

"Don't know what to tell you. The last Thanksgiving Grandpa was alive he showed us all how to do a headstand after dinner."

"Your grandpa could do a headstand?"

"He was incredibly graceful," I say. "Never kicked anyone in the face. He was a pro."

Daphne laughs. "Are you going to brave the shopping crowds tomorrow?"

"Yep. I have a date with Mom at Walmart to score the predawn deals. Then I work at the ice rink until six, and I'm taking Megan to dinner afterward."

"So, you asked her out." I can hear Daphne smiling. *Does she sound surprised?* "What are you going to do?"

"Trying to take her to see a movie," I whisper into the phone. "I'm spending the night at Bradley's afterward, so it should work out."

Daphne sighs. "I get exhausted listening to your sched-ule. It requires more energy for you to take a girl to a movie than most people exert in their entire lives."

"Trust me. I know."

"I have to go eat more turkey now," she says. "Have a good headstand."

CHAPTER 19

"Are you gay?"

Mary Alice Sizemore has two French braids running down the back of her head. Her blonde hair is almost as perfect as her blue eyes. She is eight years old, beautiful, and loud. Very. Very. Loud.

Every head in the skate office turns toward the counter, where I am busy drying the blades on returned rental skates and tucking in laces before sliding them back into the appropriate cubbyhole.

I pause and try not to acknowledge the eyes. All the eyes quietly watching for my response. Derrick is helping out in the skate office this weekend. Carla is here, too, doing paperwork for next week's schedule.

"No," I say, rolling my eyes. *Oh you silly eight-year-old,* my face seems to say.

"Do you have a giiiiiiiiiiiiiiiiiirlfriend?" Mary Alice giggles. All her little friends giggle. Each wears a perfectly matched jacket and tights and tiny white figure skates. None of these girls is wearing rental skates. They are *members* at the Carriage Club. They've taken lessons since they were five years old. Mary Alice is already landing a toe loop.

"It's none of your business, Mary Alice," I say. *Why are you explaining yourself to an eight-year-old?*

"So you *don't* have a girlfriend?" Mary Alice persists. That's one thing about her when she's in a mood like this: Ignoring her doesn't work. "If you don't have a girlfriend and you figure skate, that means you're *gay*."

Carla, the ice rink manager, is fortysomething and curvy, with curly brown hair and a wide, kind smile. She sidles over to the counter.

"Mary Alice, do you have a lesson starting soon?" she asks.

"No. I'm waiting for my mom."

"I want to see your toe loop," says Carla.

"It's too cold," whines Mary Alice.

"It's February," says Carla. "It's crisp, not cold. Out there. Now. Let's see your toe loop."

She smiles as she grabs her jacket and follows Mary Alice out toward the ice rink sandwiched between this clubhouse and the tennis courts. "God, these little rich bitches are tap dancing on my *last nerve*."

Carla steps outside and watches Mary Alice and her friends practice their tentative toe loops. Mary Alice lands a jump, and Carla claps and gives her a thumbs-up.

I breathe a sigh of relief and continue stuffing laces in

skates. Derrick comes over to the counter, grabs a towel, and starts wiping down blades.

"So..." he says.

"So, what?" I ask.

"You gonna spill the beans about this girlfriend who is none of Mary Alice's business, or am I gonna have to ask you questions?"

I smile in spite of myself. Derrick is twenty-five years old. He's shorter than I am, but muscular and handsome. He used to be a cheerleader at the University of Kansas. I've seen a couple of pictures of him lifting really pretty girls high into the air with one hand on their privates. He's shadowing the general manager of the Carriage Club this semester to earn credit for his master's degree in business.

"C'mon, Hartzler." He bangs into me from the side with one of his thick, former-gymnast shoulders. He catches me off guard, and I stumble sideways into the counter.

"Hey!" I laugh. "Knock it off."

"She hot?" Derrick gets a dimple on either side of his mouth when he gives that square-jawed grin of his. He has perfect white teeth.

"Her name is Megan, and she's not my girlfriend," I say. "We've gone on a few dates."

"Attaboy. Make her work for it." Derrick nods as Deena swings through the door into the lodge area, her cheeks pink from the chill.

"Who are you making work for what?" she asks.

243

"Aaron's breaking hearts," Derrick says.

"Really?" Deena pulls off the headband that covers her ears, and pats a mittened hand over her long blonde French braid. "Who's the lucky girl?"

"Her name is Megan, and it's nothing serious."

"Wait—was she in your musical last fall?" Deena asks.

I nod. "She was one of the girls who did the jig," I say. "Not the lead or the little old lady, but the other one."

"Curly hair?" Deena had come to see the play with her kids and Carla.

"That's her."

"She's beautiful!" Deena says with a grin. "And sort of mysterious." She elbows Derrick. "You'd like her."

"When was this play I wasn't invited to?" Derrick asks.

"Last fall," I explain. "Before you started here."

Derrick turns to Deena. "Was he any good?"

"Good? Aaron was great!" Deena is pulling off her skates after four half-hour lessons in a row. "The music was awesome, and he was the best dancer. It's no wonder he's so good on the ice."

I smile at Derrick. "It wasn't *dancing*. It was *choreography*. It's a very Baptist school."

"You are getting really good out there," Derrick says.

"I saw you working on a toe loop," says Deena. "And your spins are looking good, too. Did somebody help you with those?"

"Mary Alice." I sigh. "Every time I ask her for help she shows me how to do it, and then when I try it she yells, 'You SUCK.'"

"That little girl is gonna be a total ballbuster," says Derrick, laughing. He tosses the wet towels into a laundry bin and then grabs his coat. "I guess you'll have to bring this Megan chick to the ice show party so I can meet her."

"Oooooh, that's a *great* idea," says Deena as she tosses her skates into her bag. "Bring her to the party."

The Carriage Club Ice Show is a big event every February. It's a recital for all the kids taking skating lessons, and there's always a big party for the rink staff afterward. Usually, they have it at the bar upstairs, but this year is different.

"I'm not sure I'm even going to be able to come to the party this year," I say. "My parents aren't wild about me going to a bar with everybody."

"Oh! Fuzzy's South is a restaurant, too. They serve food and everything," says Deena. "I'll call your mom and tell her that it'll be okay. I'm going to be there with the girls, so I'll keep an eye on you."

"Will I be able to get in even though I'm not twenty-one?"

"Sure, man." Derrick grins. "You're cool as long as you're sitting at a table on the restaurant side."

"Sounds good. Sure you don't mind talking to my mom, Deena?"

"Of course not. I'll catch her tomorrow at church. Is your dad preaching again?"

I nod. "I think they're going to make him the interim pastor until they find somebody to take the job full-time."

"That's great!" Deena seems really excited. Everybody

loves Dad's preaching. He's actually really good at it. He's more of a teacher than a preacher, plus he's funny and has good, clear outlines. People always line up afterward to tell him how much his message touched their hearts.

"Son of a preacher man, eh?" Derrick smirks as he zips up his jacket. Deena covers a laugh with her hand.

"What...?" I ask.

"Oh, it's an old song," Deena says with a smile and a wink at Derrick.

"What song?" I hate not knowing the songs everybody else knows. I always feel like I'm missing out.

"Dusty Springfield," says Deena.

Derrick sings into an imaginary mic: "Only man who could ever reach me..."

Deena joins him: "Was the son of a preacher man...." They both dissolve into giggles. I smile and feel myself blush. I've never heard this song.

I guess that means that preachers' sons are...sexy?

Derrick sees the look on my face and punches me on the shoulder as he heads out of the skate office toward the parking lot.

"You are so *set*. This Megan doesn't stand a chance."

Megan is flying toward the ceiling of the gymnasium, high enough that I hold my breath a little.

Blastoff!

I smile as she lands in Heather's and Angela's arms, and the crowd at the homecoming game goes wild. It was a perfect basket toss.

"That's Hartzler's woman." Bradley nudges his friend Jacob, a tall guy with dark red hair who graduated from Tri-City last year. He's flown back from Stanford for the weekend to see his little brother play in the postseason basketball tournament. Turns out our younger brothers are in the same class. Bradley is watching their JV game with us before he plays with the varsity team.

"Wow. Little Megan is all grown up." Jacob smiles at me. "Nice work. Funny how people change."

I blush a little in spite of myself and smile. *What does* nice work *mean? I didn't do anything....*

"Awww. Look at Hartzler, all smitten and smiley." He laughs. "Putty in her paws."

Erica is wearing a gold-and-white-striped rugby shirt tucked into a long, straight purple skirt. She waves at Jacob and comes running up to say hi with Janice.

"Erica Norton," Jacob says. "Way to sport the purple and gold."

Erica smiles and points to me. "Aaron won class theme day. Our theme was 'Take Me Out to the Ball Game.'"

"You had the best baseball uniform?" Jacob asks.

"He came as a carton of popcorn!" squeals Janice. "With brown grocery sacks of real popcorn stapled inside. We ate out of him all day long!"

"Wow," says Jacob. "That's impressive."

247

"Mom and I were up until two AM popping popcorn." Late night arts and crafts is one of Mom's special skills. Since the Native American outfit covered with fringe we made when I was in fourth grade, Mom and I never have more fun than we do staying up late making costumes and class projects that win awards. Mom and I craft to *win*.

"See? That's the kind of stuff that girls totally go for," Bradley says. "Your mom helped you land Megan."

When Erica hears this, she's ready to move on. "Nice seeing you, Jacob," she says. "C'mon, Janice. Let's go get seats on the front bleacher so we don't miss anything."

Janice smiles and waves good-bye, oblivious to the reason they're leaving. As they go, Bradley lets out a low whistle. "Wow. Hartzler, you're killing me with this."

Jacob frowns. "Wait. What just happened?"

"Love tri-an-gle." Bradley emphasizes each syllable. The horn for the fourth quarter of the JV game sounds, and Bradley gets up. "Okay, boys. I gotta head to the locker room now for Coach's pep-talk-slash-prayer-meeting."

"I've seen your jump shot," says Jacob. "It's the other team that needs the prayer."

Bradley smiles. "Hey, Jacob, try not to let Hartzler break any more hearts tonight, will ya?"

Jacob laughs as Bradley leaves. "Love that guy. Now, what's going on with Erica Norton?"

I smile grimly. "Nothing. And that's sort of the problem."

"Megan more your type?" he asks.

"Something like that." I'm never sure how to answer questions like this one. Megan is beautiful, but so is Erica. There's something about Megan. I see it when other guys look at her, too. Sometimes I think Megan looks even prettier to me because other guys find her so attractive, which makes me feel strange. *Am I dating her because I think she's pretty or because they think she's pretty?*

Jacob turns out to be a great guy. Smart, funny, well read. After the games, I meet his parents. Our moms are already acquainted from being at our brothers' soccer games. This is perfect. He'll be one more friend Mom and Dad approve of.

Jacob is flying back to Stanford tomorrow. He gives me his phone number. "I'll be back this summer. Keep in touch."

"You'll be home by eleven?" Mom asks. I'm shoring up plans for the Carriage Club Ice Show party tomorrow night.

"Yes, ma'am," I assure her.

"Remember we have church the next morning."

Mom hasn't said so, but the look on her face and the struggle to score this "yes" makes me certain that she's letting me attend this party against her better judgment. She doesn't want me around people who are drinking in a bar, even if I'm sitting at a table across the room.

A few months after the drunk driver hit our car when I was in sixth grade, my teacher gave us a blank sheet of paper with random lines drawn across it at different angles. The places where the lines crossed created little spaces, random angled windows all over the page. Our teacher asked us to draw a different pattern or picture in each one. I loved this assignment, and in a window toward the very center, I drew a waiter, from his bow tie to his cummerbund. On the silver tray in his white-gloved hands rested a martini.

At the time, I wasn't sure exactly what a martini was. I only knew it came in a strange triangular glass, and there was usually an olive floating in it. Something about it seemed exciting and grown-up. Drinking martinis was something rich, interesting people did in exotic places around the world—places very different from Kansas City.

I'm not sure how I knew this. I had never actually seen anyone drink a martini in real life. Maybe I'd seen it in an old episode of *Perry Mason* or a movie on TV at Nanny's house.

When Mom saw this art project, she zeroed in on the cocktail. "Aaron, what's in that glass the waiter has?"

I looked up from the page. "A martini."

"That's an alcoholic beverage," Mom said. "Why would you draw someone serving alcohol?"

I looked back down at the paper. It just seemed glamorous at the time—something a man in a tuxedo would be serving on a silver tray.

"I don't know," I said.

"Where have you seen people drinking martinis?" she asked.

"I haven't," I said.

"Drinking alcohol isn't pleasing to the Lord, Aaron. What do you think Jesus would want you to draw in that space?"

"But, Mom! I'm almost done with it. It looks so good!"

"Why don't you turn the martini into a milk shake?"

I didn't want to, but I obeyed. I extended the sides of the martini glass up into a parfait glass and was able to nearly mask the line of the martini glass by drawing whipped cream and putting a cherry on top. Still, it wasn't the same drawing anymore. For some reason, it didn't look as cool.

Now, as I take the car keys off the hook in the kitchen, Mom has the same look on her face as she did when she saw the martini glass on my sixth-grade art project.

"Remember, Aaron: The eyes of the Lord are in every place, beholding the good and the evil."

"Got it, Mom." I give her a peck on the cheek and head toward the garage.

"Need anything?" Derrick is heading to the bar.

Everybody from the Carriage Club was already there when I arrived. We ordered food, and Deena raised her glass to congratulate everybody on a great season at the ice rink.

There are about fifteen of us in all at several tables pushed together on the restaurant side of Fuzzy's.

I look down at my full glass of Diet Coke. "No, thanks. I'm good."

Derrick smiles and jerks his head toward the bar. "Come with me," he says, and winks.

I look down at Deena. She's laughing and talking with the other ice pros. She blows me a kiss and shouts over the music and ruckus, "You were great last night in the ice show!"

I smile back at her, then get up and follow Derrick around to the front of the bar. Derrick is shorter than I am, but I notice how much space his muscular shoulders clear in the crush of people watching basketball on the monitors. Several women turn to watch us as he maneuvers through the crowd. He stops in front of a cute blonde girl who is pouring drinks.

"What can I get you, sugar?" she asks.

I'm keeping my eyes on the screen over the bar. I'm terrified she's going to ask to see my ID. *Is it okay for me to even be standing here? Is it against the law?*

I can't hear what Derrick orders, but I glance down as he puts a crisp twenty-dollar bill on the bar, then leans back toward me. "Hey, man." He grins. "Wanna Bud?"

My stomach drops, and I can't tell if I'm excited or scared. Or both.

I smile back at him and glance around. I really want to try it. I really don't want to get caught.

"Drink it here, before we go back to the table," he says, reading my mind. "Nobody will know."

Don't think about it.

I know if I don't do it quickly, I won't do it. And I want to do it. Bradley drinks, and it doesn't hurt him. I want to see what the fuss is about.

"Sure," I say. I reach for my wallet. "Let me give you some cash."

Derrick laughs and shakes his head. "It's on me."

He leans back toward the bartender and I see him hold up two fingers, doubling his order. When he turns back around, he's holding an extra-tall pilsner glass that's so cold it's fogging up on the outside. There's about an inch of white foam on the top.

"Cheers, bro." He hands me the glass and then clinks the rim of his against it. "Bottoms up."

I lift the glass to my lips.

And swallow.

The cold liquid hits my tongue. The carbonation is familiar, but the taste is not. It isn't sweet; it's sort of tart and sour.

Now I know why they call this an "acquired taste."

Derrick is watching me with a delighted grin. "How is it, man?"

I lick the foam off my upper lip. "Well, it tastes better than it smells. I'll say that."

Derrick laughs. "You're a good kid, Hartzler."

I feel a rush of excitement and a sense of belonging, like I've been waiting out in the cold for a long time, and now I've been welcomed into the club. I understand beer commercials all of a sudden—drinking this bitter golden liquid together makes you more than acquaintances, somehow. It makes Derrick my friend.

As we stand by the bar, laughing and drinking, Derrick points out the girls who are looking our way.

"Wait—really?" I ask. "Where?"

He laughs at me for not noticing.

"Those chicks behind you are totally checking you out," he says. "Girls like tall guys."

I glance over my shoulder in time to catch one girl with curly red hair turn away in a hurry. Her friend waves at us and giggles.

I stand in the bar with Derrick until we've finished our beers. The taste isn't great, but it doesn't take long before I've gulped it down, leaving some suds at the bottom of my glass.

"You feel buzzed yet?" Derrick grins.

"I'm not sure," I say. "Maybe."

When we go back to the table, our food has arrived, and as I eat, I keep waiting for the beer to kick in. I'm not sure what a "buzz" is supposed to feel like. I don't feel especially woozy or dizzy or anything, but my cheeks feel flushed, and there's this sense of intense excitement in my chest, like the thrill I got when I landed the lead in the school play and saw my name on that list taped to Miss Tyler's door. It's the same thing I felt when I bought that movie ticket in Nebraska and when I spent the night at Bradley's for the first time. It's the feeling of freedom I get every time I make my own decision about something.

I'm not sure if it's the beer or the giddiness, but I'm

starving again. Derrick orders more burgers after devouring his first, and insists I eat one, too. French fries have never tasted this good, and I stuff myself until it hurts to breathe. I play darts with Carla and Derrick, and as the party winds down a couple hours later, Deena comes to our end of the table.

"Hey, mister. I promised your mom I would keep an eye on you." She smiles. "Derrick isn't corrupting you, is he?"

"Nah." Derrick smirks. "Just one beer's worth."

I freeze. *Is Deena going to tell on me?*

"You okay to drive?" she asks me, eyebrows raised.

"He's fine," Derrick assures her. "It's been a couple of hours. Plus, I made him eat a second burger. Need to get this kid some protein so he can pack on some muscle."

"Be careful," Deena commands. "Your mom will kill me if anything happens to you."

"Really, I'm fine," I say, and I'm telling the truth. Any trace of a buzz from my single beer has drifted away. Crossing the line and having a drink feels exciting and dangerous, but my head is clear. Still, as I leave the bar and reach for my keys, I remember the accident on the first day of sixth grade—the crunch of the metal and the spray of the glass—and a shiver of caution rolls through my chest that has nothing to do with the low temperature of a blustery February night. *Is this how drunk driving begins?*

I turn the key in the ignition and remind myself to watch my speed. I dig a lemon wedge I grabbed from the table out of my pocket and chew on it as I drive down the highway toward home. Mom will be up waiting, I know, and I want to make sure she doesn't smell my first beer on my breath. It's freezing out, but I keep the windows rolled down as I drive, to air the cigarette smoke out of my clothes.

Mom is in the kitchen when I walk in to hang the keys up on the hook.

"How'd it go tonight?" she asks.

"It was fun," I say. "Deena says hi."

She reaches in to give me a hug, and I inhale deeply as she does, hoping the air flowing in will keep any hint of beer from flowing out.

"I'm glad you had a good time, honey."

"Thanks for letting me go, Mom."

I walk up the stairs toward the bathroom to brush my teeth.

"Aaron?"

I stop on the steps. My stomach drops. *Here it comes.*

"Yes, ma'am?"

"Sleep tight." She smiles at me and turns off the light in the hall.

CHAPTER 20

There's a gay pride parade in my Bible class.

The video on the screen up front shows a guy wearing a black leather harness and a pink Speedo with leather chaps—the kind a cowboy might wear when riding a horse in the Old West, only this guy isn't riding a horse. He's riding a float surrounded by lots of guys who look very similar to the He-Man action figures I used to covet in Randy's bedroom when I was a kid.

Mr. Kroger's latest video series is called "Having a Christian Worldview," produced by a televangelist with a syndicated Christian news show. Today's segment is about what a born-again Christian's response should be to the hot-button topic of sexual immorality.

The televangelist has orangey makeup and a big blond hairdo left over from the eighties. This isn't the first time I've heard these words. He leans toward the camera and proclaims: "God's plan for human sexuality is one man with one woman, for life."

Dad has said this for as long as I can recall, but the time I remember most clearly was when he took me on a road trip in eighth grade. He'd been asked to speak at a Christian boarding school in Nebraska, and he'd decided I was coming with him. The year before, when I was twelve, he'd given me a book called *Preparing for Adolescence* by James Dobson, the host of the Christian radio program *Focus on the Family*. I was supposed to read the book, and we were supposed to have special father-son meetings to talk about it. Those meetings had gotten lost in the shuffle of our busy schedules, and Dad saw this trip as his chance. Before we left, he handed me a special workbook companion to *Preparing for Adolescence* complete with fill-in-the-blank worksheets and charts of the human body.

I was *mortified*.

Dad was two years too late. I'd read everything I needed to know about the mechanics of sex under "Reproduction" in the *R* volume of the *World Book Encyclopedia* when I was ten years old. I didn't want to talk about sex with my dad. I didn't know why, exactly. It felt *weird*. I didn't want to know about his sex life. Why was he so intent on talking to me about mine?

But as we sped along the highway, I was trapped. Dad had me read sections of the book aloud, and then we'd talk through the questions in the workbook together. These chapters covered the gamut from male anatomy to masturbation to a simple, somewhat cryptic description of intercourse.

I was relieved to read that Dr. Dobson thought masturbating was a normal thing that most guys did. It was strange to read the word *masturbation* aloud to my father, but he seemed to think this was important, so I soldiered through my embarrassment. At least Dr. Dobson didn't think jerking off was anything to feel guilty about.

I, for one, certainly never felt guilty about it, but I'd always assumed Dad and Dr. Dobson would say it was wrong.

"Aaron, are you struggling with masturbation?"

I felt the blood drain from my face.

Did he really say that out loud?

"What?" I asked.

"Are you struggling with masturbation?" he repeated.

I had no idea where to even *begin* with a question like that. I opened my mouth to answer, but nothing came out. I closed my mouth again. *Am I* struggling *with masturbation?* Even his phrasing made me angry. It insinuated that somehow masturbation was wrong, and this made my blood boil. I wanted to open the door and roll out onto the shoulder of the road to get away from my dad—to get away from everything. I did not want to have this conversation. Dad was prying his way into the most deeply personal thing I had ever experienced.

That first night on the bottom bunk when I was twelve years old, it all happened so fast. Afterward, I lay there, not moving, surprised and vaguely terrified, until I remembered the *World Book Encyclopedia*. Words from those old musty pages, like *arousal* and *plateau* and *climax*, flashed to life like flares hissing around a collision on a rain-soaked exit ramp, finally defined by experience instead of the dictionary.

If there was ever a moment when I felt I was in touch with

a capital *G* God, that was certainly it. It was incredible—an experience that had changed me fundamentally, somehow. I had no idea that my body was designed to feel pleasure so intensely.

I stared out the window, trying to avoid Dad's question. Nebraska in February sped by: frozen dairy farms and gray cornfields as far as the eye could see. I felt so tired of having to hide something at every turn: movies, music, magazines. Every corner of my life seemed to require a compromise, but this?

Not this! I wanted to scream at him. *Not this, too!*

Again, Dad asked the question: "Aaron, are you struggling with masturbation?"

I didn't scream. I didn't open the door and leap from the car. I opened my mouth and gave the most truthful answer I had ever uttered:

"No."

I wanted to say more. I wanted to tell him, *No. Jerking off is the easiest thing I've ever done in my life. It's no struggle at all.* Instead, I stared out the window and silently prayed that God was on my side about this. I begged the gray expanse of heaven over Nebraska to let this moment pass quickly.

Please, God, let him drop it.

"Mom told me she found some socks behind your bed the other day that had dried semen on them."

"*Dad!*" I yelled. "This is none of your *business*!" When he said that, suddenly I was almost crying. *Why won't he stop?* "I'm not talking to you about this."

"We *need* to talk about it, son. I disagree with Dr. Dobson on this point in his book."

"Got it," I snapped. "You think I *should* feel guilty about jerking off."

"I want your thought life to stay morally pure. Jesus said if you even *think* of lusting after a woman in your heart, it's the same thing as having committed adultery with her."

I closed my eyes and took a breath. "Dad. I am not having sex with anyone. Can we please drop this?"

"It's not only about having sex, Aaron. If you're engaged in sexual fantasy during masturbation, you're being controlled by impure thoughts and not by the Holy Spirit of God. Until you meet the one woman God has chosen to be your wife, you should be striving to keep your thought life pure."

Back in my Bible class, I'm feeling the same discomfort with this video that I felt when Dad asked me about jerking off. The guy in the chaps on screen may not be controlling his thought life, but he *is* controlling his massive pecs, making them bounce to the rhythm of the dance music playing in the background at the gay pride parade.

The televangelist narrates this segment with Bible verses about how it's an abomination for a man to lie with a man as he does with a woman, but I can barely hear him. There's something strange about watching this scene. It transfixes me. I can't imagine wearing a pink Speedo and a leather harness in Central Park or dancing on a float with a bunch of oiled-up bodybuilders, but as the camera pans away from the burly man in the chaps, it passes over many others—thousands of them—and focuses on two guys hanging out in the park with a couple of beers.

These two are younger than the men on the float, probably only a few years older than I am. They are wearing jeans and tank tops. One of them has a Kansas City Royals baseball cap. They're both tall, tan, and muscular. They're not really dancing. They are simply standing there, watching the festival, and as the camera focuses on them, I see a thing I've never seen before.

They're holding hands.

My heart speeds up, and I feel a lump form in my throat. There's something about this image I can't put my finger on. It makes me feel something I don't have a word for—like the sadness I feel when I think of a good memory from far away, or when I laugh so hard that I cry. It's a fleeting warmth I grasp for but can't quite catch, a slow, delicious heartbreak.

The guy wearing the KC ball cap whispers something to his boyfriend, who smiles and kisses him on the cheek.

Suddenly, the camera zooms in and freezes on this simple kiss. With a screen wipe of wild angles, the video turns to black and white, then flashes to a color reverse image, making the image of this kiss appear to be an X-ray. A red title flies across the screen:

ABOMINATION

Erica is sitting one row up on my right. Her eyes are wide, glued to the screen. She slowly shakes her head in a daze, as if she can't believe what she is seeing.

An old panic pings up my spine and tightens my shoulders, but I'm not sure why. These guys are different from the men on the floats. They aren't wearing crazy costumes and don't have anything pierced. They're not made up like Jezebel or dancing like Salome. They look so... normal.

They look a lot like me.

The video quickly cuts to a Bible verse from the New Testament about men burning in their lust toward one another not entering the kingdom of heaven. Now the televangelist is talking about AIDS, and there are images of men marching in the parade who do not look like me. They seem old and angry. They are shouting and raising their fists. They are skinny and pale and appear to be terribly ill.

I can't stop thinking about that guy in the baseball cap. Something about it sticks in my head. The way he laughed with his friend reminds me of the way I laugh with Bradley. The kiss he gave his boyfriend on the cheek didn't look like anything evil. I kiss my dad on the cheek like that. And I've seen him kiss his brothers on the cheek the same way.

How are those guys an abomination?

The televangelist keeps saying the words *homosexual* and *gay*, hurling them away from his mouth like slurs, as if he is in a hurry to get the syllables off his lips; as if simply saying these words might somehow infect him. I think about Chad Paddle asking me if I am a girl, and Mary Alice asking me if I am gay at the ice rink. Somehow, I knew these things were connected, but this is the first time I've really thought about what these words *mean*. Before, I've been able to pretend these words refer to something abstract—to people who live far away and do vague, terrible things. *People who are not like me.*

Today, they are used in reference to those two young men laughing together. *Guys who look a lot like me.* What did these guys do that was terrible? Stand there holding hands? Was it the kiss on the cheek? Nothing looked so awful about them to me. It looked like they were nice guys who were nice to each other.

I glance around the room, suddenly afraid someone might have heard this thought in my head. *They must be able to tell.*

Megan is sitting next to me. She glances up at Mr. Kroger, then slides a scrap of notebook paper onto my desk. My heart is pounding.

The note reads: *What are you doing tonight? You should come over.*

I smile at her, relieved. She's right.

I should.

"How was the ice rink party?"

Bradley and I are walking toward our lockers. We have different class schedules, and it's the first time I've gotten to see him all day. I've been dying to tell him about my first beer, but I haven't had a chance. My smile is cautious as I glance both ways over my shoulder.

His eyes narrow and a smirk creeps across his face. "What?" he asks.

"I had a beer," I whisper.

"No *way*!" Bradley laughs and holds his hand up for a high five. "That's awesome, man!"

"What's awesome?" It's Erica at my locker, smiling. We're going to rehearse after school for a scene we're performing in chapel next week.

"Nothing," I say quickly. "We're planning the weekend."

"What's going on this weekend?" she asks.

It's one of those awkward moments when I don't understand why Erica can't read social cues. *If we wanted you to know, we would tell you.*

Bradley seems immune to moments like these. It's one of the reasons I like him. He grabs his gym bag and closes his locker.

"This weekend, Erica, the party is *on*." He grins at me and says, "Call me later, man," then disappears down the hall toward the gym.

Erica is quiet as I grab my script and walk back toward the church auditorium, where we're rehearsing. I head up onto the stairs that stretch across the front of the sanctuary leading up to the platform and choir loft. The scene we are rehearsing is staged with me on one side and Erica on the other. We are talking to each other but facing out toward the audience.

Instead of heading to her side, Erica follows me slowly up the stairs. "So, there's a big party this weekend?"

"Oh, I don't know." *Downplay. Change the subject.* The last thing I need is another lecture from Erica about Bradley.

Erica looks at me almost curiously and opens her mouth to say something, then thinks better of it. She heads over to her side of the stairs at the stage.

"Should we run it from the top?" she asks.

Relieved, I begin the scene. It's a conversation between a guy and a girl, teenagers, who have been on a date. They talk back and forth about the evening and how it was going: the party, how handsome he looked, how beautiful she was, and then on the way home—a car wreck.

As the scene progresses, you realize that the characters can't see each other now, because they were killed in the accident and are now in the afterlife. She's on her way to heaven, and he is on his way to hell. The final minutes of the scene are the guy tearfully asking the girl why she didn't tell him about Jesus so that he could have gone to heaven. The last line is her explaining why:

"Because I didn't want to lose you...as a friend."

The irony implied is that the girl lost her friend for all eternity because he died without trusting in Jesus as his savior. My dad had signed us out of classes last week to come to the chapel service at the Bible college and perform the scene for his students. We're doing it in our chapel service here at school tomorrow.

Erica is a great actor. It's one of the reasons I love performing with her. When we're done running the scene, she wipes tears from her cheeks.

"That went pretty well," she says, and smiles, her bright eyes rimmed with red.

I smile at her and nod. "You're terrific."

"Thanks."

We sit on the front pew for a second in silence.

"It's such an important scene," she says. "I love doing it because of the message."

I quietly begin gathering my books. I feel like I'm tiptoeing through a minefield. I love this scene because it's dramatic and it moves people. I can feel Erica's eyes on me now. I know she wants me to say something.

"Don't you think it's important, Aaron?"

I look up at her and smile. "Yeah. Of course."

"I worry about you," she says.

"Worry about me?"

"Yeah. Your dad was so proud of you last week when we did this scene at the college. Does he know that you're going to these parties at Bradley's house?"

I want to yell at Erica: *This is none of your business!*

But I don't. This isn't her fault. She's just doing what her character failed to do in the scene we rehearsed. It's the thing we're all told to do: Exert positive peer pressure. Encourage your friends to stand up for what is capital *R* Right.

"Erica, nothing bad is going on at these parties."

"You have such an opportunity to win souls for Christ doing scenes like this," she says. "I don't want to see you ruin your Christian testimony by hanging out with the wrong crowd."

All I can hear is my dad's voice when I was a little boy: *reaching lost souls with quality biblical drama*. Sometimes it feels like all the people I know are trying to hold me against a wall with everything they've got—afraid if they let go for a single second, I'll float away forever like a balloon in an updraft, soaring past the three-cross steeple four stories over our heads.

Erica is right about one thing: If it gets out that I drink, I'll be kicked out of school. No one will give me special privileges like performing in front of the student body or the Bible college if that happens. Still, even though I know it's risky, all I want to do this weekend is hang out at Bradley's house.

As I stand here looking at Erica, I realize my friendship with Bradley has become more important to me than anything else. It's more important than performing a scene in chapel or winning souls with the Good News. Bradley and I share so much more than just our faith. We share more than a place we hope to go when we die. For the first time, I have a connection with a friend in the here and now that feeds my soul in a way I've never felt before—in a way my beliefs never have.

I take a deep breath to steady my voice. "Erica, I think the scene is great. I think the message is very important. I'm not doing anything that is going to ruin my Christian testimony."

Erica doesn't buy it. She shouldn't. I'm lying. My friendship with Bradley may very well ruin my Christian testimony, but I don't care. She gathers her books and heads toward the doors of the church auditorium. Something stops her, and she turns around.

"Aaron, you're so good at this. You're the best actor I've ever seen. I'm realizing you're so good at it you never stop. You're acting all the time—onstage and off."

I feel my face flush. *How dare you?* I open my mouth to retort, but I know my anger could blister the paint on the walls, and I catch myself just in time.

Erica smiles at me sadly. "When we do this scene...do you even believe what we're saying anymore?"

I am silent. I can't answer her. Erica shakes her head, then turns around and pushes through the double doors. I throw my backpack onto the floor. Hard. Tears cloud my eyes. Suddenly I'm crying, and I'm not sure why.

Why is this so important? Who cares if I go have a beer with Bradley? Or make out with Megan? Or think there's nothing wrong with those guys in the video holding hands?

When I told the story of Speckles two summers ago, scaring those kids about hell made me feel so guilty. It's exactly the same feeling I have when I perform this scene. *Shouldn't I be making people feel better, not worse? Doesn't God want us to feel good?*

I sit down on the front pew and stare up at the cross hanging over the choir loft. It's empty, just like the one at my church. My eyes wander up to the peak of the ceiling that stretches high above the balcony. I think of the excitement I felt as a little boy to blast off through the roof, and wonder where it went.

"Jesus, if you're really coming back, help me believe it." I whisper these words up at the towering ceiling above the empty cross. I wait for some feeling to come over me, some sense of peace or wonder—the excitement of my eight-year-old self.

It doesn't.

As I sling my backpack onto my shoulders, I glance back at the cross. *Where is the Jesus I used to be excited about?* I feel my chest tighten around all the things I can't say out loud, the ones I'm too afraid to pray about.

CHAPTER 21

"I'm *in*."

Bradley is grinning ear to ear and shoves a piece of paper in my direction. The University of Iowa's logo stretches across the top.

We are pleased to inform you...

I pause and take a deep breath. I know how badly he wanted this.

"That's awesome!" I am smiling on the outside, but on the inside I want this year to slow down. *How will I make it through my senior year without you?*

We are walking toward the building from our cars. There is one month of school left. Jacob gets back from Stanford in three weeks, and we're already planning a big graduation bash at Bradley's place.

"Did you hear back about your PSAT scores yet?" Bradley asks.

"Yeah. I'm a National Merit semifinalist."

"That's great. You should be able to score a scholarship to a good school with that. Where are you applying?"

I blink at him. College seems so far away, and Bradley has been way more focused on the application process than any of the teachers or my parents are. I've started getting catalogs from colleges all over the place—beautiful, glossy brochures in thick envelopes with applications and pamphlets about financial aid.

"I don't really have a lot of choices," I say. "I have to start with a year of Bible college first."

Bradley stops short. "You're kidding me."

I shake my head. "Nope. Dad's rule: One year of Bible college first, then I can transfer anywhere I want to."

"Yeah, but that's suicide. All the scholarships go to freshmen." Bradley sounds truly dismayed, but I can't even get worried about it. When I think about what happens next, I feel overwhelmed and exhausted. I want to go to college somewhere that has a great acting program, but Dad and Mom don't have enough money to help me with college because Dad has always taught for Christian schools.

"I get free tuition at the Bible college where Dad teaches," I say.

Bradley rolls his eyes. "Don't they have curfews and crazy rules like this place? You have to get out of the house. Go live a little."

I shrug. I feel trapped. It doesn't matter that I've gotten straight As or that I score well on tests. There's really no money to go anyplace else. "It's sort of a money thing," I say.

"But you've gone to a Christian school since you were in kindergarten." Bradley is adamant. "You know everything there is to know about the Bible by now, don't you?"

I smile. "Yeah, the Bible doesn't change much after fourth grade."

Bradley keeps talking about an application for federal student aid, and getting a loan, and how I have to start thinking about it now; but all I can think about right now is how my best friend is leaving for Iowa.

This place will be hell without you.

"Hell is real, young people—an actual place created by the One True God, and I'm here on his behalf today to ask if you are *sure* about where you will spend eternity after you die."

It's the last week of classes, and an evangelist named Todd is preaching in today's chapel service. He is a short man with a tall pompadour and a practiced, rhythmic cadence that you can tell he really enjoys hearing. He's preached this sermon hundreds of times; his memory is perfect, his pauses placed with surgical precision. He's wearing a polyester blazer, and the louder he gets, the redder his face becomes.

"Young men and women of God, make no mistake that hell exists, but each of you has a *choice* to make. I warn you now that if you slip into a Christ-less afterlife, you will find your nostrils filled with the putrid stench of eternal death, where the sulfurous fumes of damnation turn the very tears you shed into streams of acid that burn rivulets into your cheeks as you cry out for a drop of water to quench your eternal thirst. But there will be no reply, young man. There will be no relief, young woman. This is what will happen if *you* go to *hell*."

"If You Go to Hell" is the name of this sermon, and every so often Todd says these words as a frightening form of punctuation. It already has several of the teachers shouting out "amen."

I hate sermons like these.

I've grown up with my dad preaching in churches, and his dad before him, but their sermons are different—thoughtful and passionate without being brash and showy.

Grandpa Hartzler was a cabinetmaker who'd only gone to school until eighth grade. Years later, when Dad was a little kid, Grandpa had taken night classes at the same Bible college where Dad now teaches and become the pastor of a tiny Mennonite church. I don't remember Grandpa ever yelling when he preached, but I do remember the way he prayed—standing in the pulpit, talking to God with his arms stretched out and his head raised to heaven, asking for healing and goodness and love, tears slipping down his rough-hewn cheeks.

During the summer before my fifth-grade year, Grandpa asked the whole family to come to the church he pastored for a special healing service. He'd been diagnosed with pancreatic cancer, and he humbly explained to the congregation that he was asking for healing, but he only wanted God's will for him. If the Lord had chosen this as his time to pass on, then he was ready to meet Jesus.

"'It is appointed unto man once to die,'" he quoted, "'but after this the judgment.'"

My dad and his brothers joined the other men from the church and walked up the aisle to meet Grandpa in front of the pulpit. Grandpa pulled a small bottle of Orville Redenbacher popcorn oil out of his suit jacket pocket and handed it to my dad. There was nothing special about the oil. I knew it wasn't blessed or considered holy or anything; it was just used as a symbol of what the apostles used to do in biblical times.

Grandpa knelt on the floor, and the men gathered around to anoint him. His skin had already turned a toxic yellow-green from jaundice, the same color as the oil Dad dribbled into his hair. Each man in the circle laid a hand on Grandpa's head, or his shoulder, or the shoulder of the man they were standing next to, and many prayers were said for his healing.

As I watched, I couldn't help thinking this seemed like a long shot. Other healing attempts were under way as well. One of my uncles had filled Grandma's meat-and-potatoes kitchen with macrobiotic foods like seaweed and kept talking passionately about how God would heal Grandpa to prove his wonder-working power.

Six months later when Grandpa died, the people he had helped over the years packed the funeral home for his visitation. People our family had never met or heard of spoke about how he'd changed their lives with a tiny act of kindness: fixing their tractor or the leak in their roof, or visiting their sick mother. No one mentioned how enthusiastic or polished or well rehearsed his sermons were, but person after person talked about his prayers. "Every time he prayed, I felt like I was in the presence of God."

I know Grandpa Hartzler believed hell was a real place, but I don't ever remember him trying to scare anyone with it. By contrast, Evangelist Todd is marching back and forth across the stage in the chapel, waving his arms and shouting. He will *not* be ignored.

This is good, old-fashioned fire-and-brimstone preaching, and it's working. No matter how often I question whether our theology makes sense, sermons like this scare me senseless. Any logical question as to whether Jesus is *really* coming back, or whether that oil could be an agent of symbolic healing, fly right out the window. I feel guilty for having ever asked such questions in the first place. My stomach is quaking, my heart is pounding, and a single question drums in my brain:

What if I'm not really saved?

I remember asking Jesus into my heart, but it was the week before my third birthday, so it's mainly snapshots, most a little hazy. I remember setting Josh up in his carrier and playing with the flannelgraph board, teaching him about Jesus with Mom's figures—pictures of Jesus, crucified and bleeding, flocked on the back, fuzzy under my fingers. Pressing them against the soft felt on the board so Josh could see them, telling him the words Mom had said to me so many times: *sin, heaven, Jesus, wash away, born again, heart, saved....*

I remember asking Mom again if I could be saved. Playing with my Lincoln Logs until Dad got home from work.

Sitting on the couch with Mom and Dad, bowing my head in prayer, asking Jesus to forgive me for all my dark sin and to come into my heart so I could live forever with him in heaven.

It's hazy, but I remember bits and pieces. Mom wrote down the words I prayed that day in the front of my tiny blue New Testament. She and Dad have assured me many times that once I sincerely trusted Jesus as my personal Lord and savior, I was saved from hell for all eternity. Jesus said in the Gospel of John that he gives those who trust him eternal life, and that "no man shall be able to pluck them out of my hand." It's a doctrine called "eternal security," which means once you sincerely trust Christ as your savior, you're always saved, no matter what. Still, every time I hear a sermon like this, I doubt my salvation.

When I was in fourth grade, Dad rented a TV for the holidays, and Channel 50, the Christian TV station in Kansas City, played a movie called *A Thief in the Night* that we watched as a family. The movie was made in the sixties, about a group of friends who get left behind after the Rapture because they aren't saved when Jesus comes back. The Antichrist comes to power, and one of the girls refuses to take the mark of the beast, so the Antichrist sends out his soldiers in big white vans that read UNITED on the side to hunt her down.

I was so scared after that movie that I asked Jesus into my heart every night before bed for quite a while: *This time I* really *mean it.*

I feel the same gnawing doubts in my stomach right now

as Evangelist Todd pleads with us to come down the aisle, kneel at the front, and "get right with God." He's not quiet about it, the way my grandpa used to be. This guy is all bombast. His altar call has the texture and subtlety of a commercial for the Labor Day blowout at a used-car lot.

Of course, it works. Even with my head bowed and my eyes closed, I can hear the rush of other students making their way down the aisle toward the front. It even works on me, but I don't move. This sermon, these scare tactics, aren't about a relationship with God. This man is scaring us into re-upping a contract for services, pure and simple. This is fire insurance.

There are plenty of us still glued to our pews, shaking on the inside, perhaps, but not moving on the outside. Without leaving my place, I silently pray one more time:

Dear God: If I haven't been sincere enough before, or if for some reason it didn't work, please come into my heart. I'm sorry for all the sin in my life—lying to Mom and Dad, going to movies, thinking about sex, jerking off, drinking. I believe that your Son, Jesus, paid the price for all those sins when he died on the cross. Please forgive me and wash my sins away so that I can spend eternity in heaven with you. In Jesus's name, amen.

Even before I'm done praying, I feel silly.

Do I need forgiveness for those things? Are they really wrong? Plenty of kids in this room have parents who let them go to movies and do all sorts of things my mom and dad don't allow. There are all sorts of Christians with all sorts of different rules, not to mention other people who believe in other religions. What about all the people on the other side of the world who believe as strongly in their God as we believe in our God? Are they going to go to hell because they were unlucky enough to be born in the wrong place?

A crowd of students kneel on the stairs at the altar and drape themselves across the front pew. They're praying for forgiveness, crying, talking with teachers, and hugging each other as the rest of us file out of chapel. Bradley falls into step with me as we lead the ashen-faced unrepentant out the back doors of the auditorium and return to class.

"*Jesus*," he says under his breath. "What was *that*?"

"The Good News." I sigh.

He shakes his head like he's trying to clear his brain of the last hour. "What are you doing tomorrow night after graduation?"

"I have a date with Megan."

"You're still coming to my party afterward, aren't you?"

"Wouldn't miss it." I smile. "After that sermon? I need a drink."

My friend Eric and I are the junior marshals at the graduation ceremony. We line up with Bradley and the rest of the seniors in the choir room. I'm wearing a black gown and carrying the American flag down the aisle of the auditorium and up to the stage, stepping slowly and deliberately to the rhythm of "Pomp and Circumstance."

Next year I'll be wearing purple and getting my diploma.

After the ceremony, I join the pandemonium in the foyer of Tri-City Ministries, taking pictures with my friends in their purple caps and gowns. I confirm with Bradley I'll be spending the night at his house, then Megan and I head to Fuddruckers for burgers.

"That'll be *us* next year," she says.

"Unless Jesus comes back first."

She laughs. "Oh, c'mon. I'm guessing we get another year at *least*."

"It'll happen the very second Principal Friesen hands me my diploma," I say. "A cosmic joke by Jesus, the moment I graduate."

Megan dips a fry in some ketchup and chews thoughtfully. I love the way she cocks her chin and narrows her eyes when she's considering a proposition.

"Do you really believe Jesus is coming back?" She squints at me through her long lashes.

I swallow a bite of my cheeseburger. "Do you?"

The question hangs in the air, unanswered. We both take a sip from our straws and change the subject.

I'm kissing Megan on the couch in her living room, which is bizarre because her mom and dad are on the other side of the wall, in their bedroom. It's only the two of us now, lit by the glow of the TV screen. This has happened before, but

I'm still getting used to it. The idea of making out with a girl on the couch at my house is unthinkable. My parents would never go to bed and leave me alone with a girl on the couch. Megan's mom hung out with us and talked for a long time after we got back from the movie. Megan curled up against me on the couch and held my hand while we chatted like there was nothing weird about the fact we were touching in front of her mother.

Maybe there is *nothing weird about it.*

After her mom went to bed, Megan and I chatted while the credits rolled on *90210*. I was in midsentence when she pulled me down on top of her. "Shut up and kiss me," she whispered.

So I did.

We haven't stopped kissing for a long time.

Her hoodie smells like fabric softener, and we are pressed up against each other like we're trying to meld our own unique, individual bodies into one organism. Her breath is heavy, and when I slide my arm under her back to pull her closer into me, I feel strong and powerful.

Our legs are intertwined, and everything is positioned just so. Our mouths are locked together, and I feel her hands trace down my back, then slide under the waistband of my jeans. Her hands are cool on my butt as she pulls me into her even more closely.

This is that moment my dad talks about. I get it now. This is where we're supposed to back the truck up and park a long way from the brink.

But we don't.

She grabs me by the hand and leads me downstairs to her bedroom instead. She has an enormous room with the biggest king-size water bed I have ever seen, and as we climb into it, I ask, "Is your dad going to come down here with a shotgun?"

Her giggle is raspy and warm. "Of course not. They don't care. I mean, they *care*, but they know I'm not going to have sex."

She pulls my clothes off, first my sweater, then my shirt. She loosens my belt, and I stand there at the edge of the bed. *Frozen.*

"Aaron. It's fine. They trust me."

Slowly, I crawl onto the bed, onto her. She pulls me close again, arching her back and breathing deeply as I unbutton her blouse. The more time I take, the more she seems to want me to hurry, and I smile as I look into her eyes.

Huh. So that's *how this works. I'm going to take my time.*

The water beneath the sheets lifts and falls in a lilting rhythm as we obey only the letter of the law. We slip off our underwear and pull the truck right up to the edge of the cliff.

We don't make love.

But we make waves.

As I step inside Bradley's front door I can hear the party already in progress. There is music playing, and Mrs. Westman meets me at the top of the stairs with a smile, a hug, and a shoe box:

"Keys, please, handsome man."

I drop my car keys into her shoe box, and she winks. "You can have these back tomorrow morning. Jacob and Bradley are in the kitchen with Drake."

Jacob is adding an empty can to a stack that is already several feet high on the counter.

"Hartzler!" he yells, almost sending the cans flying all over, and races over to give me a sideways hug. "How was the date?"

I smirk and shoot an eyebrow up. Jacob lets out a hoot.

"That's trouble if I've ever seen it." Drake is leaning against the island in the kitchen, stubbing out a cigarette.

"Aaron, don't let these boys corrupt you." Mrs. Westman is pouring a glass of red wine at the island. "Bradley, who are all those girls in the hot tub?"

"They are young women of the public-school variety," Bradley says. "Paula, Pamela, and Tamara."

"Where are all their cars? I don't want anybody driving home intoxicated."

"Already taken care of, Mom. Tamara's sister is home from college. She'll be coming to get them in a couple of hours."

"In that case, enjoy yourselves, gentlemen." She raises her glass. "I'll be curling up with a book. Drake, I trust I'll see you shortly?"

"If I know what's good for me," he says drily, pinching her on the butt. She laughs and heads up the stairs toward her bedroom. He turns to me. "Wingman, I need to know two things before I follow her."

"Yes, sir." I salute.

"First: Where did you leave this Megan?"

"Tucked into her king-size water bed."

There is a chorus of shouts and catcalls from Jacob and Bradley.

Drake nods his head. "Nice work. Second: What can I get you to drink? Bradley tells me you've recently expanded your beverage repertoire."

"Check it out, buddy." Jacob swings open the refrigerator door. It is packed with mixers and three cases of Budweiser. Someone has written a name on each with a black marker.

Bradley.

Jacob.

Aaron.

"Of course, there's plenty of vodka if you'd rather." Drake smiles. "Help yourself."

I eye the tower of cans on the counter. "Looks like we're drinking beer tonight." I open the case with my name on it, pull out a can, and pop it open. There's an excitement that courses through me as I raise my can to meet the other three that fly up in an impromptu "Cheers!"

We all take long drinks from our beers, and as the tart, terrible taste runs over my tongue and down my throat, I feel something click in my head.

This is what it means to belong.

This is the closeness I know my dad must be trying for by sharing Bible verses, and singing in church, and talking about masturbation, and all those other things he does with me. I know he means well, but it feels so embarrassing, so difficult.

There's something effortless about talking with Bradley and Drake and Jacob. Our friendship isn't based on sharing a faith or a big plan for eternity. It's based on sharing a beer and the big plan for tonight. With these guys, I'm good enough just as I am. I don't feel self-conscious or strange. I don't endure their presence, wishing like mad I could be somewhere else.

It feels good to be chosen.

Drake claps me on the back and heads to bed with a smile. "You boys don't do anything I wouldn't do."

It's an old line, but I hear it for the first time as the admonition of someone who wants me to make my own decisions and be responsible for my own life.

Jacob grabs a case of the beer as Bradley slides open the door to the deck, and the three of us head toward the public-school girls in the hot tub.

Paula is bright, but not sweet.

Pamela is pretty, but not bright.

Tamara is sweet, but not pretty.

By two AM the six of us have finished off the case of beer that Jacob hauled out to the hot tub. The beer and the warm water seem to have had an effect on my brain: Namely, I don't remember being this funny before. Everyone is laughing at everything I say. I've never been quite this witty.

Naturally, a game of truth or dare breaks out in the hot tub, and soon Pamela has taken off her bikini top, marking the second pair of breasts I have seen on this particular evening. Bradley and Jacob are eager for dares, but even with three beers in my system, I can still feel how chapped my lips are from kissing Megan for hours.

I decide to stick with the truth.

Eventually, both Jacob and Bradley have kissed all three girls, Pamela has licked Jacob's left nipple, and Bradley has made a lap around the backyard sans swim trunks. After this brazen show of masculinity, Bradley decides that if he has to be naked in the hot tub, all the guys should be naked in the hot tub. Jacob protests loudly, and I shock him by sliding off the trunks Bradley loaned me and tossing them at his head.

"Holy shit!" Bradley dissolves into laughter, forgets that he's naked, and stands up to give me a high five. The whole Jacuzzi gets an eyeful.

"Aaaaaugh, jeez!" Jacob covers his eyes, laughing. "Put that thing away!"

At that moment, Tamara's sister shows up to drive the girls home. She is sweet, bright, *and* pretty. She is also easily convinced by Jacob to let him ride along in her car while she drops the girls off.

"I'll be back later," he says to us in a voice that's meant to be a whisper. Bradley and I snort with laughter as they all pile into Tamara's car and pull out of the driveway.

Then it's only Bradley and me. Naked. In the hot tub.

It's quiet, and the outside air is cold. I slide down so the water comes to my chin, and as I lay my head back against the edge of the tub, a jet blasts me full-on in the crotch.

I sit up. Quickly.

"Whoa—what's up, man? Something bite you?" Bradley cracks open another beer and hands it to me.

"Um, well..." I smile. "I sort of...found a jet."

Bradley laughs. It's dark, but the light from the kitchen bounces off the water and I can see that his eyes are glassy and bright.

I wonder how many beers he had before I got here?

"Hot-tub jets are the best, man! Have you ever held your dick up to one?"

"I think I sorta just did."

He laughs. "See? Did it make you hard? Sometimes when you're drunk you can't resist a hot-tub jet, you know? I've been sitting next to this one for the last ten minutes."

A mischievous grin spreads across his face, and Bradley thrusts his hips up, letting his legs float out in front of him. His erection breaks the surface of the water. "Woo-hoo! Hot-tub boners!" Bradley laughs like it's the most hilarious thing ever, and I join him.

Maybe it's the beer, or the thrill of being *part of*, or simply a crazy night—I'll never know why—but I follow suit. Bradley hoots again when I flash him my hard-on.

"Woo-*hoo*!" Bradley is a little loud for two AM, but we can't stop laughing. He raises his beer to me. "Hartzler, you're awesome. I don't know how I would've survived this year without you." Bradley's words are starting to slide into each other. "So! Tell me what happened with Megan tonight. I want *details*."

My face is flushed. My heart is pounding. My whole body is electric right now. What just happened feels somehow more intense than what happened with Megan earlier—and that was *intense*.

Maybe it's the beer.

When Jacob finally comes back, we all crash: Jacob on the couch in the family room, me on the bed next to Bradley. I wake up to a Spanish omelet and a steaming mug of coffee from a smiling Mrs. Westman. My car keys are next to my plate.

This is the way the rest of the summer goes: dates with Megan, late nights with Jacob and Bradley. I get a job at the mall selling suits and ties. At some point, we have one last party, and the next morning as I'm helping Bradley load up his car, I promise his parents I'll still stop by to visit while he's away. After everything is loaded up, Bradley pulls me in for a hug, kisses his mom good-bye, and gives his dad a high five. Then he drives away toward Iowa City.

As I watch his car disappear around the corner, I wonder how I'll survive my senior year without him. I wonder if I'll ever be able to stop replaying that scene from the hot tub in my head, or if the awful, empty ache in my stomach will ever go away.

It hasn't happened yet.

CHAPTER 22

Years ago, Mom stitched two small embroidered needlework samplers. Both are framed and hang in the corner of our living room. One reads: THERE ARE TWO GIFTS WE GIVE OUR CHILDREN: ONE IS ROOTS, THE OTHER IS WINGS. The second reads: PLAN AHEAD. IT WASN'T RAINING WHEN NOAH BUILT THE ARK.

As the window of my brown Toyota Tercel breaks against the asphalt, the glass slices through the sleeve of my white shirt and cuts my elbow. The car tumbles end over end in slow motion, and the windshield crinkles like an accordion. Strangely, I'm not afraid. All I can think about are Mom's needlework samplers.

Plan ahead. It wasn't raining when Noah built the ark. But it *was* raining when Josh and I left the school after our final Saturday rehearsal, and I should have planned to take that curve more slowly.

There are two gifts we give our children: One is roots. The other is wings. This car has wings right now. I hope we find our roots again, soon.

My Toyota has made a complete revolution, and we land right side up, facing the opposite direction. For a moment, there is complete stillness. I feel dazed, but nothing seems to be broken.

"Aaron, I *told you to slow down*."

"I know. I'm sorry. Are you okay?" I ask. Josh isn't bleeding anywhere I can see.

"Yeah, I'm fine. Just feel like I have something in my eye."

Josh and I both look at each other, strangely calm for just having survived my car rolling end over end. "That was close," I say.

"Too close," he agrees.

My knees are so weak from the adrenaline I can barely stand up when we get out of the car. The driver of the sedan we narrowly missed hitting looks as if he's seen a ghost. A woman in the house at the corner calls the police and my mom. Josh keeps his eye closed until the paramedics show up. When they arrive, they clean out Josh's eye and check the scrape on my elbow. Other than that, we are unscathed.

We stand and stare at the crumpled brown Toyota, and I am stunned. The driver's seat, where I was strapped in, skews at a strange angle, and the roof of the car is creased only a few inches from where my head must have been.

"The Lord was merciful," Mom says softly.

The wreck when the drunk driver hit us in sixth grade comes flooding back to me now. The impact, the slow-motion float of the station wagon, the blood on Miriam's cheek and Caleb's forehead, and something else:

Mom's beautiful soprano, singing.

After the car skidded to a stop and Josh had taken off his shirt to stanch the flow from Caleb's forehead, as we waited for the ambulance to arrive, Mom had said, "Let's sing."

> *Jesus I am resting, resting*
> *In the joy of what Thou art*
> *I am finding out the greatness*
> *Of thy loving heart.*

Maybe this is where the calmness I feel now comes from. Mom has always been great in a crisis. I realize she's taught me how to handle emergencies with grace—and a song.

Songs! My tapes!

While Mom is still talking to the paramedics about Josh's eye, I grab my secret box of cassette tapes from under the seat of the totaled Toyota and stash them beneath the seat in her car.

As I traipse along the shoulder of the road picking up the items that were flung from the car, I can't help remembering the story about Mom's friend from high school who got shot while he was hitchhiking. Was this a message from God? A sign? A warning to straighten up? To quit drinking? Bradley has been in Iowa for six weeks. Since then I've had a beer out of the fridge Megan's dad keeps stocked in their breezeway, but other than that there are no parties planned until Bradley comes back for Thanksgiving.

Soon the tow truck has dragged away the wreckage, and

we are headed home. When I walk through the front door, I head into the living room and stare at the needlepoint hanging in the corner. I say a silent prayer, a prayer thanking God for keeping me alive, and promising to straighten up if he continues to, but as soon as I say "amen," guilt begins to pool in my stomach.

The God who is part of my roots knows everything. He knows I'm just bargaining. "No drinking" for a get-out-of-wreck-free card seems silly. I may be able to fool Mom and Dad, but how could I fool God? The things my parents have taught me to believe seem to make less and less sense to me, and all at once the ideas of roots and wings seem at odds with each other. What good are wings if your roots won't let you off the ground?

Mom calls us all to the table for dinner, and I walk into the kitchen wondering how I'll ever fly very far at all.

"That poster really looks like you!"

Jacob has flown back from Stanford for the weekend to see his little brother in the school play. I got the lead this year, and Jacob is genuinely impressed that Mrs. Hastings had an artist draw my likeness on the posters for her new musical about the life of Joseph.

"When my mom told me they were doing *Joseph* for the school musical, I almost fell over," he says, laughing.

"Yeah, our Joseph is not of the Amazing Technicolor Dreamcoat variety," I say.

"Can you imagine if Tri-City did the Andrew Lloyd Webber *Joseph*?" he asks. "All those shirtless slaves, and you in hot pants."

"I think the building would fall down and crush us. It would wind up being more like a musical about Samson."

We are sitting in IHOP at midnight on Friday. I'm spending the night at Jacob's tonight. His family falls somewhere between Bradley's and mine on the Christian school continuum. There's no beer or Absolut at his place, but plenty of movies in the family room. After the play, we had watched *The Terminator* and *Terminator 2*, then decided we had to get some food.

"You were really great in the show, by the way. How many more performances do you have?"

"One more tomorrow night."

"Big plans for the holidays?" he asks.

"We're going to Memphis, like we always do." Papa Davis is losing his battle with emphysema. No one is sure how much more time he has, but Nanny says this will be his last Christmas with us.

"You okay?" Jacob asks as the waitress places a cheeseburger in front of him and a turkey club in front of me.

"Yeah. A little sad about my grandfather," I say. "He's not doing very well."

Our conversation turns to Jacob's plan to finish his degree, then join the armed forces as an officer so the military will pay for him to go to grad school.

"I'll be able to retire in twenty years with a pension," he says, "and they'll pay for everything."

Talking about a pension as a sophomore in college strikes me as strange—almost like having a death wish. I suppose I understand putting things in order for the future, but I don't want to think like that. It feels like Jacob is planning to be an old man before he's even out of college.

I've never really imagined my life past twenty-five. If I try hard, I can imagine myself living in Los Angeles, in a cool apartment. I have furniture with clean lines and no floral prints. There is art on the walls, and I have a martini set on the bar, but the rest of the details are hazy.

Jacob asks about my college plans, and I tell him I'm probably headed to the Bible college across town to get my first year out of the way.

"After that, I'm not sure," I say.

"What do you want to major in?" he asks.

"I want to be an actor, but I also want to get a music major," I say. "I want to keep playing the piano."

"How are you going to make money?" he asks.

"I want to be on TV," I say. "Or do musicals on Broadway."

"Do you have a Plan B?" he asks. "In case that doesn't work out?"

I like Jacob, but something about this question bugs me. "I'm not going to plan for it not to work out," I say. "I don't know exactly what my life will look like in twenty years. I think I'm good at lots of things. I'm going to carve my own niche."

He smiles at me and nods. "Just make sure your niche has a salary expectation."

I suddenly wish I could go to Stanford. I wish I could fly to California on the next plane out with Jacob. The idea of going to the Bible college feels easy, but it doesn't get me any closer to where I want to be. Jacob's green eyes light up when he talks about college. He wears preppy suede Bass shoes and V-neck sweaters.

How did you get to Stanford? I wonder. *And how am I going to get out of here?*

"The deer ran into me!"

"Aaron, how is that even *possible*?" Daphne is laughing so hard she can barely drink her chocolate malt at Winstead's. Both of our schools are out for Christmas break, and it feels good to be done with finals.

"I'm just telling you what happened. I wasn't even going that fast."

"And a deer appeared out of nowhere to commit suicide against your car?"

I nod. "It was terrible. And it's the second accident I've had this year."

"Well, the dent didn't look that bad when you picked me up," Daphne says. "At least you can still drive the car this time."

She makes a good point. Bradley got back from the University of Iowa last night, and Jacob got back from Stanford this morning. Both of them called me and said the same thing: "Let's party." Plans are under way for a New Year's Eve celebration that will be remembered by future generations as the stuff of legend. Mom and Dad have decided I can go. They think I will be ringing in the New Year playing board games with nonexistent members of the youth group Bradley does not attend at the Westmans' fictional church.

"How's Megan?" asks Daphne. "It was good to see her last week at the basketball tournament."

"Skiing with her family in Colorado."

"She's quite the little athlete, isn't she?"

"I think she's an adrenaline junkie. She was last seen wearing a T-shirt that read FASTER, FASTER, FASTER, UNTIL THE THRILL OF SPEED OVERCOMES THE FEAR OF DEATH."

"She certainly has moved in on you pretty quickly." Daphne smirks. "How is it going with her, anyway?"

I blush in spite of myself. "She's . . . fun." I never know how to answer Daphne's questions about girls. I can talk to her about Jacob and Bradley until her ears bleed, but for some reason, I clam up on the subject of Megan.

Daphne shakes her head and waves her straw in a circle, indicating my general vicinity. "Trouble," she says. "You are nothing but trouble."

I'm the first to notice that Dad isn't driving our van toward home after church on Sunday afternoon.

"Where are we going?" I ask him.

"Stay in the buggy and find out." He grins from the driver's seat, and Mom lets out an excited giggle next to him.

"Ho, ho, ho!" she says, her eyes shining brightly. "It's a merry Christmas surprise!"

Mom is not making a joke. She's genuinely delighted. She says things like "merry Christmas surprise" all the time. Christmas is not a joke to her. When it comes to celebrating Jesus's birth, she's a professional, right down to the decorations.

Every January as Mom packs away the decorations from the previous year's festivities, she takes an exhaustive inventory of every single lightbulb, icicle, green wreath, scrap of tinsel, and ornament hook that needs to be replaced for next year. The items she can't find on holiday clearance at Walmart or Target are very carefully logged on a single four-by-six index card, which is then fastidiously paper-clipped to the November page of the calendar for the New Year that hangs on the inside of the cabinet door in the kitchen. The next year, on October 31, before going to bed, she flips that calendar page and her holiday decorating list is ready to go.

There are always surprises at Christmastime. Mom makes sure of that. It's one of the things I love about her. Both she and Dad are tireless surprise planners. They want to make sure we know we're loved—not because they say it, or hug us, or kiss us, all of which they do often. They want us to *experience* their love. They want us to see it in action.

Today, that action takes the form of tickets to the Missouri Repertory Theatre, the biggest professional theater in Kansas City. Mom and Dad have a savings account they've been trying to fill for a while now to replace the living room furniture, but they tend to break down and spend it on cultural events for us, especially around Christmastime. Last year it was *The Nutcracker* at the Kansas City Ballet; this year it's Missouri Rep's annual production of *A Christmas Carol*. The Rep is a beautiful theater, and I've been here for events before, but as I watch Jacob Marley pop through the floor of the stage in chains and beg Ebenezer Scrooge to reconsider his miserly ways, I realize there are teenagers onstage in the opening scene, and a thought crosses my mind:

I should be one of them.

As we leave the show, I stare up at the banners hanging from the ceiling of the theater lobby. Each one bears the name of a different play or musical that will be performed this season: *Death of a Salesman. The Fantasticks. A Midsummer Night's Dream.*

I make a conscious pledge to myself: *The next time you come back to this theater, it's going to be for an audition.*

It's getting dark by the time the matinee ends, and Dad takes us to see the Christmas lights at the Country Club Plaza, an outdoor shopping center not far from the Carriage

Club. The man who developed most of Kansas City was named J. C. Nichols, and he backpacked through Europe when he was twenty-one. Upon his return to the Midwest, he developed huge swaths of Kansas City with buildings in the style of the neighborhoods he'd seen in Europe.

The Country Club Plaza has large, sweeping boulevards with beautiful classical sculptures and giant, ornate fountains. It was one of America's first outdoor shopping centers, and the buildings are scale models of the architecture J. C. Nichols loved in the city of Seville, Spain. Every year, every inch of these buildings is outlined in solid-colored Christmas lights, and thousands of people jam into the space of several city blocks to count down the lighting of the Plaza on Thanksgiving night.

Dad drives us slowly through the Plaza, and we ooh and aah at the lights.

"Oh, isn't this wonderful?" Mom says. "It's so fun making memories." The radio is tuned to KLJC, which started playing Christmas songs this week. She reaches over and turns up the volume on an orchestra playing a beautiful carol, and starts to sing.

> *O come, all ye faithful*
> *Joyful and triumphant*
> *O come ye, O come ye, to Bethlehem*

One by one we join her, first my dad then me, then Caleb, Miriam, and Josh. My mother's beautiful, light soprano drives the melody, and even Dad's attempt at harmony, which can sometimes make my brothers and me call out in protest when we're rehearsing a special number for church, sounds rich and full and right on pitch.

It's already getting down below freezing at night, and there are snow flurries swirling in the air. The frost and steam on the van windows make halos around the Christmas lights, and I look up at the outline of a star strung in lights from the top of a cupola at Seville Square. Even an ordinary shopping center seems transformed in the light of Christmas. As the song crescendos, we sing out another stanza:

> *Sing, choirs of angels*
> *Sing in exultation*
> *Sing all ye citizens of heaven above!*

And that's really what the Christmas story is all about: this idea that the pure light of perfect love can make the lowliest feed troughs a sacred place and fill the bleakest sky on the coldest night with the brilliant warmth of harps and angels.

> *O come! Let us adore him, Christ the Lord.*

Mom's eyes are shining, almost brimming over with tears, and she grabs my dad's hand in between the front seats of the van. She turns to us, smiling, and says, "'And Mary kept all of these things and pondered them in her heart.'"

It's one of her favorite verses. She says it all the time

around the holidays. It's the verse that ends the traditional Christmas story in the middle of Luke, chapter 2. After the angels appeared, and the shepherds came to the stable and went out to spread the good tidings of great joy, Mary quietly pondered these events; she kept them close in her heart.

Mom seems acutely aware that we won't all be here in this family forever, and it's something that I forget sometimes. When she quotes this verse about pondering, I am reminded she's storing up memories.

Before we leave for Memphis in a couple of days to spend Christmas at Nanny and Papa's, she'll bake a red velvet birthday cake for Jesus, iced in white. We'll invite the neighborhood kids over for a special Christmas edition of Good News Club. There's usually a manger scene on the cake, little cutouts of Mary and Joseph and Jesus. We'll sing "Happy Birthday to Jesus" with all the kids, and blow out the candles.

As Mom hands out slices of red velvet cake, she'll explain to the boys and girls that the cake is red because it represents Jesus's blood that he shed for our sins on the cross. This is the reason that Mom says she's so serious about the holidays and making them a special, joyous time: because Jesus was born to die. There isn't only a manger in her Christmas story; there's a cross as well, but the Good News is that Jesus is coming again soon, not as a baby in a manger, but to take us home to heaven.

She tells the boys and girls that the reason we give gifts at Christmas is not because of Santa Claus. It's because Jesus was God's love gift to us. His birth offered the gift of salvation to sinners like herself and you and me—a simple, elegant gift of grace.

"'For God so loved the world, that he gave his only begotten Son...'"

The idea of atonement is always easier to swallow with a slice of her homemade red velvet cake, and as I smile back at Mom from my seat in the van, I try to quiet the nagging voice in my head and the strange twist in my stomach that these thoughts are making me feel.

For tonight, I'm going to focus on the beauty of the lights and bask in the glow of the miracle—angels appearing to shepherds. There is something strange and wonderful about the idea of a deity being born in a barn among commoners.

Even better than that, I realize that there is something truly wonderful about my family and our togetherness in this moment. As Dad turns the van toward home, I stare back out at the lights above the Country Club Plaza and tuck this feeling away to keep for always, to ponder deep in my heart.

Nanny has gathered us all in her living room in Memphis. Mom is staying behind to spend a few more days with Papa, who is back in the hospital. Dad loads the rest of our luggage into the van. He's driving us back to Kansas City so we can start school next week.

Earlier, we said good-bye to Papa. Nanny hasn't missed a beat the past few days. She is cheerful, even though I know she must be tired, and I have never felt closer to her. She always has a smile for me. We've laughed about something together every day, and as she calls us all into the living room, she hands me a box of mud pies.

"For the trip," she whispers with a wink.

We stand in a circle around the den, coats buttoned, bags packed, ready to go. The only thing left is for Nanny to say the prayer she always gives before we drive away.

She grips my hand, closes her eyes, then raises her head and her voice. "Father God, we thank thee and praise thee for the gift of this time we have had together celebrating the birth of your Son. We know that this may be Papa's last Christmas with us, but we commit him to you, and we know that you have a plan for each of us—a plan of good and not of evil, to give us a future and a hope.

"Now, Father God, I pray for your blessing of safety upon my precious grandchildren; that you would send your angels to make the car run smoothly, and bind Satan from the engine block. Put an angel on the hood of the car, Lord, and one at the back; an angel on top and underneath, and one on each tire, so no harm will come to my children. We ask all of this in the name of your Son, Jesus, who loved us so much he gave his life for us. So we say, 'Come quickly, Lord Jesus,' and it's in his name we pray. Amen."

As we walk toward the carport, Nanny wads three twenty-dollar bills into my hand while she hugs my neck and whispers into my ear, "Sit up front and watch your daddy's eyeballs. Make him pull over and let you drive if you see him start to nod off. Last thing I want is you gettin' to heaven before I do."

I could spend eternity talking to Nanny. It's all the heaven I'd ever need.

Bradley's New Year's party is *packed*.

"Who *are* all these people?" I ask Jacob. I met him at the front door a half hour ago and still haven't seen Bradley.

"Who *cares*?" Jacob grins. "This is the Bradley Westman Public-School Girls Network. Don't change the channel."

When we finally make it to the kitchen, I see that Drake has stocked it with enough alcohol to get us through tonight, New Year's Eve next year, and quite possibly an unforeseen zombie apocalypse. The music is loud, and it's cold outside, but the keg is on the deck, and people are already in the hot tub.

Sure beats praying in the New Year at church during the midnight watch service.

"It's a beer-free evening, gentlemen!" Bradley sees Jacob and me headed to the fridge and directs us to the drink-mixing operation he has arranged at the wet bar in the downstairs family room. I've never really experimented with hard liquor before, but Bradley has a new cocktail recipe book his dad gave him for Christmas, and sets to work making one of almost everything.

"Did you see this?" Jacob hands me a brochure for the

University of Iowa. Bradley stares off into the sunset on the first page, his square jaw set with determination to tackle the future.

"They made you the cover model for your college?" I cannot stop laughing.

Bradley nods slyly. "Yep. And female enrollment is already up by twenty percent."

"How was your Christmas, Hartzler? Any good loot?" Jacob slides me a screwdriver to begin.

"My parents gave me luggage." I smile and raise my glass.

"Subtle," snorts Bradley. I clink my glass to his, then Jacob's, and take a big swig.

Bradley whoops from behind the bar and begins to mix another round immediately. "Gentlemen! Start your engines."

By 11:30 PM my whole body is buzzing, and I've learned I like simple drinks the best: vodka and tonic, scotch and water—two ingredients at most, and nothing sweeter than rum. Jacob has determined he prefers doing shots of anything Paula, Pamela, and Tamara will let him pour into their belly buttons while they lie on the family room floor, giggling, their tops pulled up to reveal their stomachs.

"My sister is coming back for you," squeals Tamara as Jacob runs his tongue down toward the button on her jeans. "You'd better watch it!"

As if on cue the doorbell rings.

"I'll get it." I jump up with my rum and Coke.

"Hartzler! Grab me a bag of ice up there. I'm almost out." Bradley is shaking martinis now.

"Roger, that." I head up the stairs and pause on the landing to throw the door open to let Tamara's sister in.

Only it's not Tamara's sister.

It's Tyler Gullem.

My stomach lurches, and suddenly I feel dizzy. My church smile kicks into overdrive automatically.

"Hey! Tyler!" I say brightly, and I hope loudly enough that Bradley can hear me. I swing the door closer to myself from its thrown-wide-open position, trying to block the scene behind me down the stairs, and play it off like I'm cold. "Yikes! It's freezing out here. I didn't know you were coming."

Tyler's eyes move slowly from my face down to the glass in my hand and back. "I'm not coming," he says without a smile. "I'm looking for Janice. I called her place, and her mom said she was at a party. I figured it was this one."

"Nope, no Janice here." I smile, not moving an inch.

"I need to talk to Bradley," he says.

Mayday. How do I keep him outside? If he walks through the front door, the jig is up.

"Bradley's not here," I lie. "He's on a pizza run."

Tyler looks at me hard, like he's trying to see into my thoughts.

Keep him on the sidewalk.

I broaden my grin into the friendliest smile I can muster. "He'll be back soon. You should come in and let me get you a drink," I say.

306

As the words fly out of my mouth, I know I've taken a huge gamble. *What if he takes me up on the offer?*

Tyler glances down at my glass. "Diet Coke?" I ask, lifting it toward him, grin firmly in place.

"Doesn't sound like Tri-City–approved music is playing in there," Tyler says.

"Well, Bradley isn't a Tri-City student anymore. Really, man. You should come in and hang out."

Tyler shakes his head, and backs down the front steps. "Will you have Bradley call me when he shows up?"

"Sure thing, buddy."

Tyler turns to walk down the driveway toward the sidewalk.

"Happy New Year!" I call after him. He stops for an instant. I think he might turn around. I think he might say something else. Instead, he keeps walking.

"Holy crap!" Bradley is wide-eyed. Even the girls are quiet. The rest of the party is raging upstairs, but Jacob and Bradley are both staring at me like they've seen a ghost.

"So, who cares if this Taylor guy saw you here?" Paula isn't quite as smart when she's plastered.

"Tyler," says Bradley, correcting her.

"You were holding your drink?" Jacob starts laughing. "Did his head explode?"

"He didn't know there was anything in it," I say. "It's not like he knows for sure we were drinking."

"Who cares if you're drinking?" Tamara is genuinely confused.

"The school," Jacob explains. "If it gets back to the administration that he was here drinking, he'll be kicked out."

"Why did Tyler come over?" Bradley asks.

"Said he was looking for Janice. Then he asked for you."

"What did you say?" Bradley doesn't even look worried.

"Told him you were making a pizza run. Then I invited him in and offered him a Diet Coke," I say, raising my glass.

Bradley's eyes go wide. "Oh, my God. Are you *serious*?"

"It was the only way I knew he'd leave."

Jacob and Bradley collapse into laughter. "Man!" Jacob says, shaking his head. "You've got balls of steel."

"I need to sit down." I slide down the wall next to the bar, and land on the carpet.

"Barkeep!" Jacob shouts at Bradley. "Get this guy a drink."

Bradley mixes me a fresh rum and Coke. Jacob leads the girls upstairs to the hot tub as Bradley hands me the drink and sits down next to me on the floor.

"I don't think you need to worry about Tyler. Even if he did want to get you in trouble, he doesn't have any proof."

He doesn't need any, I think, but I smile at Bradley and nod. The rum makes me feel like everything is going to be okay. Bradley's here, we're hanging out, having some drinks. That's all I've wanted since he was here at Thanksgiving.

We clink glasses and wish each other a Happy New Year,

then Bradley stands and offers me a hand. When he pulls me up, he keeps my hand clasped in his, between our chests like we're arm wrestling, and he pulls me in toward him.

"I've missed you, Hartzler."

I am so close to Bradley at this moment I can feel his breath on my chin. My whole body is electric again, like that night in the hot tub. The air is thick in the family room, and I search his eyes for some flicker of recognition, some sign that he might feel something similar.

Bradley smiles, then drops my hand and heads up the stairs. "C'mon, man. Can't keep the ladies waiting."

I take a gulp of my rum and Coke as I watch him go. All at once, I'm worried about what just happened. I'm so buzzed everything is hazy right now. *Was that weird?* Maybe I'm just feeling paranoid. I feel hot and my head is spinning a little, so I pause and grab the banister to steady myself for a few seconds. Then I take a deep breath and follow Bradley up the steps to the party above, the hot tub out back, and the New Year beyond.

CHAPTER 23

It is appointed unto men once to die, but after this the judgment.
I am the resurrection and the life....

Seven days after Bradley's New Year's bash, I am back in Memphis, standing on the frozen lawn of a cemetery next to my cousin Sadie. Papa died on Monday, and Dad drove us all back down to Memphis for the funeral.

The minister wraps up the graveside service with Psalm 23, and at the final "amen," I turn and walk with Sadie back toward the warmth of our cars, waiting in the parking lot. Tears slide slowly down her cheeks, and I reach down to take her hand. At some point in the past ten years we stopped climbing the trees in Nanny's front yard, but we still tell each other secrets.

"Remember that time when we were kids and Uncle Hank gave us the stickers out of the price gun from the grocery store? We pretended Papa was sick, and you were the nurse. He let us stick those little price tags all over his forehead."

Sadie laughs and wipes her eyes. "I'm so glad we'll get to

see him in heaven," she says. "Just think! The next time we see Papa, he won't have smoker's lungs anymore. He never has to struggle for breath ever again."

I'm quiet as I consider this. I can't imagine seeing Papa again. I know everyone here would tell me the *real him*—his soul—is up in heaven. They'd say that's only his *body* in the coffin being lowered into the cold, hard clay behind us. Will there really come a time when we all see each other again in heaven? When I was in fifth grade and Grandpa Hartzler died, I didn't think about it much. It was a given: When Christians die, our souls go to heaven, and our physical bodies will be resurrected on the day Jesus comes back. I accepted as fact that we'd all see Grandpa alive again. But today, I feel something different.

My mental image of Papa and Grandpa coming back to life and shooting out of their graves to meet Jesus in the clouds during the Rapture makes me angry. This idea seems to mock the man we've laid to rest, a man who taught me how to make life a little more beautiful one loop of yarn at a time. I haven't cried since Papa died, but now I feel the tears on my cheeks, and Sadie stops to hug me.

"I can't remember what I said to him last week before we left," I tell her. "Did I whisper good-bye? Did I say I loved him? I'm not sure that he heard me."

"He can hear you now," Sadie whispers. "He can hear you now."

I want to believe her.

But I don't.

Help thou my unbelief…

I can see my breath as I whisper these words. A white cloud of steam escapes from my lips, then floats away on the breeze like a puff from the tip of every cigarette that brought us here in the first place.

Bradley is back in Iowa by the time we get home from Memphis. January and February are cold and gray. I turn eighteen, but without Bradley to throw a party, it feels anticlimactic.

By early March, the Carriage Club ice rink is dead. No one is in the lodge area or on the ice. It's only me and Carla on the final Saturday night of the season.

"You wanna go home early?" she asks.

It's only eight o'clock. I'd be home by eight thirty. *And then what?*

I feel a familiar ache. I wish Bradley were still in town. Only two more weeks and he'll be home for spring break. Megan is visiting her brother in Nebraska this weekend, my homework is done, and I've already practiced the piano today. At least if I stay at work, I can ice-skate.

I shrug. "I could use the money," I say.

"You should go skate," Carla says, smiling. "Somebody should be using the ice."

I lace up my black leather figure skates and walk outside to the rink. Peter Cetera and Chaka Khan are singing a duet on the loudspeakers over the ice. The music is one of the reasons that Dad was hesitant about letting me work here, but as I step out onto the smooth, white expanse and practice back crossovers, Dad and Mom and all the rules seem to leave my head.

I love these moments at the ice rink. When it's only me, and the music, and the sound of my blades scraping over the ice. Picking up speed as I come back around to the door, I see Carla standing at the windows watching me. I reach back and stretch into a waltz jump as high as I can leap. It's a beginner's jump, but impressive enough with the speed you can muster on a rink free of six-year-old girls. As I sail backward into the landing, I hear shouts and cheers.

I turn to see two girls and a guy clapping and cheering as they walk down the sidewalk toward the rink lodge.

"That was awesome!" The guy has an infectious smile.

I laugh at myself, embarrassed. "Sorry, didn't realize anyone was here."

I skate over to the break in the wall of the rink, step off the ice, and hold the door to the lodge open.

"You guys here to skate?"

"Yes," says one of the girls. "Skate, then have a drink at the bar."

Carla and I get their skates, trading in sizes for one of the girls, helping the other pull her laces tighter.

"Looks like you're all set," I say as the three of them wobble to their feet.

"You're coming back out there with us, aren't you?" the guy asks.

I glance at Carla. "Go," she says. "There's nothing to do in here but the crossword."

Out on the ice, the girls hang on to the railing and each other at the edge, flailing and laughing until they are red in the face. The guy skates toward me clumsily, his ankles collapsing in toward each other in the plastic rental skates. He slips about three feet away from me, and I reach out and catch him. His arms grab at my waist, and I hold him up as I feel him struggle to regain his footing.

"I'm Kent," he says, straightening up and extending a gloved hand.

"Aaron." I smile.

We shake, but when I try to drop his hand, he holds on to mine. I feel the air grow heavy around me as if a message is hanging there between us in a frequency I cannot hear.

"Thanks," he whispers in a tiny puff of breath that steams against the cold night air. I can see his words.

"You're welcome," I say, and smile. I take my hand out of his and do a couple of back crossovers away from him.

"Whoa—hang on! Where you going?"

I look over my shoulder. He is standing on the ice, arms outstretched, gloved hands hovering at his sides about waist level. He looks like he's trying to keep his balance on a rope bridge that might give way at any moment, his whole body locked, like he's bracing for an impact.

Frozen.

"C'mon." I laugh. "You gotta learn to do this on your own sooner or later."

"If I move one inch, I swear I will fall down."

The girls have their backs to us, clutching the rail, hauling themselves around the ice like bulldozers, dragging the load of their legs and floundering skates behind them. I circle back to his right side. As soon as I'm close, he grabs for me in a panicked tremor. I hold my arm firmly up against his grip.

"You're fine," I say. "Take little steps. Think of marching." This is how we teach the three-year-olds in tot classes. "Gliding comes later. You just need to feel your edges."

I do a quick outside turn so I can skate backward in front of him. He grabs both of my hands in his and hangs on for dear life.

"Relax." I smile. "Don't watch your feet. Look up." He does exactly that. His eyes are the brightest blue I've ever seen.

"You're right," he says, and smiles back at me. "That's a much better view."

I feel myself start to blush, and I drop my gaze.

"Uh-uh." He laughs. "Don't watch your feet, Aaron. Look up."

I'm short of breath, but I haven't been skating hard. We come to a complete stop on the ice, and I raise my eyes to meet his. I feel silly, standing here, staring at him, but I can't look away.

The girls are squealing and giggling as they reach the door in the side of the rink.

"Hey, Kent! We're going up to the bar. We're freezing, and I'm getting a blister."

He doesn't look away from me. "That's cool," he says. "I'll meet you guys up there in a minute."

I hear the door to the lodge open, then close. It's completely quiet on the ice now. I can hear my heartbeat in my ears.

"Let's try again," he says, softly.

My mouth feels dry and hot. When I try to speak, I croak, then cough.

"Try what?" I finally ask.

"Another lap."

There must be a reason to say no. It feels like there should be, but I can't think of what it is.

We start to skate again, this time side by side. Kent takes my hand in his, tightly, and when he does, I feel my knees go shaky over my skates, like I've been skating for many hours. I'm afraid someone is going to see us holding hands on the ice.

And think ... what?

"You live around here?" Kent asks.

"Lee's Summit. You?"

"Not far—over on the Plaza. Studying music at UMKC."

"Cool. You're a musician?"

"Dunno about that," he says. "I play the cello."

"You grow up here?"

"No. My dad's the music pastor at a little church in the middle of Missouri. Got to the city as soon as I could."

"My dad teaches at the Bible college in Belton."

Kent glances over at me and smiles. "So, we've got a lot in common."

We talk and skate around the rink for a long time. He's still holding my hand for stability. I keep my arm bent tensely at the elbow to give him some support. Slowly, but surely, he gets more comfortable on the ice. He stops looking at his skates and leaning on me heavily. Gradually, my arm relaxes.

But he doesn't let go of my hand.

After another few laps around the rink, Kent looks up at the bar and sees his friends in the window over the Zamboni garage waving him up.

"Guess I should go meet the girls," he says.

I check my watch. "Yeah, I have to get ready to close up."

"You should meet us up at the bar when you get done," he says.

Then he lets go of my hand, skates effortlessly across the rink, and throws his hips sideways in an expert hockey stop, sending a spray of ice into the wall. He looks back at me over his shoulder with a mischievous smile.

"Thanks for the lesson, handsome."

He disappears into the warmth of the lodge, leaving me in the middle of the ice. My heart is racing, but the rest of my body is unable to move.

Frozen.

"He seems like a nice guy."

When I walk into the skate lodge, Carla says this with a smile, like it's a statement, but there's a question in her eyes.

"Yeah, he is." I unlace my skates, put on the blade covers, and zip them into my bag.

"You should go upstairs and hang out with them." Carla is pulling down the door that covers the window at the skate counter, and locking it into place.

"Nah," I say. "I need to get home. My parents will wonder where I am."

In the parking lot, I reach into my coat pocket for my keys. I pull them out, along with a folded piece of paper. It's a corner torn from one of the bright pink ice rink schedules we keep in a brochure holder at the rental counter. I open it, and see a phone number scratched out in pencil beneath the name *Kent Harris*.

My heart is a Geiger counter ticking like mad over this radioactive scrap. I stare at the handwriting for what seems like a very long time: the sharp angle of the *K*, the hurried *R*s, the graceful swish of the *S*. Finally, I fold it up, slip it into the hip pocket of my jeans, and get into the car.

I put the key in the ignition, my hands on the wheel, and my foot on the brake, but I can't move. I sit in my parking space staring out the windshield. Beyond the trees at the edge of the parking lot are the lights of the deserted ice rink, sandwiched between the skate lodge and the bubble that covers the tennis courts during the winter. Carla's is the only car left in the lot. All is quiet, except the thoughts in my head.

Kent Harris gave you his number.
He called you handsome and held your hand.

You thought he was handsome, too.

As if a dam has broken, an explosion of images bursts across my brain, and it all comes rushing in: Bradley in the hot tub, Megan on the water bed, Ashley up against the car, Dad's masturbation talk, Derrick handing me a beer, the image of the guy at the gay pride parade leaning in to kiss the boy in the ball cap.

I rest my forehead against the steering wheel and close my eyes. When I look up again, the lights of the skating rink have gone dark. I turn the key in the ignition as I step on the clutch, then I put the car in reverse and drive toward home.

CHAPTER 24

When I walk in the kitchen door and see my dad holding the blue metal bin of tapes that should be under the front seat of my car, my first thought is a single word:

Crap.

I'm always so careful. I forgot to move the tapes out of Dad's car after I drove it the other day.

Shit. Shit. Shit.

Dad is sitting at the kitchen table. Mom is standing by the sink. The light on the ceiling fan in the kitchen bathes the room in warm light, and as I hang the car keys on the hook by the door, my dad says my name.

"Aaron."

He says it almost wistfully somehow—like he remembers another son, the son I used to be before he found my secret stash of music.

"Son, are these your tapes?"

Something strange happens when I look at him. I feel so sorry for him and for Mom. For all of us. I feel tired. I feel like this is going to keep happening forever. That I'll try to protect them from who I am for as long as I can, but eventually they'll know everything.

They already know about the music. Maybe I should tell them about everything else: the movies, the making out, the drinking—get it all over with. Get it all out in the open. The idea of not hiding anything anymore slaps me in the face like a snowball, startling me back to reality. I can't tell them about everything. I don't know what would happen.

Who would I be if I wasn't hiding from them?

"Be honest." Mom's voice isn't angry. It isn't anything.

"Yes, Dad. Those are my tapes."

I say the right words, but the tone of my voice comes out all wrong. I meant it to sound tired and penitent. Instead, it sounds like I'm annoyed with him. This situation calls for "I'm sorry," not "I'm angry." If I know anything, it's how to get through moments like these quickly. The fastest way out is to be as contrite as possible as soon as possible, to act sorry, even though I'm not.

So I apologize. "Wait. I'm sorry. I didn't mean it like that."

"How *did* you mean it, Aaron?" Dad's voice is so sad. He looks at me, wounded, bewildered. Something about it makes me want to explode.

"I meant, I'm sorry, Dad. I meant these are my tapes, and I'm sorry I like this music, but I do."

"Aaron, this music is secular rock music by men and women who do not love the Lord."

"Not all of it," I say, grasping at straws. "Amy Grant is a Christian singer."

"Aaron, you know there is no such thing as Christian rock. You cannot put God's words to the devil's music."

I take a deep breath and try to stay calm. "It's not the devil's music, Dad. *Heart in Motion* is her crossover album, but she's still a Christian singer."

Dad shakes his head. "Son, I understand Amy Grant has crossed over, but I want to know: Did she bring the *cross* over?"

Dad pulls each tape out of the holder and stacks them on the kitchen table one by one. "It's not just Amy Grant, Aaron—not that she's okay. What about this Bon Jovi fellow?" Dad holds it up and reads the title on the single. "'Blaze of Glory'? This is hard rock, son. This is the music of rebellion."

I lose my grip on my emotions. My voice turns snide and exasperated. "Dad, I'm sorry. Maybe when you were a teenager in the sixties, this music was 'rebellious.' News flash: Rock music is not the music of rebellion anymore. It's just the music that *is*; it just *exists*."

Dad lunges across the kitchen at me and I duck into the dining room door behind me so quickly that I stumble, off balance, across the chair at the end of the dining room table, knocking it over, and struggle into the living room. It happens so fast I don't feel anything, or hear anything, or see my brothers and sister run to the landing over the entryway at the other end of the living room.

All I know is that suddenly, my dad is sitting on top of my

chest and I'm lying on the living room floor. I'm not actually sure how we've gotten here. It happened so fast. One moment I was standing up in the kitchen. The next I am lying here, with his face in mine.

He is not yelling, but his voice is firm, and he's grabbing me by my shoulders. Hard.

I don't know what you're saying. I can't hear you even though you're so close.

I can't make out the words he's saying, but I can feel his panic. This is a feeling I understand. Dad is desperate: desperate to save me; desperate for me to understand him; desperate for me not to want to listen to this music.

But it's too late. I *do* want to listen to this music.

"Do you hear me, Aaron? Look me in the eye, and tell me you understand."

My brain feels all fuzzy, like when I was little, and he asked me to tell him what I did wrong before he spanked me with the paddle or his belt or a switch off the weeping willow tree in Nanny's front yard.

"Yes, sir," I say, and I realize I am crying. "I hear you."

But I don't know what you're saying.

Then I hear my mom. She's calling my dad's name. I look up at her, and only then do I realize how close Dad and I landed to the leg of the sofa in the living room.

It's a good thing I didn't hit my head.

Dad rolls off me. I lie there while he sits on the carpet for a moment, his head hanging down. We are both breathing heavily from the adrenaline of tumbling through the dining room from the kitchen. The noise of our clash has turned into a bottomless silence. Finally, he turns and looks at me with eyes full of hurt and remorse and confusion.

Once when I was in the fourth grade, Dad was spanking me with his belt when I broke away from him and tried to call the police. I raced into the kitchen and made it to the white phone hanging on the wall before he got to me. I had the receiver in my hand, my finger on the nine.

"Go ahead, call the police," he said when he saw me. "They'll send social workers who aren't Christians here, and they'll take you away from us and put you with a family who doesn't love Jesus. Is that what you want? To live with a family who won't follow the Bible and discipline you when you sin?"

I felt so scared at the idea of going to live with a family who didn't love Jesus, I hung up the phone. Loving Jesus meant we were doing the right thing. It meant we believed the right thing—that Jesus was coming back to take us to heaven. It also meant Jesus was on board with my being spanked with a belt. If I wanted to go to heaven, I had to accept that Dad was doing what God told him to do.

Dad has strict rules about spanking that he teaches to other parents. He quotes lots of Bible verses from Proverbs that direct parents to teach their children the fear of the Lord by using "the rod." Dad calls these passages "the biblical basis for spanking."

"Be sure to use an inanimate object to spank," he teaches. "You should use a paddle, a belt, or a switch." Dad explains these items will sting your child's bottom but not leave a permanent mark. "Hands are made for loving," he says. "You don't want your kids to flinch when they see your hands coming toward them to give them a hug or a caress."

Dad used to warn us that we were going to get a spanking if we "crossed the line" as kids. As I lie on the floor in the living room, I think of the argument over my boat shoes so long ago, when he told me to put on socks or he'd have to "blister my bottom."

I consider this phrase: *blister your bottom*. I imagine the heat and intensity of a spanking that would cause actual blisters to rise on a child's bottom. I never had an actual blister from a spanking, so it must be a figure of speech.

Dad was usually so *loving* when he spanked me.

"Son, I don't like to spank you," he'd say, often with tears in his eyes. "But the Bible commands me to discipline you. I have to break your will so you can grow up to love the Lord and be more like Christ."

He'd make sure I understood what I'd done wrong; then he'd make me bend over his bed, and he'd give me swats with a paddle or his belt. As he hit my bottom, he'd talk over my cries.

"Cry quietly, Aaron," he'd say as he swung his belt. "When you cry out loudly because you're angry you're being spanked, I know I haven't broken your will. I'm going to spank you until you cry quietly, son. Cry quietly, Aaron."

Sometimes Dad breaks his own rule. Every once in a while his anger over what one of us has done wrong will get the best of him. When this happens, the worst part isn't his fury; it's the apology that always comes on its heels.

Like now.

Dad crawls over to where I am lying on the floor by the couch. "I'm so sorry, son," he says. He wraps me in his arms and squeezes tightly, as if he's trying to keep something from slipping away. "I shouldn't have tackled you like that. I was wrong to discipline you in anger. Will you please forgive me?"

The last time Dad asked my forgiveness for his spanking me in anger I was in eighth grade. Sitting here on the floor, his arms around me, I can't recall why Dad spanked me with his belt that day four years ago, only that the strokes came hard and fast, and later he returned to my bedroom to apologize.

I'm so sorry, son. I shouldn't have spanked you in anger. I should have waited until I had cooled off to discipline you. Will you please forgive me?

That day, I looked him right in the eye, and for the first time I said no.

Dad fell to his knees and, as he did, took off his belt. He handed it to me. Then he bent over the bottom bunk in my bedroom and began to plead with me.

Oh, Aaron, I'm so sorry. I've sinned against you and against God. I don't deserve to be your dad. Please, hit me, Aaron. I deserve to be spanked.

I was crying and wanted him to get up and leave. I told him I didn't want to hit him—that I couldn't. It felt like the house had turned upside down and was flinging me in all directions. *Please get up*, I'd said over and over. *What are you doing?*

He continued to beg and plead. *Please, Aaron, whip me. I've been a bad, bad daddy. I deserve to be whipped.*

Did I take a halfhearted swing at his backside before I threw down the belt and ran out of the room? I don't remember now.

Dad is still holding me close to him while Mom goes back into the kitchen. I can hear her righting the chairs we must've knocked over as we wrestled across two rooms. Something about Mom picking up chairs causes my chest to tighten, and I feel an old hopelessness—the one I feel each time Dad breaks his own rules and my heart.

"I'm so sorry," Dad whispers again, and I know he is telling me the truth. I am sorry, too. I hate feeling like it's my fault when he gets upset over things like finding tapes in the car. This is why I lie to him: to protect him from who I am, and to protect him from who he becomes.

Dad helps me to my feet and puts a hand on my shoulder. "Will you forgive me, Aaron?" he asks.

I look into his eyes, and as I say yes, I feel determination best my hopelessness. *Let's get through this.* "It's okay," I say quietly, with all the sincerity I can muster. "I'm sorry I hid my music from you."

"Aaron, we need to destroy these tapes."

"Sure," I say. "Throw them away."

"No, son. I want you to go to the garage and get a hammer."

"A hammer?"

"Yes, son. I want to go out back with you, and we're going to smash these tapes."

"Really?" I am confused. "Why can't we just throw them away?"

"We are going to smash them as a symbol of you smashing your rebellious will."

"Isn't that a little...dramatic?" I ask.

"Aaron, it's a very dramatic, fearsome thing to commit yourself to God's will for your life. It is not something to be taken lightly. It's the most serious thing that you could ever do."

"And that's what I'll be doing by smashing these tapes?"

Dad looks at me with tears in his eyes. "Son," he says, "I can only tell you what to do. You can answer to please me, and still carry your rebellion in your heart. Or you can answer to please Almighty God, who knows your every thought and hears your every word."

I walk under the balcony landing, where my brothers and sister are watching wide-eyed. I walk down the stairs to the garage. I open Dad's gray metal toolbox and take out the hammer. Dad meets me at the door with all my tapes in the box.

Without a word, I take them from him and walk out the back door of the house. Then I kneel down on the concrete sidewalk next to the garbage cans and reach for a tape.

Amy Grant's *Heart in Motion* is the first one I grab. This is the first album I ever bought, when Jason drove me to Walmart in his sports car one night. I raise the hammer over

Amy's picture on the cover. She is looking down at a heart-shaped locket she clasps in one hand. I can hear her voice singing the song "That's What Love Is For," and my eyes well up with tears as I bring the hammer down.

Crash.

Suzy Bogguss is next.

Crash.

Bette Midler.

Crash.

Wilson Phillips.

Crash.

One by one, I bring the hammer down on the plastic cases and paper liner notes, sending splinters of clear acrylic showering over the sidewalk, ricocheting off the nearby steps. The pounding hammer creates its own rhythm.

Crash.

One day...

Crash.

I will listen...

Crash.

To anything...

Crash.

I want.

Crash.

I will...

Crash.

Not live here...

Crash.

Forever.

As the beat of the hammer holds steady, a melody rips through my chest and blends with the roar of the rage in my stomach. This new harmony swells into a raucous symphony of resolve.

Finally, each tape is smashed to smithereens. Dad helps me collect the shards of plastic and spools of black magnetic tape—the guts and organs of my love songs. He holds the dustpan as I sweep up the final pieces, and when they are deposited in the trash can, he hugs me close and whispers, "I love you, son."

I understand he is doing what he thinks is best for me, but I also know it will not accomplish what he wants. There will be more music. There will be a day I no longer have to hide it. My tapes may be crushed, but my will is not broken, and I have finally learned not to give myself away. I make no move to break from his embrace. Instead, I stand and let him hold me while I cry.

Quietly.

CHAPTER 25

The Mid-America Association of Christian Schools Fine Arts Competition was held on a beautiful spring day fraught with nerves and tension. Besides performing with the high school choir, the high school band, and the senior high select vocal ensemble, I sang a vocal solo, played the Khachaturian Toccata in E-flat Minor in the classical piano competition, and performed a humorous interpretation called "Before a Bakery Showcase," in which I played four different characters reacting to what they see behind the glass at a bakery. These included an obese woman and a four-year-old boy.

When I won in all three categories, vocal, piano, and acting, I had to make a difficult decision. The rules stated I could compete in only one of these events during the national competition at Bob Jones University.

The vocal solo had been an afterthought. I love to sing, but I knew the guys I'd be up against at nationals would all be classically trained, and the competition would be stiff.

Besides, the guy I'd beat out for first place wouldn't be able to go to nationals if I went, and singing was his life.

I'd worked hard on the piano solo, and I knew I could probably win at nationals, but the nervousness I feel when I sit down to play a piano solo in competition is unparalleled. My palms drip sweat onto the keyboard, and my knee trembles so badly it causes my foot to shake on the damper pedal. I don't feel like I'm in control of my fingers sometimes. There's more margin for freak error at the piano—more of a chance my nerves will make my brain hiccup and my fingers slip onto the wrong keys.

More than anything else, I wanted to act at nationals. The rush of being onstage in front of an audience was something I could never get enough of. So I made my decision, and after two days of sleeping on school buses, we arrive at the campus of Bob Jones University, a college in Greenville, South Carolina, well known for losing its tax-exempt status in the seventies by refusing to allow interracial dating.

The college allows students of different races to date now, but the place is permeated with an air of cheerful fascism. The dress code is strict, and the students aren't allowed to leave campus unless they sign out and sign in at a guard station. All dates between students must be chaperoned by an approved staff or faculty member. Even the grounds seem manicured in a way that feels unnatural. It's as if the leaves fall directly from the trees into plastic bags every night.

On the second day of competition, I perform "Before a Bakery Showcase" for the judges in the school's studio theater. Every audience I've performed for so far loves this piece, and this day is no exception. My characterizations are well drawn, the laughs I get are plentiful, and the applause enthusiastic. The winners in every category of the competition are announced on the last night of our stay during a huge Command Performance, which features the best of the competition in all disciplines. When the list of the performers is announced, my name is on it.

That night, I perform in front of nearly four thousand students and faculty. It is my largest audience to date.

As I begin the piece with the fat lady, the crowd goes wild with laughter, and for a few minutes in the spotlight, I am a star. After a standing ovation, I find my seat next to Erica. She is wildly proud of me.

"That was amazing!" she squeals.

The girl who follows me plays a piece by Khachaturian on the piano—not as difficult as the toccata, and the audience isn't into it. Her incredible technique and amazing effort are met with polite applause, and I know I made the right choice for me. I could tell it disappointed my mom when I didn't choose to take the piano solo, but acting is where my heart is.

When the awards are announced, I am given second place, but I don't care. The performance was the real prize. The laughter and applause of four thousand people will ring in my ears long after a plaque or a trophy loses its luster.

Besides, when I get back to Kansas City, I have an audition.

After weeks of looking, I finally found the notice I had been waiting for under the "Auditions" posting in the back of the Arts section of the *Kansas City Star*:

MISSOURI REPERTORY THEATRE
Non-Required Equity Principal Auditions
Prepare two contrasting monologues, not to exceed 2 minutes.
Bring your picture and resume, stapled together.
Please call for an appointment.

I called the number. I gave my name. I booked a time after school the following week.

"You've got an audition at the Rep?" Erica's voice is almost awed.

"Yep." I can't stop smiling.

"What are you auditioning for?" asks Megan.

"It says that they're holding auditions for the season, so I think that means they'll consider me for any part I may be right for."

Mom and Dad are more cautious about this development.

"What kind of play are you auditioning for?" Dad wants to know.

"It's not an audition for one play. It's every play in their next season," I explain. "I mean, I don't even know if I'm right for one of the parts, but it's still good to have the experience."

Dad looks less than certain.

"But what if the plays aren't good shows?" he asks. "Not everything they do at the Rep is going to have a good message like *A Christmas Carol.*"

Be patient. Breathe. I could feel my annoyance creeping into my throat. "I may not get offered any part. I just want to go and audition."

"What monologue will you do, honey?" Mom asks.

"It says two contrasting monologues, so I think I'm just going to do two different characters from 'Before a Bakery Showcase.'"

"I think that's a great idea," she says, and smiles.

Dad glances at her, then back at me. "I guess it's okay," he agrees. "What time is your appointment?"

"It's at four fifty, so that should give us plenty of time to get there after school."

I decide to wear a colorful tie to the audition. I'm not sure how you're supposed to dress, but I want to look nice, and stylish. I have a new tie from Banana Republic that has a bright abstract print on it. I iron and starch my favorite white dress shirt and pick out a pair of brown corduroy slacks. I feel great in this outfit: confident, handsome.

By the time Dad comes to pick me up, I feel like I might crawl out of my skin.

"You okay, son?" he asks.

I nod. "A little nervous."

I smile at him as we head toward the theater. It's on the campus of the University of Missouri at Kansas City. I've been there lots of times. When I was in grade school and junior high, Dad finished his PhD in education here. The theater is in a lovely part of the campus, surrounded by trees. When Dad parks, he asks if I want him to come in.

"No," I say, spotting the stage door and a sign pointing toward the check-in for the auditions. "I'll be fine."

"You will be fine." He smiles. "You're the best actor I've ever seen on a stage. Doesn't matter what these yahoos say."

Actually, it only *matters what they say.*

This is the first time I've acted in front of a professional director—somebody whose job it is to hire and pay professional actors.

What if I'm not really any good? What if I've been told I'm good by people who don't know what being good is?

My heart is racing as I step inside the stage door. I am seeing the guts of a professional theater for the first time: the rigging for the fly system that moves all the drapes and scenery; the back areas of the stage.

A young woman sees me and smiles. "Are you here to audition?" she asks.

"Yes."

"Name?"

"Aaron Hartzler."

She finds my name on the list, makes a mark next to it, and asks for my head shot and resume.

Head shot.

I've never heard that word before. Makes sense. An actor's picture must be his head shot. I hand her the resume I printed up. It has all the shows I've ever done, starting with the one where I played dead when I was three years old. Most of them are Christian musicals I've done at school. I also listed that I won second place at the National Fine Arts Competition for my humorous interpretation. Attached to the resume is a wallet-size school picture of me. I notice that the other photos in the stack she has are glossy, black-and-white eight-by-tens.

Crap. I don't even know how to bring a head shot.

The young woman with the clipboard and the stack of photos hands me an information sheet to fill out, then walks behind a curtain toward where the stage must be.

I sit down and fill out the form. Name. Address. Phone number. Age. Height. Hair color. Previous experience.

Suddenly, I'm terrified. I don't know why I came. I'm out of my league. It's one thing to sing songs and do scenes in church for people who are amazed when anyone memorizes lines and manages to quote them in order without forgetting.

What am I doing here?

I consider turning around and walking back to the car, but before I can, I hear my name being called. She's back. With the clipboard. And she's smiling and motioning for me to follow her.

I stand and hand her my information sheet.

"Oh, no. Take that to the woman in the front row," she says, smiling. She holds back the black curtain at the side of the stage and indicates I should walk through it. "Break a leg!"

I take a step forward. I feel like I am going to throw up. Two more steps forward, and I see a handful of people sitting in the empty theater. Instantly, I feel my church smile snap into place.

Breathe. Shoulders back. You know how to stand on a stage.

There is a silver-haired man with a strong jaw sitting near the seats where I watched *A Christmas Carol* with my family. He seems to be in charge and has a couple of assistants. When he sees me come in, he looks away from the younger man who is whispering in his ear, and tilts his head toward the stage, but says nothing.

A woman in the front row calls out "Hello!" with a smile, and steps toward the stage. I walk to the edge of the platform and hand her my information sheet. She consults it briefly, then calls back to the silver-haired man. "This is Aaron Hartzler."

"Hello, Aaron," he calls out. "What are you going to perform for us today?"

I take a deep breath and call back in a strong voice that fills the space:

"I'll be performing a selection from a humorous interpretation I did recently at the National Fine Arts Competition. It's called 'Before a Bakery Showcase.'"

"Very well," says the man.

I see there is an X made of tape near the center of the stage.

That must be where I'm supposed to stand.

338

I walk toward the X until I am standing directly on it, and bow my head for a moment. I take a deep breath. When I raise my head, I am the fat lady from the piece, and I perform exactly as I have every other time.

Only this time is different.

This time no one laughs.

I try to assure myself it is because there are only four people in the room. Or perhaps it's because they've seen this piece before. I try to stay in the moment of the piece. I try not to think about what they're thinking about, but it's almost impossible.

I had planned to do two characters from the piece, and when I'm done playing the fat lady, I bow my head and prepare to switch characters. Before I can begin the second character, I hear a voice from the seats in the theater.

"Aaron?"

I raise my head.

They're going to tell me to leave.

The man with the silver hair smiles at me from his seat, and holds up a finger. "One moment, please."

He turns and whispers something to the woman sitting behind him, and then leans over to the younger man at his left, who picks up a legal pad and a pencil.

He turns back to me.

"Aaron, thank you for sharing that with us. Would you mind coming down here for a moment?"

My knees almost collapse.

"Sure," I say. My heart is racing. I can feel sweat trickling down my back under my white T-shirt and white dress shirt and Banana Republic tie.

I walk back to where the man with the silver hair is sitting. He indicates the seat next to him, and when I sit, he extends his hand to shake mine.

"Aaron, I'm George Keathley," he says. I recognize his name instantly from the *Christmas Carol* playbill. He not only directed that show, he's the artistic director of the entire theater. He's directed shows in New York, and even a soap opera for several years. His voice is rich, and up close he seems younger than I expected him to be. His smile is kind and handsome.

I shake his hand. His assistant hands me the legal pad and offers me a pencil.

"Aaron, this is highly unusual. Typically, I don't stop auditions like this, as we're on a tight schedule, but I felt perhaps you could use a little direction. After all, I'm a director." He smiles. "It's what I do."

"I'm all ears," I say. He nods. I can tell he likes me.

"You are a good-looking young man. You have a presence on the stage and appear to be someone who may have a future in this business."

I blink at him and smile, cautiously.

"Aaron, you should never perform that piece at an audition again. Whatever they have you doing in your high school drama class is one thing. In the theater, I can't cast you as an obese woman, so there's no sense in you coming here to play one for me."

I feel my cheeks flush, but I immediately know he is right. *Of course.*

"If you're going to be a serious actor, you need to be reading plays," he continues, "especially plays that have characters in them who are your age—characters I could cast you as. Those are the monologues you should be looking at."

I nod again.

"Write this down," he says.

I ready the pencil.

"Go to the library," he instructs. "Check out the plays of Neil Simon. You'll want to read *Brighton Beach Memoirs* and *Biloxi Blues* to begin."

As I write down his instructions, my hand is shaking. I feel like I might cry with relief.

"Start there," says George Keathley. "Find a monologue that's one or two minutes long. Work hard. Come back. Audition for me again."

"I will." I tear the sheet from the legal pad and hand it and the pencil back to Mr. Keathley's assistant. "Thank you," I say. I stand to leave, and as I shake his hand I meet his gaze. "Thank you for taking the time."

His eyes are kind and deep, like Mrs. Westman's. They are full of a meaning I can't quite decipher. I know somehow this man with the silver hair and the strong jaw cares about me.

"Aaron, if you want this, don't let anyone try to stop you."

"I won't."

He smiles and I climb the stairs back to the stage. As I

walk through the wings, I gaze up into the rigging that towers over me in the fly space. There is something different going on here, I realize. Something better than "quality biblical drama." There's a deep importance about being on this stage I have never felt before on any other. The stage at the Missouri Repertory Theatre leaves me with a feeling of awe.

All the other stages on which I've acted were in a church or a Christian school. This stage is the first I've ever performed on that was not co-opted for theater from a Sunday sermon about Jesus. This is not a place where theater is a tool for telling stories about God. This is a stage where the craft of theater is foremost, and used with reverence for telling the stories of humanity, stories where an audience member can see himself in a character on the stage and know he is not alone.

I want to come back to a stage like this, to perform for a director like Mr. Keathley; to be seen and accepted in this world of professional actors. This audition was my first tiny taste, but I am hooked. All I want now is more. As I step into the parking lot, I realize I meant what I said to Mr. Keathley.

I won't let anyone stand in my way.

"How'd it go?" Dad asks as he turns the car toward home.

"Okay. The artistic director actually called me down from the stage to talk to me."

"What did he say?"

I tell Dad about Mr. Keathley's directions and the plays he said I should read.

"You need to be careful about the advice you follow, Aaron. Those plays may not honor the Lord."

My heart sinks. On the way to the car, I somehow hoped Dad would be as excited by this development as I am. Tears of frustration spring up in my eyes. I turn and look out the window at the trees whipping by above us, and I try not to be angry with Dad.

I wanted him to be a part of this audition. Acting is something we've always shared—something we've always done together. This is the next step, the part where I take everything he taught me and venture into the professional world. I want him to come with me on this journey so badly, to always be my partner.

We are in the same car, but we are heading in different directions. There was a turnoff back at the Missouri Rep, and it's the one I'm taking. I want to be as excited as I was walking across that stage moments ago. Instead, I feel like I'm losing my dad. He gave me my start, but he can't come any farther. This is where I finally leave him behind. Acting will now be one more thing we don't share.

"I'll be careful," I promise him.

And I will be. Careful not to let him find the plays by Neil Simon when I check them out at the public library. Careful not to mention this again. Careful not to tell him anything that will give him the chance to say no.

CHAPTER 26

It's seven AM on Sunday morning, and I have made it home from Bradley's.

Barely.

He got home from Iowa for spring break on Friday and threw a huge party last night. I am standing in the bathroom, staring at my reflection in the mirror. My head hurts so badly, I think I might start throwing up again. When I opened my eyes, I was lying on the couch downstairs in Bradley's family room, and the ceiling spun around so hard that I had to clamp them closed again for a minute to keep from barfing.

It's Palm Sunday—the week before Easter. This is the day when we celebrate Jesus's "triumphal entry" into the city of Jerusalem the week that he was crucified. This is the day when the disciples "borrowed" a donkey and Jesus rode into Jerusalem in a massive crowd of people waving palm branches and shouting "Hosanna!"

My face looks very pale in the mirror. It reminds me of that urban legend Bradley was talking about last night: waking up alive in a bathtub of ice to find a note that reads CALL AN AMBULANCE. YOUR KIDNEY HAS BEEN REMOVED.

Anyone in that situation could not look paler than I do right now. I lean in a little closer to the mirror.

Am I…green?

I turn on the cold water and splash it across my face. Mom is already up. I can hear her in the bathroom getting ready. She'll be on her way down to fix breakfast, and drizzling green icing across her signature Palm Leaf Pastry within the hour.

I open the medicine cabinet and down a couple of Tylenols with a slurp of water from the sink. My tongue is a thick, fuzzy piece of shag carpet. I get into the shower with the water as hot as I can stand it, and brush my teeth while the jets pound my neck. When I close my eyes, I can see the print of the shower curtain in Bradley's front bathroom, where I spent at least an hour bent over the toilet, barfing up tequila sunrises last night. The light orange and purple flowers on the gray fabric materialize and expand like fireworks behind my eyelids: the Jose Cuervo garden of earthly delights.

After the shower, I'm still moving slowly. The Tylenol has started to kick in, but I feel the throb of the headache, muted, lurking somewhere in the very center of my skull. When I walk down the stairs to breakfast in my shirt and tie, my stomach lurches.

The last thing I want to do is go to church.

Or play the piano.

Or eat.

345

But that's what we do here in the mornings: eat. As a family. And before the Palm Leaf Pastry, there are hard-boiled eggs.

I look down at the yellow plastic tumbler next to my plate thankfully. Maybe some milk will help settle my stomach. I take a big swig and then realize that the creamy liquid floating before my lips is...green.

"Mom! Why is the milk green?"

"Oh, sugar, it's only food coloring." She smiles brightly. "Happy Palm Sunday! Green reminds us of new life in Christ."

I wipe the corners of my mouth and rub my temples. "Green in my milk reminds me of mold."

Dad laughs. "C'mon, Aaron, you'd better wake up! You've got some hymns to play."

"Don't remind me."

My piano teacher usually plays the piano for the congregational singing, but she's covering for the organist today. I'm being tapped to fill in for her at the piano. It's nerve-racking under the best of circumstances. Doing it hungover feels like sheer folly.

"Are you okay, honey?" Mom asks. "This is what I was afraid of if you went to Bradley's and stayed up too late." She kisses the top of my head and offers me more eggs. I smile, then cut into the Palm Leaf Pastry. My brothers hold their plates. I make them wait until I've given Miriam a slice.

"Thank you for being a gentleman." Miriam smiles triumphantly at Josh and Caleb.

I smile back at her, and suddenly I feel like a fraud. Now

the guilt is as strong as the nausea. In her clear blue eyes, I can see how much she loves me, how much she admires me. I'm a liar and a cheat.

The ride to church in the station wagon does nothing for my stomach, and the nerves of getting every note perfect at the piano make me sweat in my suit jacket and tie. After I get through the first hymn, the pastor makes some announcements, and I look out over the four hundred people in the congregation.

I wonder if they can tell I'm hungover?

Several of my friends and their parents are smiling up at me. Everybody thinks I'm this great guy because I'm only in high school and I'm playing the piano in church.

If they only knew.

That afternoon, Bradley calls. "Hey. I just woke up."

"I don't even want to hear it," I say. "I was at church at nine AM playing the piano for congregational singing with the worst headache I've ever had."

"Oh my God. I wondered why you were gone already when I woke up."

"I told you I had to play in church this morning."

"Really? When?"

"Last night," I say, "while you were pouring grenadine into twenty-seven glasses of tequila."

"Was that before or after the hot tub?" he asks, groaning.

"Yes."

"Ow, *ow!* Don't make me laugh," he says. "My head hurts so bad."

"I was playing the piano, afraid that God was going to strike me dead with an electrical jolt from the nearest microphone."

"I wish somebody would strike me dead." Bradley groans again. "I am wrecked."

I smile. "Brad?"

"Yeah?"

"Last night was a blast."

"It was, huh?" he says.

"Thanks."

"For what?" he asks.

"For having me over. For being my friend."

"Whatever, man. Wait'll I'm back this summer. Your graduation party is gonna be *epic*."

"I'll have to check my schedule," I say.

"Shut up," he says, and laughs. "See you in May."

Mr. Friesen finds me in the hall between classes the next day.

"Aaron, we need to talk."

In his office, he takes a seat behind his desk. He leans back in his chair, sizing me up.

"While the kids from Bob Jones University were all home for spring break, Tyler Gullem and Dr. Spicer's sons came to see me."

Tri-City students are encouraged to go to college wherever the Lord leads them, but you can tell that most of the teachers and the administration hope that the Lord leads you to Bob Jones.

"It seems Tyler Gullem is really concerned about some things that are going on here at Tri-City. Namely, students not living for Christ."

I am not smiling anymore.

What does this have to do with me?

"Tyler told the Spicer twins he saw you drinking alcohol at a New Year's Eve party at Bradley Westman's house."

As soon as he says it, I have a strange sensation—a sort of knowing: *This is the beginning of the end.*

"Really?" I say. My face is incredulous, puzzled, perfect. "That's strange."

"Are you saying that you didn't have a drink at the New Year's party, Aaron?"

"No. I had plenty to drink—Diet Coke, all night long."

Mr. Friesen chews his front lip, then sits up, takes off his glasses, and rubs his eyes. When he looks up at me, he seems tired.

"Why would Tyler lie about something like this?" he asks.

"I'm sure he doesn't mean any harm." I smile. "You know Tyler. He always wants to do the right thing."

"Aaron, this is a serious allegation," he says. "You don't seem concerned."

"There's nothing to be concerned about. I wasn't drinking at Bradley's party."

"Tyler seems to be under the impression you go over to Bradley's to drink often."

349

I give a single, silent laugh. "Don't know what to tell you, Mr. Friesen. I haven't seen Bradley very much this year."

"You know that if you were drinking, that's grounds for expulsion."

"So why would I drink?" I ask him.

He is quiet again for a moment, then puts his glasses back on.

"I'll be calling your dad."

"Please do," I say. "I'm sure he'd be interested to know that somebody who never liked me that much has decided I was drinking at a party four months ago."

It's a challenge, pure and simple. I almost can't believe I said the words. I've never talked back to an adult authority figure like this.

I stand up to gather my books. "I'm also sure he'll be interested that you're more inclined to believe Tyler Gullem than me."

Am I shaking with anger or fear? I can't tell. I am barely able to hold on to my stack of library books. I'm writing my senior thesis on Oscar Wilde and want to get a little reading done in journalism next period.

"We're not done yet, Aaron."

"Oh?" I ask.

"Senior trip is next week. I'm not sure I'm going to allow you to go."

"Why would that be, Mr. Friesen?"

"I don't like the attitude I'm getting from you about this."

Will there ever be a day when I'm not being questioned by adults?

"Maybe I've misunderstood." I smile broadly to mask my rage. "I'm not going to be able to go on the senior trip because the pastor's sons say Tyler Gullem thinks he saw me drinking at a party?"

Even I am surprised at my tone. It's not respectful at all. *Who is this person? Where did the guy who plays the game go?* I can't seem to stop myself. When Mr. Friesen is silent, I pepper him with questions.

"Is there any *evidence* I was drinking? Is there some way to *prove* that there was anything in my glass other than Diet Coke? And if there was drinking going on at the party, what was Tyler Gullem doing there?"

Mr. Friesen glances down at his desk and moves a pencil back into place with several others that are lined up in a military roll call at the edge of his blotter. He straightens his tie clip. He looks back up.

"Tyler and the Spicer twins will be home from college by the time you return from the senior trip. At that point, I'll need to meet with you and your parents. Then we'll see what he has to say."

"We certainly will," I say, smiling. "I'm so curious to hear all about this."

The adrenaline surges through me as I walk out of Mr. Friesen's door and down the hall to class. I am still shaking as I sit down in journalism class and flip open my copy of *The Picture of Dorian Gray*, but I can't see the words on the page.

All I can see is Tyler Gullem in the doorway at Bradley's New Year's Eve party, looking down at my cocktail.

Mom is putting the finishing touches on the Empty Tomb Cake when I walk in the door from school, and I remember that it's Good Friday.

The Empty Tomb Cake is one of Mom's specialties, a cake in the shape of the grave where Jesus was buried after he died on the cross. It's usually chocolate cake with gray frosting, the color of stone. She puts shredded coconut into a plastic Baggie with green liquid food coloring and shakes it onto the plate around the cake so it looks like grass. She adds a round Hostess Ding Dong to the front as the stone that seals the door of the tomb, and stands a little cross ornament in the frosting on the top.

The cake will sit in the middle of the table tomorrow as a centerpiece, then late tomorrow night, after everyone has gone to bed, Mom will steal into the kitchen under cover of night and roll the Hostess Ding Dong away from the door of the Empty Tomb Cake. She'll retouch the frosting and add her small black Bible to the display, the book open to the passage where the angel speaks to Mary in the garden:

Why seek ye the living among the dead? He is not here, but is risen.

I feel like a dead man.

I have to tell Mom and Dad about Tyler Gullem and the conversation with Mr. Friesen. I decide to wait until after dinner.

When I get to my room, I close the door. Mom has left

some clean laundry folded on my bed. I open the top drawer of my dresser and put away my socks and underwear. In the back of the drawer, underneath some T-shirts, is the tiny pink scrap of paper with Kent Harris's phone number. I pull it out.

I walk into my parents' bedroom, and sit on the bed next to the phone on Mom's nightstand. I pick up the receiver and dial the numbers.

My heart races as I wait for a voice to answer.

What if he actually answers? What will I say?

An answering machine clicks on, and when I hear his recorded voice on the message, my stomach flips, and it's hard to catch my breath. I can see Kent's clear blue eyes staring at me at the rink last month. I can feel his hand in mine.

When I hear the beep, I pause for a split second, then hang up the phone.

Idiot. You're an idiot. *What are you doing?*

A new book in the stack on Mom's nightstand catches my eye. The picture on the cover is a silhouette of a child walking on a balance beam. The title says something about raising children in a risky world. I flip the book open to a bookmark stuck in the pages. The chapter is about helping young men remain morally pure. The word *homosexual* jumps off the page at me.

Is this the chapter that made Mom and Dad want to get this book?

I'm afraid Mom might walk in on me reading this page, but I scan through the chapter, skimming the information from the Christian author, hoping. Maybe there is something here that will make it okay, explain it, ease my mind. As I read, words pop out at me one after another—*abomination, agenda, molested, predatory, sin, pedophiles, addiction*...

The phone rings. I jump at the sound. My stomach fills with dread.

What if Kent is calling back?

Quickly, I close the book and slide it back into place. I slip the pink scrap of paper into my hip pocket, then head back to my bedroom and close the door. As I am hiding Kent's phone number under the T-shirts in my underwear drawer, I hear Mom call up the stairs:

"Time to eat."

"That was Mr. Friesen on the phone before dinner," Dad says.

"I thought it might be," I say. "He called me into his office today to tell me that Tyler Gullem told Dr. Spicer's sons I was drinking at Bradley's New Year's Eve party."

Stay calm. It's your word against Tyler's. You've won this game before.

"Were you drinking at the party at Bradley's?"

I act astonished. "What? No! Dad!"

"Well, son, why would this rumor be going around if it weren't true?" Dad stares directly into my eyes, his gaze heated, unwavering. I feel like I've been kicked in the stomach. *Why are you surprised? He has no reason to trust you.*

"I don't know."

"Were other people drinking at this party?" Mom looks stricken. "Do his parents drink? Do they keep alcohol in their house?"

It's time to give them a little bit, so that they buy it. I can't escape this totally unscathed.

"Yes, ma'am."

"You never told us that, Aaron," she says. "You knew we wouldn't want you spending time around people who drink."

"I'm so disappointed in you," Dad says.

I'm angry now, and I don't have a leg to stand on. "We go to Royals games all the time, Dad. They have beer there. You don't drink it. I don't drink it. Besides, it wasn't like Bradley's parents were drinking every time I was over there." My voice is unwavering. I've become an expert liar.

"But people were drinking at this party at Bradley's over New Year's?" Dad asks.

"I don't know," I insist. "I wasn't."

"What do you mean you don't know?" Dad is firm.

The fury of the situation bubbles up inside me again, and I have to tamp it down. *Do not blow your cover.* I speak slowly. I try to keep the sarcasm from creeping into my voice, and only barely succeed. "We all walked around holding glasses of liquid. Everyone was drinking *something.* The only thing in *my* glass was ice and Diet Coke."

"Were there other students at the party from Tri-City?" Mom asks.

"It was mainly public-school kids—friends from Bradley's old school. I was the only current student." There were a

355

couple other guys there from the basketball team, but Mom and Dad certainly don't need to know that. If this all goes south, the last thing I need to deal with is a witch hunt.

Dad looks at Mom, then shakes his head. "This is exactly the kind of situation that happens when you don't avoid the appearance of evil," he says.

"Dad, nothing evil was going on."

"But was anything *good* going on, my son?" Mom's eyes are sincere and search mine for an answer.

CHAPTER 27

I am stuffing graduation announcements into envelopes at the dining room table. There are two envelopes for each announcement. I'm writing the mailing address on the outer envelope, the first names of the people at that address on the inner envelope. The announcements are embossed on the front with a loopy purple foil that spells out a shiny GRADUATION '93 over the Tri-City Christian crusader and shield in gold.

I have fantastic handwriting. I taught myself calligraphy in third grade with the Sheaffer fountain pen calligraphy set that Mom got me for my eighth birthday. I used to sit at the desk by the window in my bedroom during the summer, practicing calligraphy and listening to the Kansas City Royals game on the radio. As I write addresses in my angular script, the phone rings.

Mom answers. It's for Dad.

Each invitation has a feathery edge along the bottom, ragged, like it was torn. I insert a tiny name card into the precut slots of each announcement, then stuff it into the inner envelope.

Dad takes the call in the kitchen. It's Mr. Friesen.

After a while, I hear Dad hang up the phone, then I hear him talking to Mom quietly. Both of them come into the dining room. Dad sits down at the head of the dining room table. Mom crosses her arms and leans against the doorframe, as if she's bracing for what may happen next.

"That was Mr. Friesen," Dad says as I lick a stamp and press it onto the envelope of another completed announcement.

There is silence for a moment as Dad decides what to say next. I continue to put little cards into precut slots.

The Senior Class
of
Tri-City Christian School
announces its
Commencement Exercises
Saturday afternoon, May twenty-ninth
Nineteen hundred ninety-three
two o'clock

"Pastor Spicer wants to meet with us tomorrow morning. Tyler Gullem will be there, too."

I pick up two senior pictures and put them into the announcement I'm holding. Friends and relatives who live far away are getting two senior pictures. Both are wallet-size.

One is a profile picture of me in my purple cap and gown. I lick another envelope closed, then take up the pen to write an address.

"I'm ready to go in there and go to the mat on this with them."

The tone of Dad's voice makes me pause and lower the pen. He is looking me directly in the eyes. "I think they're going about this the wrong way."

I glance at Mom. She is watching intently from the door.

"I think they mean well, but, Aaron, if you say you didn't drink, I believe you, and they should, too. Before I go in there and defend you, I'm going to ask you one last time: Did you drink at that party?"

There's no proof. It's my word against Tyler's.

I try to imagine the meeting tomorrow. Dad and Mom and me and Tyler and Dr. Spicer and Mr. Friesen. I would maintain that there was only Diet Coke in my glass. Dad and Mom would stick by me, but Tyler would be telling the truth, and my parents would be sticking up for my lies.

I run my finger along the feathery edge of an announcement on the pile.

Torn.

I look up at my dad. I love him so much. He's always been on the other side of this equation, calling in students and their parents when their kids have done something wrong. I don't want him to be embarrassed.

The pile of graduation announcements under construction covers the table. At least thirty are complete: stuffed, sealed, stamped, addressed—ready to mail. It would be so much easier *not* to mail these than it would be to mail them, then have to call people and tell them not to come.

You can't hide forever.

I decide to be exactly who I am, and to let Mom and Dad catch a glimpse of who that is. I take a deep breath and look Dad in the eye. "Yes, I drank at the party."

Saying what is actually true about this situation instead of what I wish were true causes something to break free inside me. Maybe sticking to my roots has given me wings. I steel myself for their response, something big and loud and dramatic. Instead, Dad only nods, then reaches across the table and places his hand on mine. "Thank you for telling me the truth."

When I look up, I see tears in Mom's eyes.

"I'm sorry," I say quietly.

She walks over and puts her arms around me.

"Me, too, honey," she whispers. "Me, too."

In a flash, the version of myself so carefully constructed for Mom's and Dad's eyes crumbles all around me. I have let them see my truth. Not the son I pretend to be, or the son they thought I was, but the son I really am.

We all know what this means. There will be no first son's high school graduation. There will be no open house. No one will have to iron the purple gown I will never wear. The invitations on this table will not be mailed.

There have been moments prior when I have disappointed Mom and Dad, and I can feel the crush of their disappointment now, but somehow their sadness is not the main thing I feel. It's the things that are missing I'll remember most about this moment.

There is no yelling.

There is no anger.

There is no praying.

There is only "thank you," and "me, too," and hugging—a pulling together, a tangle of arms, and tears, and hearts.

For this moment, there is only love.

Dad is wrapping up his message in chapel. He's been preaching from Psalm 1, about being like a tree planted by the water that bears fruit, instead of like the chaff that the wind drives away.

We're supposed to take a lesson from this: We should want to be like trees, firmly rooted next to the living water, not like chaff, unstable, able to be blown about by the suggestion of others.

On most days, Kansas City feels like the middle of nowhere. Today, it feels like the center of everything. Dad has taken the morning off from teaching at the Bible college to speak in chapel at the school where his oldest son is being expelled. There are only two weeks of classes left, and Principal Friesen has agreed to give me my diploma if I'll apologize to the student body today. Dad could have let me do this on my own, but he didn't. Instead, he asked if he could speak in chapel today. He asked to be here so he could stand by me on the hardest, most humiliating day of my life. He wanted to be here for me, to support me, to let me know how much he loves me. He wants to be here when I say "I'm sorry."

The thing is, I'm *not* sorry. I only regret how much I've disappointed Dad.

When he's done preaching, he'll call me up to the microphone like he's done so many times before, but this time I won't be up front to sing, or play the piano, or perform a dramatic scene. There will be no music or lyrics or lines to hide behind. I'll inch past everyone sitting in this pew next to me, walk down the center aisle, step up to that mic in front of all one hundred thirty-seven students, and confess my sins. I'll let them in on my secret: I haven't been living like a tree. I've been chafflike, not Christ-like.

Or at least that's the plan.

Dad finishes his sermon. I hear him say my name. He tells the student body I'll be coming to the mic next to share something with all of them.

"But first, let's pray."

One hundred thirty-seven heads bow. Two hundred seventy-four eyes close. My dad surveys the room and sees me looking at him. His gaze lands on mine for maybe one one-hundredth of a second, but that's enough. I can see it fifty pews away. I can feel it all at once: the love, and the grief, and everything he didn't say in all the words he's spoken today. My handsome, tall, smart, charming, charismatic, well-groomed dad is one more thing today:

Heartbroken.

He bows his head, and no one but me hears the catch in his voice when he says "Heavenly Father." Suddenly, my eyes are full, and one stray drop leaps down onto my khakis.

No one else knows this is the hardest thing my dad has ever had to do. I want to spare him from the next twenty minutes. What I did in private has suddenly become about what he does in public. Now everyone will know that the guy who trains people how to teach their kids to do the right thing has a son who didn't learn the lesson. Dad follows all the instructions he gives out with his own kids. Now people will know it didn't work. I wish I could take it all back. I wish I could run down the aisle, grab the mic, and tell everyone this isn't his fault—that he did everything right. I wish I could protect him from this moment, from the shame of everyone knowing who I really am.

Before I can, he starts to pray.

"Heavenly Father, we thank you for the opportunity we have today to learn the principles from your word. We know, Lord, that we live in the end times and that your Son, Jesus, is coming back at any moment—"

If only Jesus *would* come back right now. If only we'd hear a trumpet sound and an archangel shout, and then everybody in the room would shoot out of their clothes and up through the four-story-high ceiling into the sky over Interstate 70, to meet Jesus in the air over the Independence Center shopping mall across the highway. We could forget about the confession and the cap and gown, and we would be in heaven, where God would wipe away the tears from my father's eyes like it says he will in the Bible. If Jesus came back right now, I wouldn't have to tell the whole student body about what happened at Bradley's party in December, because it simply wouldn't matter anymore.

Maybe it doesn't matter now.

I look up at the cross over the choir loft, and it hits me: I'm not so sure Jesus is coming back anymore. I don't know when it happened—it wasn't any one specific moment. Somewhere along the way this year, that certainty and excitement I once had just drifted away. I'm not saying Jesus won't come back; I've just decided I can't keep hoping to be rescued from my life. Maybe it's up to me to change things. It's time to start saving myself.

I look back up at Dad. He's still praying. Every head is bowed, every eye closed. I wonder what would happen if I got up and walked into the hall? And then into the parking lot? And then got in my car, and drove away from here, from Kansas City, from everything?

Get up now. Walk away.

Dad is wrapping up his prayer. If I go right now, no one will see me. No one will stop me.

"—and we thank you and praise you for all of this, and it's in Jesus's name we pray. Amen."

One hundred thirty-seven heads are raised. Two hundred seventy-four eyes flutter open. I'm still sitting here in the pew near the back. I've waited too long. If I walk out now I'll cause a scene. Miss Favian will look up from the papers she's grading at the end of the row. She'll follow me through the foyer in her powder blue cable-knit sweater with the collar that looks like a neck brace. She'll ask me where I'm going.

I'm stuck.

"Aaron's going to come say a few words now." Dad steps back from the microphone, and every head in the room swivels back to look at me.

I guess saving myself starts here.

As I walk down the aisle toward the front of this cavernous auditorium for the final time, I feel the three-by-five card in the pocket of my pants. It has a Bible verse written on it that I'm going to read when I make my apology speech. I practiced in my bedroom yesterday. I used my dresser as the podium and rehearsed my apology to the bedroom wall. No one was home. I don't remember where everyone was.

I don't remember writing down the Bible verse. I don't remember who told the rest of the family. Did Dad tell my brothers and sister that I was getting kicked out of school? Did Mom?

I walk past Megan, then Erica, their faces full of questions. At least Bradley is away at college. I don't know if I could have handled him watching this.

I've been in front of this crowd so many times in the last two years: every play, every musical, every choir performance, every skit, every piano solo, every song I've sung, every joke I've told, every spirit week and costume day. This time is different. This is my final appearance on this stage, my command performance.

As long as I have to do this, I'm going to make it good.

When I reach the microphone, a silent hush falls over the room. It's quieter than I've ever heard it, even during prayer. I look up at the empty balcony, then back down across the entire student body. I think about aiming both barrels at Bradley during the play last year and deafening the entire room with blanks. What I'm about to say will be more surprising than a blast from a shotgun.

I pull the card out of my pocket and lean toward the mic.

"There's a verse in Isaiah that says, 'These people come near to me with their mouth and honor me with their lips, but their hearts are far from me. Their worship of me is made up only of rules taught by men.'"

I can see Erica and Megan across the row from each other. Erica looks pale. Megan leans forward. I haven't been able to call her since I confessed to Mom and Dad. She knows something is up.

"I've been one of those people," I say. "I've stood on this stage and I've told you I am following the Lord. I've sung songs and played the piano, and I've said all the right words with my lips, but my heart has been far from God."

My voice cracks. I blink, and a single tear slides down my right cheek.

"Today is my last day at Tri-City. I drank alcohol at a party over New Year's, and I lied about it. I want to apologize to all of you and ask your forgiveness. I'm sorry for drinking, and for lying, and for not being honest about who I am."

Erica and Megan are both crying now. The whole place

is riveted. Dad is standing beside me now. I don't remember him getting up. He is saying something about praying for me. He's asking the students to pray for me and for our family. Mr. Friesen is at the microphone now as Dad pulls me over to the front pew. Mr. Friesen is dismissing the student body— everyone but the senior class.

One by one, they come up and hug me. Most of the guys are somber. A couple of them look terrified. I know they drink, too. They must be scared shitless I'm going to tell on them. I try to telegraph that I am not. Many of the girls are crying. There is a great deal of hugging, which none of the teachers try to stop, even though it technically violates the rules. There are whispers of forgiveness and the words "We still love you."

Then there is Erica, weeping, her face blotchy and red. This is not a pretty cry. She smiles ruefully at me and shakes her head.

"I asked God to convict your heart, Aaron. I asked God to bring you back to him. I guess that you had to make him do it the hard way. I hope you've learned your lesson now."

She tries to hug me, but it is awkward and strange. I am relieved when she turns and leaves the auditorium.

Megan hangs back toward the end of the line. She doesn't care about the rules. She doesn't care about the scene. She is bold and daring, wrapping her arms around me, pressing her body close to mine. To my surprise, no one moves to stop her. After a while she stands on her tiptoes and kisses my cheek. "It's going to be okay," she whispers. "Call me."

Then she is gone. They are all gone.

I sit on the front pew with Dad in the giant church auditorium. We are silent for a moment, and then I feel his arm around my shoulders.

"I'm proud of you, son."

The tears explode out of me. The anger and frustration, the fear and relief pour down my face in a torrent.

"For what?" I ask.

"For doing the right thing," he says. "For telling the truth."

CHAPTER 28

The right thing seems all wrong now.

I am standing on Bradley's front porch, pressing the doorbell. My parents are standing behind me, waiting. This is the final stop on my post–high school apology tour.

Last week after I apologized to the student body, Dad brought me home, and he and Mom and I sat down at the kitchen table. They started asking me questions. I told them the truth about everything: the drinking, the movies, sneaking out. Dad made a list of everyone I'd attended a movie with since Jason back at camp two years ago.

Almost everything. I haven't told them about Kent Harris. I can't be *that* honest with them. Not yet. I want to make them smile again so I don't have to walk around feeling like I've killed someone. The rest feels too big to think about right now.

Dad made a list at the kitchen table, and over the past week, he listened while I called every single person on the list and apologized to them. First it was Jason, and Megan, and Daphne for going to movies. Then it was Carla and Deena from the ice rink for drinking. I've made so many phone calls over the past few days, I don't remember them all. They all go the same way:

I need to tell you that I'm sorry for [drinking, going to a movie with you, etc.]. *It was wrong of me because I was being rebellious and not honoring my parents. I put what I wanted ahead of obeying my parents, and I wasn't a good example of what a Christian is supposed to be. Will you forgive me?*

Now it's Bradley's turn.

Mrs. Westman opens the door. Her kind eyes land on me, and she smiles, then swings the door wide and looks up at my dad.

"Please, come in."

She leads the way up the stairs to the living room. I see Bradley at the top of the stairs. He called when he got back from college last week, but I had to tell him we couldn't hang out. I haven't seen him since he was home for spring break.

"Hey, man." He smiles cautiously. "How are you?"

I don't know how to answer him.

Mrs. Westman calls for Drake, who comes up the stairs from his office off the family room. There are handshakes, tense smiles, beverage refusals. I can only imagine what my father must think when Mrs. Westman asks him if he'd like a drink.

Finally, we're all sitting in the living room. Waiting.

"The reason we're here today is because Aaron has something he'd like to say to you all."

Bradley looks from my dad to me. My stomach leaps into my throat. I have to force myself to take a breath. I can't hold his gaze. What I'm about to say is so humiliating. Will he ever be able to understand why I'm saying it?

I look away from Bradley, and my eyes land on Mrs. Westman. She is sitting on the couch, her elbows resting on her knees directly across from me. She's not worried. She's looking directly into my eyes, and she's got a quiet smile and a steady gaze. I see the look in her eyes—the one she had that first night I met her.

"I'm here to apologize," I say.

Dad had carefully gone over with me what I was supposed to say. We worked on it in the living room before we drove over. One more time he was coaching me on what to say, how to play dead.

"I'm sorry for drinking at your house. I'm underage, so not only was I breaking the laws of our state, but I was breaking God's law. I'm commanded to honor my parents in the Bible, and by doing something that I knew they would not want me to do, I was being rebellious and following my own way. I'm here to apologize to you for not being a better example of a Christian, and to ask you to forgive me for doing the wrong thing."

When I finish, everyone is quiet for a moment. Mr. Westman is staring at my dad with a quizzical expression, like there is a lot he'd like to say but has thought better of it. Mrs. Westman smiles at me, then turns her gaze to my dad, who is talking now, saying something that I can't quite make out.

I look over at Bradley, who glances up at me with a look in his eyes that I will never forget. It's pity, and sadness, and exasperation with my parents for me, and he's looking for a sign from me that this is going to be okay, that I'll be okay.

But I'm not okay. Something is breaking apart inside me. *This is the last time I'll sit in this living room with you.*

Before I know it, we're all standing up to leave. Our parents are shaking hands. My mom and dad are heading down the stairs. Suddenly, I don't want to go. I want to stay here. I want to go upstairs to Bradley's room and listen to his new CDs and go out back and sit in the hot tub and stay up too late watching MTV. I want to stay here with these people I barely know—people who don't care if I have a drink at a party or a kiss in the driveway. People who don't need me to be a missionary, or a Christian schoolteacher, or anyone I'm not.

"Hang in there, bud." Mr. Westman shakes my hand and heads into the kitchen.

Mrs. Westman throws both arms around me. "This is all going to be okay," she whispers in my ear. "You'll see."

She takes my face in both her hands and stares directly into my eyes. Her look tells me that she's sure this is the truth, and I desperately want to believe her.

I walk down the stairs to the front door. Bradley follows

me out onto the front porch as my parents get into the car. We stand there, looking at each other. My hands are shoved in my jeans pockets. He punches my shoulder lightly.

"Oh man," he whispers. "You must be in hell."

If I say anything, I'm afraid I will cry. What's worse, I'm afraid there isn't anything to say. My parents will never let me come back here. I look at him, swallow the lump in my throat, and nod.

He holds out a hand. When I take it, he pulls me in for a hug. "Call me when the heat dies down?"

"Sure thing," I whisper. "It'll probably be when I get back from Brazil."

"Cool," he says.

And then there's the moment when there's too much to say to try to say anything at all. So I shrug. It's the best I can do. My dad starts the car. I look at Bradley one more time.

"Thanks for everything," I say softly.

"You bet," he says, and smiles.

I climb into the backseat and close my eyes. I can't watch when we pull away. Since our friendship began, I never imagined it ending. I never imagined driving away from his house and not knowing when I would see him again. I never once imagined my life without him, or that it would hurt like this.

"You did an excellent job in there," Dad says from the front seat. I turn my face toward the window so he can't see the tears streaming down my cheeks. When I don't respond, I hear him say my name.

"Aaron, are you okay?"

I'm getting used to telling him the truth, and I do it again. The honest answer slips from my lips in a single syllable:

"No."

Megan's hand grips my arm as I escort her to junior/senior banquet through the long corridors of the Ritz-Carlton on the Plaza. Her long chestnut curls are pulled back and slightly up. She is statuesque in a formfitting gown of navy silk. The dress is simple and gorgeous, with a straight skirt—none of the poufy bows or garish colors that tend to make the average prom dress a tragedy.

"You look amazing," I say as we wait for the elevator.

She does a slight turn from me so her leg slips out of the slit up the back of the gown. There are tiny seams whispering up the back of her stockings. Her heels are high, and she handles them expertly. I drop my jaw in response, and she turns back into my arm with a little laugh. "Had my mom stitch up the slit in the back about six inches before I brought it in for dress check."

All girls have to take their dresses to school to be checked and approved for modesty before they can be worn to junior/senior. No strapless, no off-the-shoulder, all straps must be two inches wide, all skirts must cover the knee.... The requirements go on and on. Our combined armed forces have less stringent regulations for uniforms than the girls who must haul their dresses into the school in hanging bags to be modeled for a female teacher or Mrs. Friesen. Straps, hems, and necklines are checked with a measuring tape to ensure compliance.

I lean back and steal another peek at the slit in Megan's dress. "That's a pretty big slit."

"Cut out the stitches after they approved it." Megan smirks. "I figure I'll be sitting on it most of the time we're here. It's not like we'll be dancing or anything."

"I'll keep an eye out for Mrs. Friesen sneaking up with a tape measure."

Megan laughs and leans into my arm. I catch a glimpse of us in the mirror between the elevators. My black tux is crisp and classic. I am seized by the urge to take Megan by the hand and lead her out of the hotel and into the Country Club Plaza. To get away from the room full of our friends waiting for us downstairs. I'm not sure I'm ready to face the whole senior class.

The limo was a few minutes late leaving her house because there were so many people to cram into the long black car. We all split the cost of the limo, and there were so many pictures taken I still have purple splotches floating across my eyes from the endless series of flashes. I hadn't seen anyone since the chapel service, so it was a big reunion of sorts. While everyone else went inside, Megan and I hung back to make arrangements with the driver to pick us up after the banquet.

Now it's only the two of us, making our way toward the ballroom. Our grand entrance is imminent.

"I can't believe Dr. Spicer and Mr. Friesen let you come," she says.

"It was contingent on my apology in chapel."

"And how on earth did you get your parents to let you out of their sight for the evening?"

"For one night, can we not talk about my parents?" I ask.

An elevator finally arrives. We step inside, and as the doors close, she turns to face me and pulls me toward her by my silk lapels.

"We don't have to talk about anything at all," she whispers.

We kiss long and hard. This is the only moment we've been alone together since I got kicked out of school, and we don't pull away from each other until the elevator slows and stops on the ballroom level. We turn and straighten ourselves. Megan wipes at the edges of her lipstick with a perfectly manicured fingernail.

"Talking," she says, sighing. "So overrated."

I laugh as we step out of the elevator, and for the first time in weeks, I feel good. I'm glad Megan will be around this fall. We've both enrolled at the Bible college where my dad teaches. I move into the dorms at the end of August. I'll only be twenty minutes away from home, but it's a start.

As we walk toward the end of the hall, I can see the room full of our friends. I feel my stride begin to slow. I can hear music and see a flash of Erica's blonde hair. Megan turns to look at me as I stare at the light from the doorway spilling into the dimly lit hall.

"Are you okay?" she whispers.

I search myself for the answer.

What are they going to think of me? How will they look at me? Who am I now?

I don't know how things will change when college starts this fall, but I know everything will be different, and somehow, in this moment, that is enough. Like the light coming from the door at the end of this hallway, I see a light at the end of getting kicked out of high school. I don't know what's on the other side, but I know it will be better.

After all the tears and frustration and hurt, there's something inside me that remains unbroken. It's strong and whole; it's the place where the best part of me resides, and that's the part of me who is going to walk into the junior/senior banquet with my head held high in front of everyone two weeks after being expelled: the real me—the me who is learning not to hide anymore.

I turn to Megan and smile. She clasps my arm and smiles back.

"Showtime," I whisper with a wink. Then we step through the door out of the dim hallway into the light, and turn every head in the room.

"You're the only person on the planet who gets kicked out of high school, then goes to Brazil."

Daphne has a point. It does seem odd.

"Dad accepted this speaking engagement a while back,"

I explain. "A bunch of students at his Bible college have parents who are missionaries in Brazil. They're all coming into the mission compound for a retreat, and he's going to speak every night."

"Will you be near the beach?"

"Yes," I admit.

"Sounds like a vacation to me."

I wince and shift my weight on the chair I'm gingerly sitting on in the family room. "Well, the shots I got today are no vacation, let me tell you."

"When will you get home?" Daphne wants to know. "I want to make sure we get to shop for college at least once when you get back."

"We'll be in Brazil for about a month. Then we're going to Memphis for a couple of weeks to see my grandmother."

"Are you excited?" she asks.

I smile. "Yeah. Really excited. I've never been out of the country before. Well, once in Canada on a road trip to Oregon when I was little, but that doesn't really count."

"Do you have a book for the plane?"

"A couple, actually. I checked out those plays that the director at the Rep told me to read. I'm going to work on a couple of audition monologues while I'm there."

"Please don't drink anything out of a coconut on the beach," she says.

"I promise."

"When is Tri-City's graduation?" she asks.

"Tomorrow."

Daphne is quiet for a moment. "Does it feel weird knowing you won't be there?"

"Yeah," I say. "It does. They put my diploma and honor society cords in a cardboard box with the stuff from my locker. I stopped by school last week to pick it up. I hummed 'Pomp and Circumstance' on the way down the stairs to my car."

"I wish you'd never left Blue Ridge." Daphne sighs.

"But then I wouldn't have this great story to tell my grandkids."

Daphne laughs and tells me good-bye.

I hang up the phone in the family room, then gather up the piano music I'll be playing for the missionaries next week.

REVELATION

noun \ˊre-və-ˊlā-shən\: communication of divine truth; an enlightening or astonishing disclosure

"The skies in northeastern Brazil are always ranked the most beautiful in the world," says Luke. He's the son of a missionary family here, and he's showing us around. Luke is driving one of the two dune buggies we rented up the sloping side of a gigantic sand dune in a resort town called Jericoacoara. The sky is a gorgeous swath of blue crowded with cotton-ball clouds, the kind I used to search for shapes, and signs of Jesus.

When everyone piles out at the top of the dune, my brothers and sister race to peer over the edge. Luke says it's a 150-foot drop down to the flat beach below, but the fun part is that you can go running off the steep side in a free fall until you land in the sandy slope.

Luke goes first to demonstrate, and my brothers and sister follow suit. With shrieks and whoops, they land in the steep sand after a twenty-foot free fall, their legs sinking up to their knees. I can hear them giggling and squealing as I watch them tumble and slide the rest of the way down to the beach where Mom is waiting.

"Looks like it's your turn, Aaron."

I smile back at my dad. Things have been more normal this week. I'm glad this trip was planned before I got kicked out of school. Watching Dad in his element, preaching and laughing, and talking in front of a large group of people, has been good. It's reminded me how much I love him; it's reminded me that so many of my finest qualities are the ones I've learned from him. So many of the things I love—acting, singing, writing, drawing, playing the piano— are the things he taught me or encouraged me to pursue and enjoy. I've realized how much I am like him as I watch him easily chat and laugh with our friends here. I've seen myself in his mannerisms and his humor and the way he winks and laughs when he tells a joke.

I've been worried that Dad and I don't agree about everything anymore. More and more, I wonder if we agree about anything at all. I worry that the guy I am growing up to be will wind up being impossible for him to love. I fear that I'll never be able to be completely honest with him about who I really am in the deepest part of myself.

But today in the sun, under these endless skies, in a different hemisphere, a place where no one speaks English and the water circles down the drain in the opposite direction, it seems like anything may be possible. It feels like I might be able to be the person I really am right out in the open—without holding anything back. It feels like I might be able to let go of the lies that I've built around myself to protect Dad from the son that I truly am.

Maybe I can trust him to love me whether we agree or not.

"This is crazy," I say, pointing at the edge.

"Sure looks like it to me." He laughs. "But if you fall the wrong way and break your noggin, don't worry. We'll see you when we get to heaven."

Dad says this with the funny country hick accent he uses when he's kidding around, but I know he isn't really joking. This is his truth, and always will be. He believes this with all his heart, and I'll never change his mind.

What if you loved him just as he is?

It's the first time I've ever turned the question on myself. I've been so focused on him accepting me I've never stopped to wonder what would happen if I accepted him.

In spite of the temperature, a tiny chill runs up my spine at this thought. I smile at Dad in the bright sun, and he grins back at me. It's a smile I recognize, one that looks familiar because it's so much like the one I see each morning in the mirror. My smile, my laugh, my height; all these things were his before they became my own.

Dad strolls over and puts his arm around me. He stands next to me, at the edge of the continent, staring out at the sky and sea.

Thousands of miles away from the place where we live our lives, I recognize something else in his smile, and in the tenderness of his arm on my shoulders—a new sort of understanding.

I understand that my father's heart is full of answers about where we go when we die, and answers about how we should live before we do. He is sure of these things, as certain of them as he is that the sky is blue.

My heart is full of questions. I'm no longer certain about what will happen when I die, or if Jesus will really come back one day, bursting through clouds like the ones sailing over our heads right now. I have so many questions about living, too. One of these questions I'm so frightened to ask I'm not yet sure how to phrase it.

Yet somehow, as I stand here with my father in the sun, I understand that my heart full of questions and his heart full of answers are both filled with something else:

Love.

This may be the one thing of which I am certain. I know this love will keep us working to understand each other no matter how hard it gets, or how long it takes. Whether we ever agree or not, we will always stand up to defend the things we believe, our truths—even if those truths are hard, even when those beliefs create more questions than answers.

This is the man Dad raised me to be.

We may disagree about where the truth lies, but somewhere in the midst of the questions, if we fight for each other instead of against each other, our love will bring us here; to a quiet place of transcendent beauty, to a simple moment of elegance—a moment I now understand has a name:

Grace.

I can't find the words to share this with my dad. I'm not sure how to tell him all these things inside my heart. I don't know if he'll ever understand them the way I do. Instead, I slip my arm around his waist and hold him, tightly.

"You going for it, Aaron?"

"Yes!" I shout into the tropical wind whipping up the dune from the water.

Dad steps back with a smile and I run as fast as I can toward the precipice. Sunlight bursts from the edges of towering clouds, and shoots dazzling beams across the surface of the water in both directions as far as my eyes can see.

The sand is warm against my feet, and as I reach the edge I feel my body take flight. My arms spread wide, and the sweet, humid breeze sweeps through my hair. I close my eyes as I leap, sailing in a high arc as the dune drops away beneath me.

Blastoff...

I reach toward the clouds and the azure sky beyond. For a split second, as I hang in the air, I feel the awe of true mystery, the wonder of not seeing where I will land, the thrill of knowing nothing for certain.

It's a leap of faith.

It's a rush of pure freedom.

It's the feeling of rapture.

ACKNOWLEDGMENTS

noun \ik-ˊnä-lij-mənts\: things done or given
in recognition of something received

Most first-time authors feel fortunate to find a single editor who believes in their writing. I was lucky enough to have two. Thank you to Jennifer Hunt, who adopted this snarling mutt of an idea, and to Kate Sullivan, who made it behave. No book is too much for Kate. She rehabilitates manuscripts; she trains authors. She *is* ... the Book Whisperer.

Thanks also to the fantastic Little, Brown team who believed in this book and worked so tirelessly to make it the best it could be: Megan Tingley, Andrew Smith, Alvina Ling, Melanie Chang, Steve Scott, Victoria Stapleton, Zoe Luderitz, Leslie Shumate, Pamela Garfinkel, Barbara Bakowski, and Pamela Barricklow.

Thank you to my agent, Michael Bourret, for being fearless, frank, funny, and my friend.

David Lipsky once wrote, "A book, like a writer, has

friends before it has readers." Constrained by space (and under threat of the orchestra playing me off the stage), please forgive in advance this impersonal, alphabetical list of the best friends a book has ever had: Chad Allen, Gee Cee Bahador, Robin Benway, Stacie Chaiken, Rachel Cohn, Kathleen Dennehy, Anthony Glomski, Holly Goldberg Sloan, Brian Hedden, Sean Hetherington, Annie Jacobsen, Jenny Janisko, Allyn Johnston, David Levithan, Ian MacKinnon, Ken Madson, Jack Martin, John Ryan Martine, Sandy Matke, Peter McGuigan, Molly McIlvaine, Laura and Tom McNeal, Moira McMahon, Tim Miller, Michael Neely, David Ozanich, Rachel Parker, Gary Rosen, Chris Saint-Hilaire, Francesco Sedita, Julie Strauss-Gabel, Kim Turrisi, Sam Wasson, Isaac Webster, Nicholas Weinstock, Jamie Weiss Chilton, Tina Wexler, Alan Jay Williams, John Andrew Wolf, Sara Zarr, and John Ziffren. Each one of you has been pivotal at some point in the process.

Thank you to the authors whose books were my map for writing memoir: Julia Cameron, Natalie Goldberg, Anne Lamott, David Rakoff, David Sedaris, Ryan Van Meter, and Jeannette Walls. Your words were instructive whether you intended them to be or not.

Mom, Dad, Joshua, Miriam, Caleb, Elizabeth Joy, and Nanny: I hold each of you in my heart and love you more than these pages could hope to contain.

Finally, to Nathan Hatch, the man with whom I have chosen to spend my life: For words to fail me is uncommon, yet each day your love leaves me speechless.